WINTER
8000

BERNADETTE
McDONALD

WINTER
8000

CLIMBING THE
WORLD'S HIGHEST
MOUNTAINS
IN THE COLDEST
SEASON

Vertebrate Publishing, Sheffield
www.v-publishing.co.uk

BERNADETTE MCDONALD

WINTER 8000

First published simultaneously in Great Britain and North America in 2020
by Vertebrate Publishing, Sheffield, and Mountaineers Books, Seattle.

Vertebrate Publishing
Omega Court, 352 Cemetery Road, Sheffield S11 8FT UK.
www.v-publishing.co.uk

Mountaineers Books
1001 SW Klickitat Way, Suite 201, Seattle, WA 98134, United States of America.

Front cover: Ethereal early morning light on summit day, 2 February 2011. Denis Urubko, Simone Moro
and Cory Richards became the first to climb Gasherbrum II in winter. Photo: Cory Richards.

Individual photography as credited.

Extract from 'Sing You Home' reproduced by permission of The Ennis Sisters.

A CIP catalogue record for this book is available from the British Library.

ISBN: 978-1-912560-38-7 (Hardback)
ISBN: 978-1-912560-40-0 (Ebook)
ISBN: 978-1-912560-41-7 (Audiobook)

10 9 8 7 6 5 4 3 2 1

Cover design by Nathan Ryder – www.ryderdesign.studio
Design and production by Cameron Bonser, Vertebrate Publishing.
www.v-publishing.co.uk

Vertebrate Publishing is committed to printing on paper from sustainable sources.

Printed and bound in the UK by T.J. International Ltd, Padstow, Cornwall.

CONTENTS

Climbing the fixed lines on Gasherbrum I in winter 2012. *Photo: Darek Załuski.*

INTRODUCTION

The Art of Suffering

... there are men who, on the approach of severe pain, hear the very opposite call of command, and never appear more proud, more martial, or more happy than when the storm is brewing; indeed, pain itself provides them with their supreme moments! These are the heroic men ...

Friedrich Nietzsche, *Die fröhliche Wissenschaft*

He stood out immediately. Towering over many of the best high-altitude climbers in the world, Andrzej Zawada was holding court. His natty tweed jacket atop a simple black turtleneck complemented his salt-and-pepper hair. Severe black-framed glasses balanced his angular bone structure, adding to his regal posture.

Zawada was among a group of fellow climbers at the Polish Mountaineering Association clubhouse, celebrating the wrap of the 1994 Katowice Mountain Film Festival. The wintry city was enveloped in a thick blanket of smog. Although the building was dank and dingy, the windows smudged with residue from nearby smokestacks, inside was warmth, light and plenty of vodka. And stories: incredible stories of exposed traverses, high-altitude storms, desperate bivouacs and triumphant summits.

I had helped organise the festival, and knew the reputations of many of the alpinists in the room, superstars of high-altitude climbing, both summer and winter. But it was my first meeting with Andrzej Zawada, a legendary winter specialist. I asked, 'Mr Zawada, why do you prefer to climb in the Himalaya in winter when summer is so much more appealing?'

He looked down his long, aristocratic nose and said, 'Because the Himalaya in summer is for vimmen!' I spied a twinkle in his eye as he glanced around to gauge the response to his outrageous comment. Like everyone, I laughed.

But there was no questioning the respect due this man who had inspired a generation of climbers to launch their high-altitude careers in the cruellest season. The concept of winter mountaineering in the Himalaya and Karakoram was born in Poland, nurtured in Poland, and for years, dominated by Polish climbers. Almost 200 expeditions from dozens of countries have ventured into the highest mountains in Nepal, Pakistan and Tibet in winter, but the Poles, under the leadership of Andrzej Zawada, were the first to succeed in the coldest season at 8,000 metres.

Years later, Adam Bielecki, one of Poland's leading winter climbers, wrote: 'Winter domination was the fault of Stalin and Bierut[1] because they locked us in a cage. When others were doing first ascents of 8,000-metre peaks, we remained trapped behind the Iron Curtain. When it finally lifted, we jumped out of the cage. We were very hungry.'[2] It's true that after the end of the Second World War, Polish mountaineers were not part of the resurgence of activity in the Himalaya. While the Poles languished under Soviet rule, alpinists from around the world summited all fourteen of the 8,000-metre peaks. The French started it with Annapurna in 1950, and the Chinese finished the job on Shishapangma in 1964. Yet none of them were climbed in winter. Winter still offered an unexplored frontier for Himalayan climbers.

When you contemplate the reality of climbing in winter at 8,000 metres, the scale of the challenge becomes almost abhorrent. Gasping for oxygen in the thin air, throbbing headaches and retching stomachs are common at high altitude in any season, but winter accentuates the problem. As high-altitude medical expert Dr Peter Hackett explains, 'Barometric pressure at high altitude is considerably lower in winter than summer – enough to make a clinical difference.' Lower barometric pressure means less oxygen to keep warm and make progress, both of which are already harder because of the bitter cold.

Temperatures at 8,000 metres in winter defy understanding. It is so cold your lungs feel as if they are burning. Eyelashes become coated in rime and cling together. Exposed skin freezes in minutes. Your extremities are horribly vulnerable and if immobile or constricted in any way can freeze as solid as wood. Fingers and toes die, turn black and must be amputated. Stoves malfunction. Metal snaps. Cold *this* cold is brutally unforgiving. It wraps itself around you and around your mind and then begins, ever so slowly, to squeeze. It's terrifying.

Savage winter winds rarely let up at high elevations on these peaks. For weeks on end, summits are buried in the jet stream. And these winds are not simply breezy or gusty; they have the power of hurricanes. Such winds can lift a grown person and throw them down. They destroy tents, fling barrels of equipment hundreds of metres, snap guylines and polish glacial ice to marble smoothness. They drive huge quantities of snow, packing it into deadly slabs poised to avalanche at the slightest trigger. They roar and howl and scream until even the most well-balanced climber begins to feel he is going insane.

The degree of isolation in the highest mountains in winter is hard to imagine. With difficult ground access and dangerous flying conditions, any emergency quickly turns into a life-threatening situation. As winter Himalayan climber Darek Załuski explains, 'It's difficult to find loneliness under the 8,000ers except in winter. Winter is at the end of the world.'

There is little colour in the high mountains in winter, only thirty shades of white, gradations of grey and blackest black. The variations of white provide a frame of reference for snow quality, avalanche risk and all kinds of clues that can help you survive. Black is the colour of the rock-hard ice that will deflect your ice axe, resist the bite of your crampon, and glisten like glass. Grey roils in with every storm: charcoal grey, dove grey, milky grey. Rarely, the heavy sky splits wide to reveal a startling blue so deep you could drown in it, luring alpinists into action for a day or two of good weather. And then it's back to grey.

Winter is darkness. Winter days are short, and those long winter nights feel like forever. In a tent at 7,000 metres, nights are not only long but filled with loneliness and uncertainty. During an open bivouac at 8,000 metres, prolonged darkness arouses emotions that can overwhelm you: fear, paranoia, even malice.

In a word, suffering. Winter climbing at altitude is all about suffering, or as Polish climber Voytek Kurtyka described it, winter in the high Himalaya is the 'Art of Suffering'. And yet there are those who are passionate about climbing at 8,000 metres in winter, even obsessed. They crave the mind-numbing isolation. They are trained and ready to dance across ice as hard as stone, to move lightly on unstable snow, to punch thousands of steps into knee-deep drifts. They know their equipment so well it's like an extension of their limbs. They move quickly and efficiently, even while swaddled in down suits that restrict their movements and enormous mitts that render them as clumsy as infants. They recognise and react to potential threats, although they are peering through ice-filmed goggles. They understand patience. Patience to wait days or weeks, and sometimes months, in base camp, hoping for a break in the weather, that blazing blue sky, even if it's only for two days. They push their bodies to the very edge, peer over that edge, and judge when to pull back to live another day. Their dance with suffering combines instinct, ingrained mountain wisdom and a formidable will to survive. These are the 'Ice Warriors'.

It's rare to meet a true visionary, a man elevated above the ordinary. Watching Andrzej Zawada interact with the world's pre-eminent high-altitude climbers, observing their respect, their deference, their ready acceptance of the hardships, the cruelty and dangers of venturing into the highest mountains on Earth in winter, piqued my curiosity.

As I delved into the history of winter climbing, I was astonished by the scope: over a period of four decades almost 200 expeditions and over 1,500 climbers had been drawn to the coldest season, from Poland and Italy, Japan, Russia and many other countries – too many to contain in one volume. Choosing whom to include was difficult; chronicling this complex history even more so. For simplicity's sake, I decided to recount the story of the 8,000ers in winter in the order of their first successful winter ascents. It just so happened that it all started with Everest: not the most difficult 8,000er, but the highest.

Writing it in the dead of winter – in fact, the harshest winter at my home in Banff in 131 years – seemed appropriate. Huddled at my desk beneath a frosty window, swaddled in down, I tap-tapped for hours, slipping away mid-day for a sprint around the local ski trails, hoping for a glimmer of sun to melt the frost on my eyelashes. Those frigid dashes provided ample time to imagine those same temperatures – but six and a half kilometres higher – and to reflect on the resilient characters capable of functioning in such conditions.

I know, or in too many cases, *knew*, many of these winter climbers. Knowing them and their families made writing some chapters a gut-wrenching experience. But as I revisited the long conversations that led to this book, remembered that first meeting with the grandfather of high-altitude winter climbing, Andrzej Zawada, and reflected on the strong friendships that were formed in the process, it became increasingly clear that I needed to write their story. This book is testament to their suffering and effort, their triumphs and failures.

1

EVEREST

First Time Lucky

We lived with a sense of perfect freedom and deep physical
and mental well-being. We wanted nothing.
Eric Shipton, *Upon That Mountain*

There can only be one *highest* mountain on Earth, and as such, Everest has always been a sought-after objective. But for Andrzej Zawada, Everest felt more like a thorn in his side. By the late 1970s, the mountain had seen a number of important ascents. New Zealander Edmund Hillary and Sherpa Tenzing Norgay reached its 8,848-metre summit for the first time by the South Col route in 1953. An American team climbed the difficult west ridge via the Hornbein Couloir in 1963. In 1975, Japanese mountaineer Junko Tabei became the first woman to make the summit. That autumn, the British climbed the south-west face. Three years later, on 8 May 1978, Italian Reinhold Messner and Austrian Peter Habeler shattered another barrier when they climbed Everest without bottled oxygen.

Yugoslavs, Swiss, Chinese, Nepalis and Tibetans: all had made their mark on Everest, some on extremely impressive routes. But no Pole had stood on its summit, a cause for distress and even humiliation among Polish climbers.

Wanda Rutkiewicz broke the stalemate. On 16 October 1978, she became the third woman to climb the mountain, the first European woman, and the first Polish climber. Poland's leading female alpinist, Wanda possessed all the attributes of a climbing star: athletic, ambitious and famously beautiful. All of that plus perfect timing. Her summit day coincided with the election of Pope John Paul II, who hailed from Poland. Both announcements generated an explosion of joy in Poland, almost as great as in England in 1953, when news of Edmund Hillary's first ascent coincided with young Queen Elizabeth II's coronation.

Andrzej was, perhaps surprisingly, relieved by Wanda's ascent because she had unknowingly solved a problem for him. Until her triumphant climb, the Polish Mountaineering Association (Polski Związek Alpinizmu, or PZA) had been pressing Andrzej to organise a spring expedition to Everest. That would have a far greater chance of success than the winter attempt he was proposing. Andrzej resisted, arguing that since Everest had been climbed in spring or autumn by almost a hundred climbers, one more ascent would add little to mountaineering history. After Wanda's success, the committee began warming to Andrzej's plan. More precisely, two plans. The first was to climb Everest in winter; the second was to climb it by a new route the following spring.

There could be no one more qualified to carry out such ambitious endeavours than Andrzej Zawada. He was not only a climber but also a leader who could inspire, a diplomat who could open doors. He came from a long-standing Polish upper class, starting with Count Malczewski, a Romantic poet who is sometimes regarded as the first Polish alpinist, having climbed Mont Blanc in 1818. While not himself a count, Andrzej was aware of his privileged lineage: Philip, his father, had a doctorate in international law and his mother, Eleonora, was a linguist who translated both Russian and German. As reward for successfully negotiating the terms of the amorphous German–Polish border in the 1920s, Philip was named the Polish Consul. The family's diplomatic life abroad ended when Philip was struck down with tuberculosis; despite first-class treatment in Davos, Switzerland, he died in 1931. Andrzej was only three years old. Eleonora moved her two young boys back to Poland's high country, near the Tatra mountains, and by 1939 they had settled into a cosy, alpine-style chalet.

Her choice of home was fortunate: in the mountains they were relatively sheltered from the horrors of the Second World War, which was soon ripping Poland to pieces. Eleonora supplemented her income by translating at the local hospital, where hundreds of injured soldiers arrived for treatment. Although overrun with German and Russian soldiers, the area also harboured small bands of brave resistance fighters. At night, they would huddle around the fire in her chalet, planning their covert actions. It wasn't long before little Andrzej began colluding with the partisans. Still a boy, he stashed a machine gun under his desk at school and grenades by his bed at night. By the age of seventeen, he had already spent a month in prison.

Upon release, his mother whisked him away to a secure location where he finished his high school studies before going on to study geophysics in universities at Wrocław and Warsaw. Andrzej thrived in the big cities but being a mountain boy at heart he joined the local mountain clubs, taking their courses and climbing at weekends.

Although Andrzej usually played by the rules imposed by the Polish Mountaineering Association, climbing with more experienced partners until he was sufficiently skilled, he sometimes broke free of the PZA's constraints. Ignoring their warnings, Andrzej couldn't resist making in 1959 a complete winter traverse of the Tatras: seventy-five kilometres and 22,000 metres up and down on a route that was steep, airy and difficult. Andrzej saw the traverse as an important test of his abilities in winter conditions. The PZA saw it as a flagrant disregard of their rules. Polish climbers at this time had to rely on the PZA to apply to the communist government for passports to travel abroad. So it wasn't surprising that the PZA punished Andrzej by withholding his passport for an expedition he had organised to the Rakaposhi area in Pakistan's Karakoram mountain range.

Since mountaineering was considered an 'official' sport in Poland, there was an elaborate system of vetting and qualifying alpinists who wished to travel abroad. An approved project would receive funding from the PZA but their support did not include equipment. Climbers needed to be creative, finding seamstresses, bootmakers, welders and anyone else who could manufacture the specialised equipment needed to survive the harsh conditions found in the high mountains.

Andrzej excelled at these jobs. He was already a proven problem-solver, leading geophysical scientific expeditions, managing logistics, permits and equipment. He travelled widely, learnt how to navigate government bureaucracies and how to lead people in situations of significant risk. As his skills improved and his organisational experience grew, he gradually prepared himself as the ideal climbing expedition leader.

In 1971 he led the groundbreaking first ascent of 7,852-metre Kunyang Chhish, a peak in the western Karakoram of Pakistan. Buoyed by this success and his experience of winter climbing in the Tatras, he felt Polish mountaineers were now ready to stake a claim to some new territory in the high-altitude mountaineering world: climbing in winter. His first objective would be Afghanistan's highest mountain: 7,492-metre Noshaq. His plan was unusual enough for the government of Afghanistan, before granting a permit for the expedition, to demand a letter from the PZA stating they understood the implications of the Polish winter objective and took full responsibility for their actions. With some difficulty, Andrzej obtained this letter.

On 29 December 1972, the team gathered at Warsaw railway station with three tons of equipment. While he appeared confident, Andrzej journeyed with a heavy heart, worried their goal was too ambitious. Venturing into extremely high mountains in winter had not yet been done. As the train rumbled along, he stared out at the endless frozen fields, tormented by visions of blinding snowstorms, thundering avalanches and frostbitten feet.

When they finally arrived at Noshaq, Andrzej was relieved to see very little snow. But it was frighteningly cold. Daytime temperatures hovered around -25° Celsius, and at night, ten degrees lower. Hours of daylight were brutally short. As winter storms cycled through, the climbers suffered, most eventually retreating to base camp to tend their cracked lips and frozen limbs.

Towards the middle of February, Andrzej and Tadek Piotrowski, a notoriously tough Polish alpinist famous for his icy river training swims, climbed to within 800 metres of the top, but temperatures dropped even lower and the wind was howling. Then, during the night of 12 February, Andrzej woke with a start; the tent had miraculously stopped flapping. He peered out into an eerily calm night, the ebony sky studded with a million stars. This was their chance.

The two men started early next day, stopping in late afternoon to rest on a snowy plateau and make tea. Soon after, the moon rose, bathing the mountain in an ethereal glow. Since the summit appeared just a short distance ahead, they radioed down to base camp that they would push on. Yet when they reached the top, well after 9 p.m., their spirits plunged: the main summit was still more than a kilometre ahead. It was almost midnight when they finally arrived at the true summit, their faces numbed by bitter winds. At 4.30 a.m., after seventeen hours of near-continuous movement, they arrived back at their tent. Andrzej was in remarkably good shape but Tadek's two big toes were frozen like cubes of ice.

Despite the cost, the two men had set a new record: they were first to climb a mountain over 7,000 metres in winter. Andrzej was already thinking about what would be next. While resting at base camp, his mind raced with the possibilities. He later wrote: 'We began to think about our next winter expedition: but this time it would be to 8,000 metres … climbing the highest peaks of the world in winter would open a new chapter in mountain climbing … to prove that it is possible to climb under any conditions and at any time of the year is a test to sort out the top climbers from the others. It would be an achievement which would give the highest satisfaction.'[1]

Once he'd returned home, Andrzej Zawada began planning the next winter expedition. His first choice was Everest, but the PZA turned this plan down repeatedly so, for the 1974–75 season, he settled on Everest's neighbour Lhotse, at 8,516 metres the world's fourth-highest mountain. In retrospect, many consider this to have been more of an 'autumn' expedition rather than winter, since the Poles arrived at base camp in late October. And while they made a valiant attempt, described in Chapter Seven, they didn't quite succeed. It would take another five years for Andrzej to launch a team on Everest in winter, but he never lost sight of his vision. He was determined to explore the limits of what was possible, and Poland's climbers were eager to prove themselves.

As preposterous as it might seem to tackle the highest mountain on Earth in winter, it wouldn't have appeared outlandish to Polish climbers. In their home mountains, the Tatras, winter climbing was almost as popular as rock climbing. As Andrzej once said, 'There are no glaciers in our Tatra mountains, so that in order to approximate to Alpine conditions, we have to climb in winter.'[2] Winter routes in the Tatras are primarily mixed climbs, requiring high-level technical skills for both rock and ice. Equally important is the ability to protect the climber: finding cracks in which to place pitons and build safe belays, the methods used to secure a climber to the wall. A curious mix of frosted granite, frozen clumps of grass and thin slivers of ice, the walls of the Tatras in winter are difficult, both technically and psychologically: an excellent training ground for winter alpinism in the high mountains.

Another valuable skill acquired in the Tatras was how to survive a winter bivouac, a night out on the mountain with minimal shelter, either planned or, through force of circumstance, unplanned. Bivouacking became so popular with Polish climbers in the 1970s that they began competing with each other, even developing contest rules: sleeping inside a tent didn't count; subtract one point for using a bivouac sack; being content to stuff one's legs into a backpack scored the highest points. Leading the 'bivvy competition' was Zygmunt Heinrich, a notoriously tough Himalayan climber who boasted hundreds of bivouacs and who, not surprisingly, was chosen for the Everest winter climb.

Andrzej Zawada, despite his impressive reputation as an expedition leader, was an amateur alpinist, a geophysicist who climbed only when he could find the time. Even as an amateur who had to squeeze his expeditions in between job requirements, he brought a professional attitude to all aspects of expeditioning, including the equipment. But at that time in Poland, he couldn't simply saunter into a shopping mall with a credit card. There were no outdoor equipment shops and there was certainly no credit. He galvanised anyone and everyone he thought could provide him with the specialised gear he needed for the job, convincing them they were part of the team, important cogs in a wheel that would take them to the top of Everest in winter.

But there was the troublesome business of securing a permit. Even after winning over the PZA, Andrzej's compelling arguments failed to convince the Nepalese authorities. 'The highest peaks which have already been conquered in the pre-monsoon and post-monsoon seasons will be virgin peaks to winter expeditions,' he wrote in his application letter. 'Winter expeditions to the Himalayas are a natural historical consequence in the development of mountaineering progress.'[3]

The Nepalese government forced him to wait until 1979. When it came, the permit was valid from the beginning of December to the end of February, with the understanding that Andrzej's team would finish climbing by 15 February, leaving two weeks to descend and clear the mountain of equipment. Unfortunately, this precious piece of paper didn't arrive in Poland until 22 November, nine days before they were scheduled to begin. Andrzej had planned to travel to Nepal overland by truck, but that was now impossible: there was no time. Flying was the only option, but for that Andrzej needed more money. Miraculously, the PZA agreed.

He already had his team in place; there was no shortage of willing alpinists. In 1979 there were 2,400 active climbers in Poland and most were keen to sign up for anything Andrzej could envision. In choosing the team, he first compiled a list of Poland's top forty alpinists; then he created a question-naire, grilling them on their level of experience and their interest in either the winter expedition or one planned for the following spring, also to Everest. He pored over the answers late into the night, shuffling climbers back and forth: on the list, off the list, winter, spring.

Polish Himalayan climber Zygmunt Heinrich, one of the leading climbers on the Polish 1979–80 winter Everest expedition. *Photo: Alek Lwow Archive.*

Krzysztof Wielicki, an ambitious and plucky climber from Wrocław, was among those chosen for the spring attempt. When three men from the winter team bowed out for personal reasons, Krzysztof was shifted to winter. Born in 1950, Krzysztof grew up near the sea. He flourished in the natural world and was soon an enthusiastic Boy Scout. For two months each summer he was immersed in the outdoors, learning valuable skills: orienteering, camping, fishing, and getting along with people in confined spaces. When he entered university in Wrocław to study electrical engineering, he joined the local mountain club where he learnt to rock climb, as well as bivouac. 'We were like total idiots,' he said. 'The rest of our friends were at a campfire and we were shivering the whole night like Jello in our harnesses.'[4] He quickly revealed a daredevil, even reckless tendency. The elfin alpinist, his face overrun by an unruly moustache, fell and broke three lumbar vertebrae during his first season.

Krzysztof's bad luck continued. Three years later in the Italian Dolomites, he was hit by falling rock that destroyed his helmet. He lost consciousness for a few moments before continuing up to an unplanned, blood-soaked bivouac immediately below the summit. When a doctor stitched him up the following day, he advised Krzysztof to take a break from climbing until he healed. Instead, Krzysztof left for the Afghan Hindu Kush and climbed a new route, alpine style, on 7,084-metre Kohe Shakhawr. Andrzej Zawada had been tracking his career and was confident Krzysztof would make an exciting addition to any Everest team.

Another of Andrzej's choices was Leszek Cichy, a lanky, fair-haired mountaineer from Warsaw, one year younger than Krzysztof. Leszek was a university lecturer with an impressive climbing CV, including a new route on Gasherbrum II and a high point of 8,230 metres on K2. But while young and fit, neither Leszek nor Krzysztof was a likely candidate for the Everest summit team. There were more experienced climbers on the team of twenty.[5] Mountaineers like Zygmunt Heinrich who, earlier that year, had summited

Lhotse and who had reached 8,250 metres on the same mountain in winter, climbing with Andrzej. Their partnership was sealed on the summit of Kunyang Chhish, which they reached together in the summer of 1971. Zygmunt (known as Zyga) had also made the first ascent of one of the summits of Kangchenjunga, 8,473-metre Kangchenjunga Central, confirming his reputation as a first-class, high-altitude alpinist capable of performing above 8,000 metres, regardless of the season.

Thanks to the late-arriving permit, the last of the Polish team's baggage arrived in Kathmandu on 20 December 1979 and it wasn't until 4 January that base camp was fully constructed on the south side of the mountain. Yet within ten productive days, the first three camps were in place and Andrzej began to wonder why no one had tried this before.

The news from Camp 3, however, wasn't good. Above the tents reared the Lhotse wall, one continuous sheet of hard ice. They had hoped for snow, into which they could easily kick steps, but the winter winds had stripped the face down to its icy core, presenting the Poles with much more difficult climbing. When the frigid temperatures and screaming winds of January bit hard, their spirits fell. The team retreated to base camp, where the anemometer often registered 130 kilometres per hour and the temperatures fell to -40° Celsius at night. They began to understand why they were completely alone on the mountain.

To compensate for the harsh conditions, Andrzej surprised the tired mountaineers with a plastic bathtub from Warsaw. The plastic soon cracked in the cold, but Andrzej replaced it with a giant aluminium basin he had purchased in Kathmandu. A fire burned constantly in the kitchen tent, providing piping hot water for the tub, into which the alpinists lowered their weary bodies, wallowing in its warmth.

Another feature at base camp, though less popular than the tub, were two 20-metre aluminium radio aerials, the handiwork of Bogdan Jankowski, a climber from Wrocław. Bogdan was responsible for not just the aerials but three long-distance transmitters, eight radio telephones, tape recorders used to record communication between camps, a gas-driven high-voltage generator and batteries. Bogdan sent out daily bulletins to Poland so the public could monitor their progress on the mountain. Return messages reminded the mountaineers of home. Hanna Wiktorowska, secretary of the PZA back in Warsaw, was charged with communicating the crucially

Bogdan Jankowski and his communications centre at Everest winter base camp.
Photo: Bogdan Jankowski.

important newsflashes from the families to the team: 'Zosia has got one tooth up, one tooth down … Are you remembering to wear warm socks?'

For weeks, shrieking winds battered the climbers, eroding their strength and their will. From Camp 3 to the saddle of the South Col was a distance of only 850 metres, but in these conditions, those 850 metres took nearly a month to surmount. By this time, many on the team were too exhausted to continue. Others were injured. Krzysztof Żurek was knocked over by the wind and tumbled twenty metres before the nearest piton stopped his fall. He managed to reach Camp 3, but then slipped into a crevasse – twice – on his way to base camp. Both Zyga Heinrich and Alek Lwow were suffering from frostbite in their hands. The climbers' throats were inflamed from the cold, dry air and their camps were routinely destroyed by hurricane-force winds. The busiest person on the expedition was the doctor at base camp.

By 10 February only a few were still strong enough to function well in the otherworldly conditions: Walenty Fiut, the unstoppable Zyga Heinrich, and the two youngsters on the team, Krzysztof Wielicki and Leszek Cichy. Andrzej moved them about like chess pieces, looking for the magical combination that would take them to the South Col. 'I was convinced it was only a psychological barrier preventing us from reaching it,' he said.[6]

Leszek, Walenty, Krzysztof and Jan Holnicki set out from Camp 3 on 11 February. Each one climbed alone, at his own pace, immersed in his thoughts. They reached the Yellow Band, continued towards the Geneva Spur, and began a long, exposed, slanting traverse. Partway across, Jan turned back, but the others reached the South Col at 4 p.m. A breakthrough. Leszek quickly returned to Camp 3 in the face of the screaming winds battering the col. Walenty and Krzysztof battled with their four-season tent but were unable to erect it in the wind, so they settled for a small, inadequate bivouac tent. They survived the night, but spent the entire time propping up the tent pole. The thermometer inside the tent showed -40° Celsius.

Base camp was worried. They talked on the radio throughout the night with Walenty and Krzysztof, encouraging them, calming them. There was radio chatter from other camps as well, including one rather badly received message from Leszek, who was resting in relative comfort at Camp 3. When he suggested Walenty and Krzysztof should continue since they were so near the top, his comment was greeted with howls of protest from the rest of the team. The next morning, the lead climbers fled, Krzysztof to Camp 2, complaining of frostbite in his feet, and Walenty all the way to base camp.

Andrzej sensed this was a critical moment: there was a perceptible shift in mood. 'How powerless is any leader at moments like these?' he asked. 'If I wanted to save the expedition, there was only one thing to do, and that was to attempt the climb myself.'[7] Andrzej had not yet been as high as Camp 3, and now he was proposing to climb the mountain. A preposterous idea, but within two days he and Ryszard Szafirski were on the South Col.

Andrzej knew he was unlikely to go any higher since he wasn't sufficiently acclimatised, but he had made a staggering effort in order to salvage team morale. It worked. Almost immediately there was a renewed energy. Oxygen bottles were soon cached at 8,100 metres for the summit team; Krzysztof and Leszek were at Camp 3; and Zyga and Pasang Norbu Sherpa were at Camp 4 on the South Col, feeling strong and ready to try for the summit.

As it was 14 February, they now faced a bureaucratic problem that seemed insurmountable. Their permit was about to expire and orders from Kathmandu were clear: no more moving up the mountain after 15 February. After that, the only allowable activity on the mountain would be to clear their camps and descend. Since Andrzej doubted they could climb it by that date, he dispatched a porter to relay a request to the ministry of tourism for an extension. The porter had his own ideas about a permit extension: he was fed up with the expedition and wanted to go home. So, he cunningly requested only two more days. Two more days, and the suffering would finally be over. Two days was all they got.

Climbing without supplemental oxygen, Zyga and Pasang began their summit bid on 15 February. The winds had stopped, but it was snowing steadily. Zyga was known for his careful attitude towards risk, and it soon became clear from radio transmissions with Andrzej that the accumulating snow was making him nervous. They reached 8,350 metres before turning around and descending: a bitter decision, but a new winter altitude record.

There were now only two alpinists high on the mountain: Leszek and Krzysztof. With just two days remaining on their extended permit, the pressure was enormous as they left their tent at Camp 3 on the morning of 16 February, bound for the South Col.

That night, the temperature plummeted to -42° Celsius and the wind continued to roar. 'We were in a trance,' Krzysztof recalled of the following morning, the last day of the permit. 'When we left towards the summit … we already had blinders on. Only the summit mattered … when you feel the nearness of the summit, you feel that it's within your reach. And it's easy to lose your sensitivity. You stop being able to measure your strength versus your ambition. And when you pass a certain boundary, then only luck is left.'[8] They understood there was no choice: Poland was Poland, and Everest was Everest. They had to climb it.

They lightened their loads as much as possible by taking just one bottle of oxygen each. Krzysztof could no longer feel his feet but he kept plodding on, drawing on his reserves. Moving without a rope, they took turns breaking trail through the snow. The two rarely spoke. There was no need. As they climbed higher, the jet stream hit them, knocking them off balance. Krzysztof recalled that the Hillary Step, the crux on the upper part of the climb, was surprisingly easy, being completely drifted in with snow. He clipped into fixed lines left by previous expeditions and soon after saw Leszek raising his arms: he was on the summit. Krzysztof joined him and recalled vaguely that they hugged.

The rest of the team was waiting. 'The tension was unbearable,' Andrzej said, reflecting the momentary intimacy of that group of men bonded by their anxious concern. 'Hope and despair followed one another at each passing moment. As the hours passed and there was still no word over the radio telephone, our anxiety was overwhelming.'[9]

At 2.25 p.m. Leszek's voice boomed over the radio: 'Do you copy? Do you copy? Over.'

'Negative, say again. Say again.'

'Guess where we are!'

'Where are you? Over.'

'At the summit. At the summit.'

As base camp erupted into screams of joy, Andrzej raised his hands to silence the commotion. He needed to be certain they were on the true summit. His voice crackled over the radio: 'Hey you, can you see the triangle?' The Tibetan and Chinese climbers who'd summited in 1975 had left a metal tripod to mark the summit. Leszek assured him they were standing beside the tripod, and he promised to leave a maximum-minimum thermometer, a small cross and a rosary to prove they had been there, and to record some data about winter temperatures on the summit of Everest. The following spring's Polish team planned to retrieve the items, but a Basque team beat them to it. Unfortunately, the Basque climbers didn't realise what the thermometer had recorded, so they shook it and lost the minimum temperature measurement.

Andrzej radioed Hanna at the PZA, where she had been anxiously waiting for hours. 'Today on 17 February at 2.30 p.m. the Polish flag appeared on the highest point in the world. Thereby the Polish team set a record in winter climbing. Best regards from all the participants. Zawada. Over.' Both Leszek and Krzysztof later admitted if the goal hadn't been Everest in winter, they would have given up weeks earlier. But the objective, and Andrzej's leadership, had inspired them to their highest level of performance.

Yet, as with all climbs, the summit wasn't the end of their journey. Before beginning the descent, Leszek gathered a few small rocks and Krzysztof collected a snow sample, a request from NASA. By the time they reached the South Summit, their oxygen tanks were empty. Almost immediately they could feel the brutal cold deepening in intensity. Their welding goggles proved useless in the blowing snow. Then their headlamp batteries died. Forced to continue the epic descent in complete darkness, Krzysztof started lagging behind Leszek, his feet in such pain he eventually crawled. 'I completely stopped thinking about my feet,' he said. 'I knew that it could be bad, but … usually severe frostbite only happens during a big accident or with a bivvy overnight without moving. When you're moving nonstop you might have some frostbite but not amputation.'[10]

When Krzysztof reached the South Col, he couldn't find the tent. 'You go crazy in these situations, and it's easy to make irrational decisions,' he said. 'I figured that if I was heading down and the tent wasn't there, I should go left. Then I thought, no, Tibet is there, so I should go right … I started to doubt myself. Go left. Go right. Go left. Go left. Go right. In the end I almost trampled the tent but it was a close call. Each of us descended independently. Of course, the knowledge that your partner is close by, and is waiting for you, is a sort of psychological anchor. But the battle for survival had to be fought alone.'[11]

Once in the tent, they radioed base camp. They had promised to call in at the South Summit, but couldn't afford the time. 'What could we have said anyway?' Krzysztof said, laughing. 'That it was getting harder? That we didn't know if we could get down? At some point, that feeling of solidarity with base camp – their words of encouragement – stopped having any meaning or value. You completely focus on survival.'[12]

He spent the night warming his feet over the flames of the stove, desperate to save them. Over the following days, the two managed to descend the rest of the mountain to base camp, where they were received as heroes. Krzysztof later remembered the moment when he and Leszek arrived, the camp awash with tears of joy, as the most marvellous experience in his mountaineering career. 'We had the presence of mind that we were part of a tribe – an expedition tribe – and in large part, because of luck, and a little bit because of our training, it was our turn to get to the summit … Often during expeditions there are elements of personal jealousy, but on the winter Everest expedition, that didn't exist. It was obvious that there was true joy in everybody's eyes that we had succeeded. Such a pure form of joy never happened again on any of my trips.'[13]

It was quite a start to his career on 8,000-metre peaks. 'At first I thought that Everest wouldn't be a big deal in my climbing career,' Krzysztof later said. 'But in retrospect, both emotionally and in building my self-awareness as an alpinist, it was a really important moment. Having summited the highest peak in winter, I was encouraged to think that others should go fairly well … Every success strengthens a person, increasing the belief in oneself. That's how Everest affected me.'[14]

A hero's welcome for Krzysztof Wielicki after having made the first winter ascent of Everest with Leszek Cichy. *Photo: Krzysztof Wielicki Archive.*

Upon their return to Poland, Krzysztof and Leszek became instant national heroes and Andrzej was hailed a brilliant leader. They had taken a step into the unknown, and had survived. But there were misgivings in certain quarters of the international climbing community. For the next two years, the Italian legend Reinhold Messner insisted they hadn't climbed Everest in winter at all, because officials in Nepal had recently shortened the winter season to 31 January.

Messner's argument did at least focus minds on when winter begins and ends. The question seems simple but, in the Himalaya and the Karakoram, the season's parameters are debated with passion. There isn't a winter climbing specialist who doesn't have an opinion on the matter. Calendar winter begins on 21 December and ends on 21 March. Meteorological winter begins on 1 December and ends on 28 February, or 29 February in a leap year.

Karl Gabl, an Austrian climatologist who is the go-to weather forecaster for many Himalayan and Karakoram winter expeditions, says: 'The mountaineering winter starts on 21 December and ends on 21 March. There can be weather situations before and after these dates which are colder and windier than days in the astronomical [calendar] winter but this doesn't matter.'

The official winter climbing season in Nepal is currently from 1 December to 15 February, dates which contrast significantly with the accepted northern hemisphere calendar winter spanning 21 December to 21 March. Most alpinists, particularly those who are active in Himalayan winter climbing, disagree with Nepal's definition. Mountaineering historian Eberhard Jurgalski acknowledges both 'first meteorological winter ascents', between 1 December and the end of February, and 'first calendar winter ascents', between 21 December and 21 March in his reports.

Messner, who was about to mount his own winter expedition to Cho Oyu in Nepal the following year, continued discounting the Everest climb for some time. He suggested the official word on the issue should come from officials in the country in which the peak lies. Himalayan climbing historian Elizabeth Hawley, who lived in Nepal, defended the Polish claim, saying, 'I am not amongst these quibblers.' Messner then accepted the fact the Polish team had climbed Everest, but *illegally*. When Nepal's ministry of tourism produced a certificate stating they had climbed it within the 'official' winter window, Messner finally said, 'Okay, I give up. They *did* climb it in winter.'

Unlike Messner, Pope John Paul II had no misgivings about the winter triumph. He sent a letter to the team, dated 17 February 1980:

I express my happiness and congratulate my compatriots on their success in achieving the first ascent of the Earth's highest summit in the history of winter Himalaya climbing. I wish Mr Andrzej Zawada and all the participants of the expedition further successes in this excellent sport which so brilliantly demonstrates the 'royal' nature of the human being, its cognitive skill and will to rule God's creation. Let this sport, which demands such a great strength of the spirit, become a great lesson of life, developing in all of you all the human virtues and opening new horizons of human vocation. For all the climbs, including the daily ones, I bless you all.

Following the stunning success of the 1979–80 Polish climb, two expeditions headed to the mountain the following winter, both hoping to write their own chapter of Everest in winter.

Six Japanese alpinists and five scientists led by Naomi Uemura, who had already climbed Everest in spring, wasted no time in getting to Camp 3 by

26 December 1980. But on 12 January, team member Noboru Takenaka slipped from a fixed line and was tragically killed. One climber reached the South Col in late January, but the jet stream forced them back and the expedition ended without success.

Not far from the Japanese base camp was a small team from the UK. Initiated by Alan Rouse and Brian Hall, it would be inaccurate to say the expedition was led by either, since they agreed from the start theirs would be an entirely democratic approach to a climb, each person making informed and intelligent decisions based on the situation at hand.

Alan Rouse was known throughout Britain for his bold approach to alpinism. With fine, even features framed by large wire-rimmed glasses and topped by a mop of unruly hair, he looked every bit the Cambridge-educated mathematician he was. Brian Hall was a study in contrasts: compact, powerfully built, with an intensity to his gaze that confirmed his forceful persuasiveness and conviction. Adding significant colour to the team were the Burgess brothers, Adrian and Alan. Identical twins, tall, blond, with rakish good looks and identical reputations for wild living, the twins brought years of high-altitude experience and strong survival skills to the team. John Porter brought expertise as well, much of it gained while climbing with Poles in the Hindu Kush and India, a considerable advantage for such an objective. Joe Tasker was already a superstar alpinist in Britain, having earnt his reputation in India, the Himalaya and Karakoram. Along with Paul Nunn and Pete Thexton this was a formidable team with powerful climbers and uncompromising personalities. And no leader.

Joe explained the objective: 'It seemed the most obvious thing in the world that we should now look to an ascent of Everest during winter, by its most difficult route and without oxygen.'[15] He was referring to the west ridge via the Hornbein Couloir, first climbed in 1963 by Americans Tom Hornbein and Willi Unsoeld. Unlike the Poles who had climbed the mountain the previous winter, the British alpinists weren't planning to use supplemental oxygen. Nor would there be bathtubs with steaming hot water at base camp. It was a stripped-down expedition with an appropriately stripped-down budget, something which may have contributed to their failure.

From the beginning, the UK team had difficulty finding porters to carry their equipment to base camp; most porters in the Khumbu Valley were already working for the much larger and richer Japanese team. Hygiene was also a factor. Base camp was plagued with dysentery, debilitating the climbers one by one. But the biggest problem was completely outside their control: the weather. From 1 January onwards, the storms did not stop. Even at base camp, the wind roared like a hungry, uncaged beast.

The British planned to climb Everest by 31 January since they were playing by the rules of the Nepalese government, which had issued a permit ending on that day. On that same basis, Joe doubted the legitimacy of the Polish ascent, believing that 'in official terms Everest was still unclimbed in winter'.[16] What he didn't know was that the Nepalese authorities had given the Polish climb their official blessing.

The first challenge was to open the route from base camp up to the Lho La, the col below the west ridge that separates Nepal from Tibet. They needed to push through 600 metres of rock buttresses, broad gullies blocked with unstable boulders and, finally, a steep, difficult corner opening on to a ramp arcing up to the Lho La plateau. When a large Yugoslavian team had first climbed this route in the spring of 1979, they had constructed a hand-operated pulley system to hoist their six tons of equipment to the Lho La. By the time the British team arrived, the pulley had been destroyed by rockfall and avalanches, so the Brits humped loads up on their backs, staggering under the weight, using fixed lines which they installed on more difficult sections.

Back in base camp, instead of relaxing in warmth and comfort, they shivered in their small communal cook tent around one small paraffin stove perched on the table to offer some semblance of heat. When the Japanese invited them over to their base camp for dinner one night, they discovered how the other half live. Thanks to an electric generator humming outside, the spacious mess tent was a luxurious cocoon, bursting with culinary treats and flowing in *sake*. The trudge back to the British camp was both wobbly and depressing.

The British toiled all of December on the steep terrain, trying to gain the Lho La. Joe described their life, high on the mountain: 'Words do not emanate of themselves the slowness of movement, the lassitude at such heights; memory cheats and passes over the blank spaces between events; half an hour to put on boots and then strap on crampons sounds ridiculous but is normal. Life on this mountain was a slow-motion actuality.'[17]

Nevertheless, when they finally reached the true West Shoulder of Everest, and could absorb the incredible panorama of Everest, Lhotse and

Nuptse, reaching the summit still felt possible. Unfortunately, it was already 23 January, only eight days until their permit expired. They negotiated a two-week extension, having dispensed with the purity of an 'official' winter ascent. But almost impossibly, the weather now worsened. John became marooned at Camp 3 for three days, alone in a storm. 'The cold penetrated deep into my bones,' he said. 'Sleep was impossible. The moment I dozed off, my breathing became fitful and irregular.' His descent off the mountain was nightmarish, sick with dysentery, delirious from fatigue, and lost in the dark. When he finally stumbled into base camp, he described how 'the bright light and warmth hit me like the memory of a lost world'.[18]

The expedition now began to unravel. On the morning of 31 January, Paul came over to John's tent in the pre-dawn light, poked his head in, admitting a blast of -35° Celsius air. 'I've been thinking,' he said. 'We need to leave. If we don't, someone is going to die.' John agreed, later saying, 'Everyone nearly died at least once on that trip I believe, except perhaps for Joe.' By 10 a.m., the pair had gone.

The team's momentum stalled, since only Adrian and Joe remained high on the mountain. Nobody else was fit or healthy enough to climb up to support them. When they returned to base camp the final time, Adrian unleashed his anger about the lack of support. 'Somebody should have dug a cave for [Camp] 4 and others carry rope. But nobody came up. It's unfortunate that the mind drives the body and when the mind has given up, the body ceases to function.' Alan concluded that their chosen objective might be possible, but not for them. Not that year. Joe disagreed, saying, 'We didn't stick our neck out enough.'[19] The expedition was finished.

When Adrian later reflected on their experience, he accepted his statement had been made in haste and in anger. His understanding of the relationship between mind and body had evolved. 'I had not thought about how the body forces the decision upon the mind … It is a delicate balance between driving oneself to exhaustion and listening to the body as it strives to survive without oxygen, food and heat.'[20]

Nearly every moment had been a test. They had survived the harrowing conditions for two solid months. They hadn't lost control of their ambitions by risking too much. And they had all returned from the mountain with no major accidents. In contrast, the sensation that Krzysztof Wielicki described when he and Leszek left Camp 4 the last morning, heading to the summit, was 'out of control'. They got away with it, but barely. The British team chose life over luck. As Joe wrote afterwards: 'The pain is forgotten and the dream remains.'[21] But for Joe, for Al and for Pete, those dreams ended tragically in the mountains: on Everest, K2 and Broad Peak.

Winter attempts on Everest continued, year after year. The Japanese, South Koreans, French, Belgians, Spanish and Americans all sent teams, some elaborate and expensive, others lean and light. They approached from all sides: via the South Col, the south-west face, the north-east ridge and on and on. There were individual attempts in the winter of 1992–93 by Spaniard Fernando Garrido and in 2018 by Basque superstar Alex Txikon, both with Sherpa support. Japanese alpinist Yasuo Kato managed to reach the summit alone in the winter of 1982–83, but died on descent. There was even a husband and wife attempt, each leading an expedition from opposite sides of the mountain with the intention of meeting on top. Japanese and South Korean teams did succeed in subsequent years but when you consider that thirty expeditions attempted Everest in winter between 1979 and 2018 and only five succeeded, the seriousness of the objective is evident. Perhaps they thought it would be easy. After all, the Poles had climbed it on their very first try.

2

MANASLU

Zakopane Boys

You can't test courage cautiously, so I ran hard and waved my arms hard, happy.
Annie Dillard, *An American Childhood*

After the astonishing success on Everest in the winter of 1979–80, it was only a question of when another 8,000er would be climbed in the coldest season. Manaslu, at 8,163 metres, is the eighth-highest mountain in the world. Located in west-central Nepal, the mountain's meandering slender ridges lend it an elegance that belies the ferocious steepness of its upper elevations. The mountain has two sharp summits, the eastern one, somewhat lower at 7,992 metres, being an ethereal spire that pierces the sky. Together, they form a stunning panorama.

First climbed by the Japanese in the spring of 1956, the peak is often referred to as a 'Japanese' mountain in climbing circles. Fittingly, a Japanese team arrived in December 1982, hoping to make the first winter ascent. Led by the famously strong and ambitious Noboru Yamada, the ten-member team climbed steadily until high winds forced them back at 7,700 metres. Tragedy then struck when Takashi Sakuma was blown off the mountain while retreating.

The Japanese weren't the only ones beaten down by howling gales. The following winter, a four-person Canadian team led by Alan Burgess, part of the British Everest winter attempt two years earlier, turned around at 6,850 metres. They at least made it down with no fatalities. Noboru Yamada would eventually return for another try at Manaslu in winter, and succeed, but not before the intrepid Poles arrived.

Their leader was Lech Korniszewski, a mountaineer and physician who often performed double duty on expeditions. Lech's first taste of expedition life came in 1978 as doctor for the joint Polish–British team that included John Porter on India's Changabang. The invitation had come as a surprise to Lech: 'I was forty-two years old. I said to myself: "now or never".' Lech took part in another successful expedition the following year on Peak 29, also known as Ngadi Chuli. Close to Manaslu, and at 7,871 metres a true Himalayan giant, it has not been climbed since. In 1980 he was on the spring Everest expedition led by Andrzej Zawada.

Smitten by the Himalaya, when he wasn't busy with his medical practice, Lech started working on a Manaslu winter permit. He submitted his application in 1981, and Nepal finally granted permission in 1983. Along with support from the Zakopane branch of the PZA, he financed the expedition with profits from smuggling operations from previous trips. Taking full advantage of communist Poland's false economy, where products were artificially cheap, climbers routinely filled their outgoing expedition trucks with Polish goods, sold them in India and Nepal, and returned to Poland with hard currency. Every Polish mountaineer travelling abroad participated in these activities to help finance their nomadic lifestyle.

One of the eleven Manaslu climbers was Maciej Berbeka, an alpinist from Zakopane, an idyllic mountain town nestled in the Polish Tatras. Lech knew Maciej from the expedition to Peak 29, where he had become intimately familiar with Maciej's teeth, since he had been forced to extract one of them during the climb.

Maciej was born in 1954 into a respected Zakopane mountain family. His mother Elzbieta and father Krzysiek were both sporty. Living in the mountains, it was natural that climbing would be one of their activities. During their courtship, Elzbieta recalled, 'I charmed him because I was a better skier than he was.'[1] They obviously got on well, because at the age of seventeen, Elzbieta was pregnant with Maciej. Despite the scandal they caused at their local high school, they married and settled down in Zakopane, where Krzysiek became a mountain rescue specialist. Little Maciej would often accompany his dad to the rescue room, marvelling at the ropes and ice axes and all kinds of intriguing pieces of metal. 'People there served as an example to me, as authority figures, an ideal beyond the reach of a kid like me,' he said.[2]

When Krzysiek was killed in an accident in the Swiss Alps, the family dynamic changed. Elzbieta was no longer keen on Maciej spending time in

Left: Polish Himalayan climber Maciej Berbeka, who began his Himalayan winter career by making the first winter ascent of Manaslu, 12 January 1984. *Photo: Maciej Berbeka Archive.*

Centre: Ewa Berbeka, young wife of Maciej. *Photo: Maciej Berbeka Archive.*

Right: Polish Himalayan climber Ryszard Gajewski, who made the first winter ascent of Manaslu with Maciej Berbeka, 12 January 1984. *Photo: Jerzy Porębski.*

the mountains, but it was too late. By then he was destined to become a climber and mountain rescue specialist, like his dad. Both Maciej and his brother Jacek were in love with mountaineering, though they tried to restrain themselves for their mother's sake. 'We were always saying that we won't operate in the Alps, and we won't climb together,' Jacek explained, carefully excluding the Himalaya from their promise to Elzbieta.

One of Maciej's most frequent partners was Ryszard Gajewski. The two were friends 'almost from birth', as Ryszard often said. Their fathers worked together on the mountain rescue team, they were in the same grade, and they began climbing together at the age of fourteen. They would skulk around, slipping their equipment out of the door so as not to alarm Elzbieta before heading up into the hills. Both were athletic and mountain fit, Ryszard with his long and lean profile, in sharp contrast to Maciej's broader frame. While still in their teens, they travelled across Poland on Ryszard's motorbike, hunting for climbs. After they made the third winter ascent and first one-day ascent of *Komin Węgrzynowicza*, a forbidding wall in the Tatras, the climbing community began nodding their heads in admiration and the Polish climbing magazine *Taternik* wrote about them. So it was no surprise that when the PZA announced an expedition to Peak 29 in 1979, both Maciej and Ryszard were invited.

Their first Himalayan adventure was a success, although Maciej didn't reach the summit. His return to Zakopane was marred by a bout of hepatitis and the shock that his girlfriend had dumped him. What's more, he wasn't invited to Andrzej Zawada's winter expedition to Everest later in the year, something he wanted badly. Particularly since Ryszard was going.

The silver lining to all this disappointment was that he met Ewa, his future wife. Both Maciej and Ewa had studied fine arts, and it was their love of design that initially brought them together. They formed a handsome couple, Maciej with his muscular physique, his broad face and kind eyes, and Ewa the brilliant stage designer, slight and fair-haired, with fine, elegant features. As with Elzbieta and Krzysiek, the romance progressed quickly and their first child arrived early, three months after they exchanged wedding vows.

Maciej continued climbing and Ewa became acquainted with worry, the bane of all alpinists' partners. 'I was scared, but I also felt that nothing would ever happen on these expeditions,' she said.[3] His first 8,000-metre summit was Annapurna Middle Peak in 1981, a subsidiary of Annapurna itself. As expedition life intensified, he was soon spending three to five months a year in the high mountains, returning to Zakopane to recover and plan for the next trip. It was as if he had two separate lives: life in the mountains and life with his family.

Central to his existence as an expedition climber was the local Zakopane mountain club. It managed everything: the permits required to access his passport which he needed to leave the country, the climbing permits, even the special permits needed to buy expedition food. Top-level climbers led privileged lives compared to other Polish citizens, since they could travel abroad and buy scarce food products. 'We were on top of the world,' fellow climber Janusz Majer said. 'The clubs became micro-communities within the country. People worked *in* the clubs and *for* the clubs.' Alpinists spent all of their free time either with their families or with club members who had similar interests and values. They ignored the dysfunctional realities of the communist ideology and channelled their unfulfilled hopes and suppressed energies into a passionate love of mountains and adventure. Their tight mountain community provided a way to fulfil themselves and create meaningful lives.

When Lech's invitation to join the Manaslu winter expedition arrived, Maciej, of course, said yes. Ryszard didn't hesitate either, even though his wife was pregnant. His explanation was typically blunt: 'She didn't prevent me from going to the Himalaya because she knew I would go anyway.'[4]

Lech's team planned to make the first winter ascent of the mountain via the Messner route, which was of particular interest to Lech since Reinhold Messner had publicly stated a winter ascent of his line would be impossible. After eight days of trekking, they reached base camp on 2 December 1983. The elevation was rather low at 4,000 metres, so they built an advanced base camp (ABC) at 4,400 metres on the Thulagi Glacier the following day. Immediately above ABC was a wall of rock. In order to safely haul their many loads of equipment up the mountain, they installed fixed rope for the first 500 metres of steep climbing.

Steep headwall above advanced base camp on the Polish Manaslu 1983-84 winter expedition.
Photo: Lech Korniszewski.

Unfortunately, rockfall became an ongoing hazard on the wall and one of these careening stones was most likely the cause of a tragic accident. On 11 December, expedition filmmaker Stanisław Jaworski was about to descend the fixed line from Camp 1 to ABC, but mistakenly attached his belay device to an older line left by previous expeditions. The rope, which had been damaged by rockfall, broke; Stanisław fell 100 metres to his death. While the tragedy was unfolding, Ryszard Gajewski and Bogusław Probulski were erecting Camp 2 at 6,400 metres, completely unaware of what had happened below. 'We had very poor radio communication,' Ryszard said, 'and were communicating by leaving handwritten letters in the camps or at gear drops. We found out about his death on 14 December descending from Camp 2.'5

The team conducted a typical mountain burial by slipping Stanisław's broken body into a yawning crevasse, offering prayers to his memory and erecting a cross nearby. As often happens on expeditions, and as Lech later explained: 'After a short discussion, we decided to continue.' The loss was nevertheless a shock for the team; they were mostly young climbers, the average age being only thirty-one, and this was for most of them the first gut-wrenching experience up close with death. After establishing two more camps high on the mountain, everyone descended to base camp to celebrate Christmas. It's hard to picture the celebration, knowing their friend and teammate had perished only two weeks earlier.

The weather deteriorated badly after Christmas, the usual winter combination of high winds and low temperatures. The climbers had no access to weather forecasts, though they dispatched occasional messages to try and learn something about what was in store. The result was usually a five-day-old report of what had already happened. 'As if we had forgotten,' Ryszard recalled, laughing.

On 11 January, Ryszard and Maciej set up Camp 4 at 7,750 metres where, during the night, the temperature inside the tent hovered at a chilly -32° Celsius. They were on the summit the following day. The pair spent forty minutes on top, taking pictures, enjoying the view and – something almost certainly unique to this ascent – tapping out pitons left by a previous Korean expedition. They couldn't resist salvaging such expensive equipment. As Ryszard explained: 'We didn't have them [pitons] in abundance ... for climbing in the Tatras.'6

With their precious booty tucked in their packs, the two Poles now faced the descent, which proved much harder than the ascent, since hurricane-force winds were now blowing directly into their faces. They dropped to their knees at times, even crawling backwards down the slope. Ryszard laughed as he described the technique. 'If it is windy, and you can't stand, then you kneel, and if it is still windy when you kneel, and you can't go on, then you must crawl … I've always accepted the conditions in mountains with humility.'[7] It worked to a point, but Maciej suffered frostbite in his toes and Ryszard in one finger. When a second summit team set out a couple of days later, Camp 4 was nowhere to be seen. The winds had destroyed it and carried it away. The expedition was over.

The Poles had made the first winter ascent of Manaslu via a route deemed impossible in winter by the world's greatest climber. And they had done it without using supplemental oxygen, of itself an impressive achievement since oxygen is an essential tool in dealing with the intense cold at altitude in winter. Without supplemental oxygen, they had to rely wholly on their bodies' engines to keep their extremities from freezing.

The team dedicated their climb to their teammate Stanisław Jaworski, who had given his life for the ascent.

Lech's team had climbed the mountain so quickly they now had time on their hands. Their flight back to Poland was from Delhi, but rather than spend money they didn't have on expensive hotels, they embarked on a camel trek in Rajasthan. While astride their camels, two of the climbers, men who had recently battled winter conditions on an 8,000-metre peak, discussed the most terrifying moment of the expedition: a nurse's medical injection. 'I'm telling you, when she approached me with that needle, man, the world went black before my eyes, and how she stuck it in!'[8] Having survived Manaslu, the camels *and* the nurse, the team returned to Poland.

For Maciej, the experience had been a punishing one. 'Over there the altitude, plus the temperature, plus the wind, plus the exhaustion, makes us fight for every step … I think I wouldn't want to return to those nights at 8,000 metres in winter, because … it's simply a nightmare.'[9] And yet Maciej was already on his way to becoming a leading winter specialist on those same 8,000-metre peaks. Something about their cold lonely summits would keep drawing him back.

———

Even though the first winter ascent of Manaslu was no longer attainable, Noboru Yamada of the Japanese team wasn't discouraged. He returned in

1985 and succeeded in a physical and mental tour de force. He had summited Everest on 30 October and was back in Kathmandu, recovering. Not wanting to lose any acclimatisation, he and his climbing partner Yasuhira Saito flew by helicopter to Sama, and by 5 December were already in Manaslu base camp. They started up the north-east face the following day. On 14 December, they reached the summit, roped together to keep from being blown off the ridge, and were back in base camp the following day, continuing on to Sama without stopping. In just ten days they'd completed an ascent of an 8,000-metre peak in (meteorological) winter. Noboru, an almost super-human alpinist, summed up his season in the 1986 *American Alpine Journal*: 'I climbed three 8,000ers: K2 in July, Everest in October and Manaslu in December.'[10] Four years later, Noboru would be found frozen and tangled in ropes after winds of 300 kilometres per hour lashed Denali, Alaska's highest mountain.

There were plenty of winter attempts on Manaslu in the ensuing years: teams from Spain and South Korea, Japan, the Netherlands, the Czech Republic and even Denmark. In the winter of 1990–91, French climber Eric Monier tried to climb it solo, reaching an impressive 7,950 metres, before giving up. Hallucinating badly, he recalled talking to 'people' who had been accompanying him, including a woman who said she was a hundred thousand years old. 'The experience of loneliness was very intense,' he wrote.[11]

One of the successful expeditions was a team from Kazakhstan, which arrived in late 1995. On the team was the legendary Kazakh alpinist Anatoli Boukreev. With his shock of blond hair, lean physique and sapphire eyes, Anatoli made a strong impression. He moved easily, with a negligent grace. He had already enjoyed a busy Himalayan season, with a spring ascent of Everest and an autumn solo ascent of Dhaulagiri, both without supple-mental oxygen. He was back in Kathmandu, enjoying the sights and the oxygen-rich air when he met a group of Kazakhs on their way to Manaslu. They wasted little time inviting Anatoli to join them. 'I was tired, of course, both physically and psychologically,' Anatoli admitted. 'But I quickly answered yes.'[12]

It had been four years since Anatoli had climbed with his Kazakh countrymen, and during this period his country had changed dramatically: economically, politically, socially. But as Anatoli said, 'What didn't change was the spirit inside of us, which drives us to choose again and again the roads leading to the mountains, to choose difficulty and danger, and to reach beyond the material comforts of our civilised world.'[13] He was proud of the high-altitude performances of former USSR mountaineers, not only in the Himalaya, but in the Tien Shan and Pamirs as well. He rated those accomplishments equal to other great Soviet achievements: cosmonauts in outer space and the exquisite artistry of the Bolshoi Ballet. 'It was good to see this rebirth of our special breed of alpinism, and to realise that not all that was great had died, that it was still possible to see our heritage in the great powers of sport.'[14]

The expedition began in early November, too early even for the meteorological definition of a winter climb. One month later, on 8 December, eight of the ten climbers stood on the summit. Events then took a sombre turn. The two youngest members, Mikhael Mikhaelov and Dimitri Grekov, fearing the possibility of frostbite, had turned around on their summit bid. When the summit climbers reached Camp 3 on their descent, they realised the pair were missing. Base camp radioed up to say they could see them sitting in the snow on a steep face immediately below the highest camp. Something had happened, but nobody knew what.

With no rest and no time to rehydrate, Shavhat Gataoullin and Anatoli left Camp 3 and headed back up in the dark. Three hours later, they reached the two stranded mountaineers, who were now terribly cold and disoriented and needed help strapping on their crampons to descend the icy slope. They would not have survived the night out. Unlike so many other bad situations on winter climbs at high altitude, a tragedy had been averted. Anatoli attributed it to 'solidarity and collective action, the very qualities that the high-altitude climbers of the former Soviet Union had been famous for during their height.'[15]

Yet the ordeal was not over. As the four were descending towards Camp 3, two teammates climbed up to bring them some tea. While drinking it, one of the exhausted alpinists, Mikhael Mikhaelov, lost his balance and fell. He pulled off Dimitri and the pair toppled over a fifteen-metre wall of ice, pulling Anatoli after them. After twenty metres, they all came to a stop, thanks to the belay Anatoli had made to secure their descent.

Safely off the mountain, Anatoli wrote about his pride in the climb and its place in history: 'I would like to hope that it is only one of the important victories of a renewed Kazakhi team on its way to revival. Even more, I hope that the accumulated knowledge of previous generations of climbers didn't die along with the fall of the Communist era.'[16]

Anatoli was clearly instrumental in saving the lives of the two young men through his actions. Ironically, one year later, when he acted in a similar manner on Everest to save the lives of three clients caught out in a storm at the South Col, there were some in the mountaineering community who vilified Anatoli. The exuberant Italian climber Simone Moro was not one of them. He and Anatoli became close friends and frequent climbing partners. Simone had shown a preference for winter climbing at the tender age of twenty-five, making a winter ascent of the difficult south face of Aconcagua, at 6,959 metres the highest peak outside the Himalaya. It was then he discovered the beauty and solitude of approaching a busy peak in a different season.

In late 2014 Simone Moro would also attempt Manaslu in winter, with the young Italian alpinist Tamara Lunger. By then, Simone was a winter veteran, having broken the 'Polish barrier' to become the first non-Polish alpinist to make the first winter ascent of an 8,000er. The international climbing community initially thought his winter ascent of Shishapangma was a fluke, since his partner on the climb was Polish. But as Simone subsequently proved, he truly *was* an Ice Warrior, not a mere tag-along. By the time he went to Manaslu, he had already climbed three 8,000ers in winter. Tamara also boasted an impressive CV, including K2 without bottled oxygen. When Simone accepted her request to join his winter expedition, Tamara recalled how 'I was so happy and I felt so strong and it was my next step.'

Unfortunately, their arrival at base camp coincided with half a metre of new snow and ultimately it was snow that defeated them. It never stopped snowing: entire camps buried by the stuff, their time spent shovelling it off their tents. They eventually had to accept this was not the year for Manaslu.

Two years later, French alpinist Élisabeth Revol, who had already tried Nanga Parbat three times in winter and had made two solo ascents of Himalayan peaks, announced her intention to climb Manaslu in winter, solo and in alpine style: no Sherpa support, no fixed camps, no bottled oxygen, no fixed lines. 'On my return from Nanga, the idea of the Himalayas in winter would not leave me, and over the year it became almost an obsession.'[17] As daunting as it sounds, solo climbing is what Élisabeth knew and loved, but she faced a different kind of loneliness on Manaslu. On her previous solo climbs, she was near other teams. But once she launched up Manaslu, she was terribly alone, and she felt it.

Still, this petite French woman seemed motivated by the extremity of her circumstances. 'I became captivated by the situation and the challenge … I felt a boundless energy, and immense self-confidence, I felt strong … nothing seemed to exhaust me.'[18] Despite her optimism, heavy snow turned her back at 7,300 metres. 'To climb on the slopes of this mountain is the most arduous thing that I have experienced, always in a threatening atmosphere … I think I can say that this was the most committing attempt in my life.'[19]

Simone returned in the winter of 2019, announcing his intention to climb Manaslu in alpine style, without supplemental oxygen, together with Pemba Gyalje Sherpa, a Nepalese mountain guide. Once again, the dangerous snow conditions turned him back.

Of all the fine mountaineers who launched themselves on to Manaslu's snowy flanks in winter, it was only the Polish team, back in 1984, that succeeded in the true winter season. And it was those Zakopane climbers who raised the bar a significant notch, since they had done it without using supplemental oxygen.

3

DHAULAGIRI

The Looking Glass

Love unto exhaustion, work unto exhaustion, and walk unto exhaustion.
Mark Helprin, *A Soldier of the Great War*

Poland had been laid waste by the six wretched years of the Second World War. Between the German and Russian armies, the bombs and the tanks, the blood-soaked battlegrounds and grisly death camps, little was left standing. One of the most devastated areas was the city of Katowice in the south-west region of the country called Silesia. Things changed dramatically in 1950 when the Soviets introduced their six-year economic plan. One of the pillars of that plan was heavy industry – unlimited iron and steel – and the epicentre of this production was Katowice. The Soviets even constructed a railway linking Katowice directly to the Soviet frontier to transport steel from the massive Katowice works. It was in this visually desolate and polluted atmosphere that a community of hardcore climbers emerged, forged in the steelworks that gave them a living.

They didn't actually work *in* the steelworks. They worked *above* them, cleaning and painting the slippery, precarious industrial smokestacks that penetrated the leaden Katowice sky. Although the work was dangerous, it paid well, and almost every climber from the Silesian region honed his entrepreneurial skills high above the city, scraping and brushing and dreaming of the next Himalayan expedition.

One of them was Jerzy Kukuczka. Known by his friends as Jurek, he was a smokestack expert. He had to be, since he was so frequently on expedition. His understated, down-to-earth appearance belied a fierce ambition and drive.

Polish Himalayan climber Jerzy Kukuczka, whose first winter ascent of an 8,000er was Dhaulagiri on 21 January 1985, together with Andrzej Czok. *Photo: Marek Pronobis.*

Like most Polish alpinists, Jurek began by progressing through the PZA system of instruction, both theoretical and practical. After a few months he earnt his rock-climbing certificate, although he never excelled on rock. His physique wasn't suited for the delicate dance required on vertical or overhanging terrain, clinging to minuscule holds, fiddling his way up a complex wall. A former boxer, he was built for stamina, not prancing. Voytek Kurtyka, his climbing partner for years, described him well: 'Jurek was the greatest psychological rhinoceros I've ever met among alpinists, unequalled in his ability to suffer and his lack of responsiveness to danger. At the same time, he possessed that quality most characteristic to anyone born under Aries – a blind inner compulsion to press ahead. Characters like that, when they meet an obstacle, strike against it until they either crush it or break their own necks.'[1]

After passing all of his courses and climbing in the Tatras, Alaska and the Hindu Kush, Jurek began his Himalayan career. Along the way he met Celina, a raven-haired, dark-eyed beauty who, after three years of dating, became his wife. Celina sensed the depth of his commitment to the mountains, and it concerned her. 'I knew it was possible to die there … It was in the back of my mind that this sport could be dangerous.'[2] Curious, she asked to join him at base camp on one of his expeditions. Jurek discouraged her. 'A woman in the base camp was not a good idea,' he said. 'If you're alone, you can concentrate better on the mountain.' At least he was clear.

Jurek's first Himalayan expedition was to Lhotse in 1979, and by 1984 he had already climbed six 8,000-metre peaks, all but one by new routes and four in alpine style. When Adam Bilczewski, from the nearby Gliwice Mountain Club, invited Jurek to join a ten-member team to attempt 8,167-metre Dhaulagiri in winter, there was no hesitation: 'Yes, I'm in.'

The seventh-highest mountain in the world, Dhaulagiri's very name, 'white mountain', denotes its dazzling beauty. But despite his enthusiasm for this splendid peak, Jurek had a domestic problem. He had just returned to Poland from the Karakoram in September, Celina was due to have their second child in October, and he wanted to leave again in November for the Himalaya. What kind of husband does that? A husband who was in a race with Reinhold Messner to become the first to climb all fourteen of the 8,000-metre peaks. Although the race was never formally declared, every Himalayan climber knew the two climbers were vying for the honour and Jurek, the poor Pole, was clearly the underdog.

His in-laws saved the day. When Celina's parents offered to help her with the baby while he was away, Celina agreed. She didn't really have a choice. As for Jurek: 'Any feeling of guilt about the desertion of my fatherly duties evaporated as I launched myself into a whirl of preparations.'[3] Jurek had evidently mastered the art of compartmentalisation. That process included subterfuge, because Jurek wasn't being completely honest with Adam. Even though Jurek craved a spot on the Dhaulagiri team, he neither painted chimneys to raise money for the trip nor helped organise the food and equipment. He didn't have time, for the simple reason he was busy negotiating a spot on *another* winter expedition to the Himalaya with Andrzej Zawada's Cho Oyu team. It was an unheard-of and incomprehensible scheme, and at this point it was exactly that – not heard *or* understood by either leader.

When Jurek showed up in Gliwice at the beginning of November with two barrels of personal equipment, the rest of the Dhaulagiri team didn't take him seriously. A week later he learnt everything had been shipped to Nepal, except his two barrels. There had apparently been some 'problem' with space in the truck. Jurek ignored the slight and sent a message to Adam: 'Please do not cross my name off the expedition list when you are in Nepal. I will join you. I am serious.'[4]

It's hard to know what Adam thought, but he must have accepted that Jurek played by different rules. The shimmering star of Polish Himalayan climbing was no pushover. Everyone in the Polish mountaineering community knew that once he decided on a course of action there was no turning him round. If others didn't agree with Jurek, particularly while on a mountain, he pushed on anyway, even alone. His record of success in the mountains spoke for itself: having Jurek on an expedition brought confidence to every single person on the team, particularly the leader. No matter what, Jurek climbed mountains – all the way to the top. That's what he did. So, it wouldn't have been too surprising if, at some level, Adam hoped Jurek *would* show up.

Jurek travelled to Nepal alone, behind the rest of the Dhaulagiri team. But before he could join them he had important business to attend to in Kathmandu, delaying even more his arrival at base camp. He needed to talk with Andrzej Zawada about Cho Oyu. Jurek met with Andrzej and his team to continue pitching his idea of climbing both Dhaulagiri and Cho Oyu that winter, adding two 8,000ers to his collection, thereby improving his chances of winning the race with Messner. Unfortunately, he explained, he wouldn't be able to go with the Cho Oyu team to help establish camps and fix ropes because the Dhaulagiri team had already left; he needed to rush if he was going to catch up with them. He would pop over to Cho Oyu later.

The team was shocked. It was an outrageously ambitious plan, extremely dangerous, and not fair. Zyga Heinrich, one of the most experienced and respected members of the Cho Oyu team, said, 'You must realise that this will be a serious blow to *our* expedition strength. You know that we have a very hard route ahead of us, and now, right at the beginning, you are withdrawing your assistance from the hardest work, that of establishing the route … Now you want to join us later … in my opinion you are creating problems which will go against the best interests of our expedition.' Most, but not all, agreed with Zyga. Andrzej Zawada didn't say much, listening to the discussion, occasionally nodding his head, a slight frown creasing his forehead. He would think on it. The following day he announced his surprise decision: Jurek could come to Cho Oyu after Dhaulagiri as a welcome addition to the team. 'It is a great idea,' he said. 'Rather wild.'5

Grinning with delight, Jurek raced to catch the Dhaulagiri climbers. On 20 December, he boarded the first bus to Pokhara, the largest town near Dhaulagiri. On arrival, he bought a ticket on a Fokker light aircraft to whisk him to Marpha, a village much closer to his mountain. Unfortunately, flying conditions had to be perfect for the Fokker to lift off. Two days passed. No flights. On the third day, passengers piled into the plane, ready to go before that flight was also cancelled. Jurek's spirits began to sink. There he was, stuck in Pokhara in a dingy, draughty room, a bed of boards, no friends nearby, bad weather, and it was now Christmas Eve. His thoughts drifted homeward, to Celina, to his two sons and to the warmth and light and love of the family celebration he knew was taking place without him. For the first time, he forgot about camps and fixed lines and climbing and summits. He tortured himself with visions of Christmas goodies and gifts and Christmas Eve candlelight mass. Alone, he lit a candle, boiled up a packet of soup, opened a can of sardines and read a passage from his Bible.

Christmas morning found him back at Pokhara airport, seated once again on the plane. Another cancellation. Painfully aware that with every passing day the Dhaulagiri expedition was moving farther up the mountain without him, he trudged back to the airport on Boxing Day for a repeat of the ritual cancellation. Except this time his prayers were answered: the tiny aircraft lifted off, threading its way up the serpentine valley, gaining elevation, bucking headwinds, tossing and heaving like a frisky bronco. Also on board were a couple of tourists, an American soldier on leave and a few locals with honking geese in their clutches; everyone prayed.

Jurek wobbled off the plane in Marpha and immediately began searching for a porter to guide him to Dhaulagiri base camp. The route was nothing to be cavalier about: it crossed two passes over 5,000 metres, and in winter that meant deep snow. He found a young man who agreed to go with him, but at twice the summer rate. The boy seemed fit and knowledgeable and even willing to cook, so Jurek accepted the price. But he had chosen poorly. The porter didn't know the way, could barely make tea, most certainly did not know how to cook, and was too weak to break trail through the deep snow. He was a liability.

While Jurek was struggling to reach Dhaulagiri, the rest of the team had been busy. They arrived with 100 porters on 4 December. The porters dropped their heavy loads of food and equipment, stretched out tarps to shelter themselves and erected tents for the climbers on meadows at around 3,700 metres. The west face of Dhaulagiri, clearly visible in the evening light, looked nothing short of magnificent.

Everyone retired to their tents that night relieved they had reached base camp with all of their gear and excited about the adventure ahead of them. 'At 5.30 in the morning I was woken up by a terrible roar which could be nothing else but an avalanche of tremendous strength,' Adam recalled. 'A moment later the tent tumbled down on my head.'[6] Ice séracs had broken off from the west face at a height of 6,000 metres and tumbled towards their camp, picking up more snow and ice along the way. When the avalanche ground to a halt about 300 metres from base camp, the resulting windblast completely demolished their tents, engulfing them in masses of snow and ice. They later found remnants of their camp as far away as one kilometre. Miraculously, nobody was injured.

The porters insisted on moving camp lower. The team agreed and lowered the camp by a hundred metres, but they clearly needed to establish a higher base to be effective on the mountain. They managed to convince seventeen porters to carry loads up the glacier to a height of 4,600 metres, where they established advanced base camp (ABC) by 10 December. Four days later, this was also destroyed, not by avalanche but by ferocious winter winds. They moved camp again, to an ice gully that offered some protection. In the meantime, it had started snowing. Constantly. As they stared up at the north face, their planned objective, they could see the growing snowpack was becoming too dangerous to climb. Perhaps the 'normal route' on the north-east ridge would be possible.

Since Camp 1 was already in place at the base of the north face, they now had to relocate to the north-east ridge by traversing a series of vertical rock faces. One of the trickier mountaineering manoeuvres is moving sideways; doing so at altitude, and in winter, even more so. Yet the Poles managed and having established Camp 2, everyone descended to base camp for Christmas. While Jurek ate sardines in his flea-bitten room in Pokhara, the rest of the team revelled in its esprit de corps and swilled vodka. Two days later, the climbers resumed work, hauling supplies to Camp 2 and fighting the elements, as vicious winds now reached hurricane force and temperatures hovered at -40° Celsius.

On 30 December, Jurek finally arrived at base camp. The first person he encountered was his old teammate Andrzej Czok. Andrzej was a powerhouse by anyone's standards. With three 8,000ers to his name, including Everest with Jurek, the dark-haired, powerfully built Gliwice native was known for his oxen-like strength and his infectious motivation. No surprise then, that he and Jurek would be tempted to rope up on this climb as well. Unfortunately, Andrzej already had a Dhaulagiri partner – Janusz Skorek.

When Jurek learnt the team had only reached Camp 2, he was relieved; he had been fretting that they were climbing the mountain without him, and would soon be packing up for home. Not so. As he said, 'There was a lot of hard work still to do; they needed manpower, and were very happy that I had turned up.'[7] Although pleased to have the extra help, there was one small issue: Jurek wasn't acclimatised. The rest of the team had already been at altitude for three weeks, working hard, gaining height, sleeping progressively higher. Every day that passed reduced the risk of pulmonary or cerebral oedema once they moved higher up the mountain. Jurek was at a distinct disadvantage, and a dangerous one.

Having previously suffered from altitude, both in Alaska and in the Himalaya, Jurek knew the risks. Now as he fought to catch up, he faced a delicate balancing act between pulling his weight, setting up camps and fixing lines, and the clear but unspoken desire for a summit bid. Too much effort on the lower part of the mountain could jeopardise his chances. Every alpinist thought about it, mentally calculating their output, their progress, their level of fatigue, and their rate of recovery. It was all part of the strategy: save enough energy for the summit.

On 12 January, Jurek, Andrzej and Janusz Skorek carried supplies to 6,800 metres. Six days later, in an ambitious push, Andrzej and Jurek pitched a tent at Camp 4 on an icy slope at 7,400 metres. They attempted the summit next day but bad weather forced them back from their high point of 7,900 metres. Jurek chafed at the irritating weather pattern. 'Clearings lasted at most half a day, then it snowed again with a bitter, penetrating wind … endless digging around in deep snow and a visibility rarely exceeding fifteen metres.' He described the challenge of functioning in these conditions: 'You had to rely a lot on your mountain instinct, all the time plagued by nagging doubts. Sometimes you simply did not know whether to go left or right.'[8] They retreated to Camp 3.

Adam, the leader, now had to step in to determine who would be paired with whom, and in what order for the next summit bid. Perhaps instinctively, he kept Andrzej and Jurek together, pairing Janusz with another climber for the subsequent attempt. Not surprisingly, there was friction between the two rope teams, both of whom wanted to be first.

Andrzej, Jurek and Mirosław Kuras started up from Camp 2. Since Camp 3 was completely buried by snow, they carried on to Camp 4. While struggling to climb into their down suits the following morning, they were startled by a sudden, silent mass landing on top of them. The avalanche didn't destroy their tent, but as it settled, it threatened to smother them. Jurek panicked. 'Give me a knife,' he shouted. Andrzej tried to calm him: 'Take it easy, take it easy, relax, we'll manage without a knife.'[9] They leapt out of the flattened tent to survey the damage. Andrzej was so rushed he neglected to put on his boots and stood in his socks on the hardening avalanche debris. Mirosław couldn't find his mitts, so he clawed at the snow and wrestled with the tent poles with his bare hands.

It took two hours to straighten out the poles and salvage the tent. By then, Mirosław's fingers were nipped with frostbite; he had to descend if he hoped to save them. Andrzej was also in trouble, but his difficulties weren't so immediately obvious. His feet had been compromised from standing outside in his socks, plus the zip on his protective outer gaiter jammed, further exposing his legs to the cold. Although it seemed insignificant at the time, every detail mattered at this altitude and in these conditions. The flow of warm blood to his feet was reduced to a trickle, and one by one his blood vessels began closing down.

Nevertheless, he and Jurek continued up, carrying the tiny battered tent with the intention of setting up a higher Camp 4. Their world shrank to a few square metres as they plodded up, step after step. Their rhythm was determined by the firmness of the snow: kick your crampon, shift your weight, swing your ice axe, pull up, swing your second axe, kick your second crampon. Repeat. Repeat. Repeat. At 7,600 metres, they stopped and set up their tent. Andrzej was strangely quiet that evening. He turned away from Jurek and massaged his legs and feet, trying to restore some feeling.

On 21 January, Andrzej and Jurek left the tent at 6 a.m. in a snowstorm. They moved up by instinct, peering into the murky half-light. Suddenly a blade of ridge reared up in front of them. They tiptoed up this technical rock section together, placing running belays. While this method is not nearly as secure as stopping to belay one another, it seemed the only option in these bitterly cold temperatures. A series of pinnacles and dips and hidden gendarmes appeared: confusing and tedious ground. False little summits raised their hopes and dashed them, again and again. Yet at no point did they stop to discuss whether they should turn around, or whether it was too late to continue. And finally they spied a bamboo wand on the highest point. This time there was no doubt: there was nothing higher. Relieved, they waited for a brief clearing to photograph each other, their faces draped in ice. After fifteen minutes they started down, the bamboo wand taken as treasure.

Partway down the ridge, at 4 p.m., Andrzej stopped to radio base camp with the news. 'We have made the summit, made the summit, over … '[10] Four p.m. is terribly late to be on or near a summit on 21 January. Only a month from the winter solstice, days are short. Within moments of calling base camp, darkness fell. 'We did not have the faintest idea which way to go,' Jurek admitted.[11] Wandering in circles, they realised they were in danger of stumbling on to treacherously steep terrain. A bivouac in winter at over 8,000 metres was a terrifying prospect, almost sure to end badly. But they had no choice. They hollowed a small depression in the feather-light snow and sank down on to their packs. It was -40° Celsius. With nothing to eat or drink, they simply huddled together, struggling to stay awake. Jurek occasionally slipped into a dreamlike state, only to wake with horror a few minutes later, convinced that hours had passed and he was frozen in place, dead. The night dragged on. They pummelled each other to keep blood moving to their extremities. They talked, offering encouragement and hope.

Down in base camp, Adam described the scene after having received their radio call. 'For the next seventeen hours there was no other message. These hours seemed to be everlasting. That night a heavy storm was raging at the base and I didn't know what was happening higher up. After twenty-five years I started to smoke again.'[12]

When the thin dawn light crept over the mountain, Jurek and Andrzej rose from their crouched position, unfolded their frozen arms and legs and began to move. In half an hour they reached the tent. Andrzej turned on the radio.

'Base camp. Base camp. We are at the tent. We are safe. We made the summit. Over.'

'Great news. Congratulations. We were worried about you. What is your physical condition? Over.'

'Okay. But I can feel nothing in my feet,' Andrzej answered. They spent the subsequent few hours dozing off, brewing tea and rubbing Andrzej's horribly swollen feet. It was 2 p.m. before they left the tent, confident it would be a straightforward descent to Camp 2 or lower. It was essential that Andrzej reach base camp where he could receive some medical attention. But they had miscalculated how tired they were. Their downward progress slowed to a crawl. Not even Camp 3 was now within reach.

Jurek slumped to the snow in near defeat. Andrzej continued ploughing down the slope, and since they weren't roped together in this moderate terrain, they lost sight of each other. Jurek raised his weary body, prepared to follow Andrzej, but the blowing snow had already buried his tracks. He panicked. He began to traverse off the ridge, could see nothing, reversed his steps and shouted. No response. Where was Andrzej? How could he have disappeared so completely? He must be in Camp 3. If so, it must be close. But where was it?

He kept plunging down the ridge, scanning ahead, peering left, struggling to spy some movement to the right, searching for Andrzej, desperate for a glimpse of Camp 3. When darkness fell, Jurek was still on the ridge, dropping blindly down. That's when he realised he would have to endure another bivouac, this one alone. 'I wanted warmth. I wanted a drink. I was afraid that another night like the last could end in a drama, but what else remained?'[13] He scraped a small niche in the icy slope with his ice axe and opened his pack to retrieve his headlamp. It tumbled down the slope. 'I sat down on my rucksack and the great battle for survival began all over again.'[14]

In that complete and utter darkness, time becomes elastic, one hour the same as one night or one day. Drifting in and out of consciousness, he became unaware of the wind tearing at his body. Soon, the hallucinations began: Jurek is in a well-lit village at the foot of the mountain, eating and drinking, warm and safe. Now, he is transported to the Morskie Oko valley in the Polish Tatras, to his favourite mountain hut. Six friends at the table. Candlelight. Special mountain tea. Laughing, drinking, telling tales: some of them tall. Late in the evening, they lower their voices. Someone asks, 'Have you touched the looking glass yet? Have you taken a peek?' Some look confused, not understanding the question. But a few exchange knowing glances with Jurek before looking down. They have taken a look. So has Jurek. They know how it feels to approach the thin edge separating life from death. And they know they'll go back. He pours another imaginary cup of tea, warming his cold hands.

At dawn the next day, Jurek was still alive. When he staggered into Camp 2, he called out in a hoarse voice. Andrzej and the other climbers at the camp emerged from the tents, relieved to see him. Andrzej's feet were in bad shape, but after arriving at 10 p.m., he had spent a warm night in his sleeping bag. Now reunited, the climbers rested, drank some tea, packed up camp and prepared to head down to Camp 1. It would be a straightforward descent, since the wind had stopped and the sun was peeking through the clouds.

Yet snow had drifted so heavily in the previous storm that they made little progress. Sliding and leaping from one drift to another, they were forced to bivouac one more time, the third night out in as many days for Jurek. They finally reached the security and comfort of Camp 1 in the late afternoon of the following day – all except Jurek. Despite the agonies of three winter bivouacs in a row, he had other plans.

Instead of going down to base camp and walking out with the rest of the team, Jurek had struck off for the French Col and the shortest possible route back to Marpha. Since it had been snowing continuously for the past few weeks, he was soon immersed in chest-deep drifts. Acutely aware of the passing time, he pushed on, flailing in the deep snow, burrowing to create a tunnel through which he could make some progress. It was a mindless wretched fight, which at times brought him to the edge of tears. After an entire day's effort, he could still see his last bivouac site.

For two days, Jurek fought his way through the snow. Each night he examined his feet, which had become slightly frostbitten on the Dhaulagiri descent and the three nights out. Each day the blisters grew. They became infected, oozing foul-smelling pus. He cleaned them, bandaged them, and carried on.

When he reached Marpha, he stumbled into the house where he had slept on the way in to Dhaulagiri. What had seemed a wretched hovel now felt like five-star luxury. They fed him, even offered him brandy to celebrate his successful climb, and then informed him the next flight out wouldn't leave for another three days. The nightmare of frustration was continuing for Jurek. He *had* to get to Kathmandu. The Cho Oyu permit ended on 15 February. He had another 8,000er to climb.

The following morning, he convinced a porter to compress the seven-day walk back to Pokhara into three. Off they went, the young lad carrying Jurek's pack, and Jurek nursing his blistered feet. When they reached the trailhead, Jurek hailed a taxi, arriving at Pokhara station as a bus was about to leave for Kathmandu. He leapt on board and reached the city that evening at 10 p.m. He then hobbled over to the trekking agency in charge of the Cho Oyu expedition and radioed the team.

While Jurek was racing around the country, trying to reach his second mountain for the season, Andrzej, his partner, had arrived in Dhaulagiri base camp. When he removed his mitts and boots, he was met with a sobering sight. His feet and hands were badly frostbitten. The team bandaged him as best they could and began the trek out. Despite the crippling pain, Andrzej started walking with twenty-five kilos on his back. That didn't last long. Soon he was being carried, first by a porter and then on horseback. Back in Poland, he sought treatment for his frostbite. Amputations followed. He had learnt the hard way that partnering Jurek demanded a superhuman level of stamina. At any point on their ascent, they could have turned around. There were a dozen reasons for them to have done so, not least the loss of feeling in Andrzej's feet. But Jurek was focused on the summit and Andrzej was just as motivated. In that sense, they were the perfect team, loyal to each other's dream. But it was Andrzej who paid the ultimate price, with the loss of his toes.

One year later, on 8 December 1985, Dhaulagiri was climbed again in winter, albeit with an early interpretation of the term 'winter'. The climb itself was spectacular. Three Swiss aces, Erhard Loretan, Jean Troillet and Pierre-Alain Steiner, started trekking to Dhaulagiri in the middle of November. When asked why he would choose to go to a Himalayan peak in winter, Erhard replied in his characteristic tongue-in-cheek style: 'There is nothing more difficult than spending the winter at 8,000 metres, and mountaineers, who are not to be confused with masochists, love to push their personal limits … My first winter expedition confirmed these two theories – the climbing conditions were excellent, and the weather was horrific. It was exactly what I had come for.'[15]

He certainly didn't waste any time. At midnight on 6 December, they crawled out of their snow cave at the base of the east face, intent on repeating the route which his good friend Voytek Kurtyka had pioneered in 1980.[16] They carried exceptionally light packs, considering what they were planning: a snow shovel, a bivouac sack, a few bits of food and, in Jean's pack, a sleeping bag – one sleeping bag for three climbers. You can imagine the jockeying at their first open-air bivouac. In response to a query about the lightness of their style, Erhard quipped: 'It was bold, but when you remove the turtle from its shell, it becomes a hare.'[17]

They spent the night clipped to three ice screws. Although firmly attached to the icy face, the deep cold gripped their bodies. They shivered uncontrollably. They negotiated with Jean for a sleeping bag timeshare. They spooned. Jean, owner of the sleeping bag, gleefully recalled: 'The poor boys froze all night.'[18] When the sun finally pierced the Himalayan horizon, without one word of discussion, they prepared to continue up. 'We got ready,'

Erhard recalled, 'and as if none of us had even thought of retreating as we lay awake, as if the words "give up" had never been part of our night-time vocabulary, we kept going. That was a revelation for me; the fact that in spite of it all we kept going that morning helped me understand that nothing can stop a determined person. To this day, I can't believe that none of us mentioned giving up. At that moment I said to myself, "Nothing is impossible."'[19]

At 1.30 p.m. on 8 December, they stood on the summit. A few candies, and a burning desire, had fuelled their ascent. It was Erhard's eighth 8,000er and his first in winter.

A couple of years after the Swiss trio's ascent, French speed climber Marc Batard summited even earlier in the winter season. He and Sungdare Sherpa reached the top on 2 December 1987, smacked by winds that clocked 150 kilometres per hour. Marc is one of the tiniest alpinists to ever set foot on a Himalayan giant. It's hard to imagine how his light frame held to that summit ridge without being lifted up and flung to eternity.

Two days later, a Yugoslavian team led by the unstoppable Stane Belak reached the summit as well. Stane Belak, known throughout the mountaineering world as Šrauf, was obsessed with Dhaulagiri. He led a total of four expeditions to the peak, including his first in 1981 when he climbed almost the entire south face, a remarkable achievement. But the summit kept eluding him, so he kept returning: in 1985, 1986 and 1987. Not once did he consider a straightforward or previously climbed route. His last expedition, late in 1987, placed Iztok Tomazin and Marjan Kregar on the summit close to nightfall on 4 December, in winds so strong they couldn't stand up. But again, despite getting extremely high on the mountain, for the fourth time, Šrauf did not touch the summit of Dhaulagiri.

There were other winter attempts and more agony on Dhaulagiri. But the greatest prize remained with the Polish team of 1984–85. It was a prize that drove the ambitious Jurek Kukuczka to seek out even more suffering that same winter, as though it was pain itself he craved.

4

CHO OYU

Two for Two

We climb onward, toward the sky, and with every step my spirits rise … I begin to smile, infused with a sense of my own foolishness, with an acceptance of the failures of this journey as well as of its wonders … I know that this transcendence will be fleeting, but while it lasts, I spring along the path as if set free.

Peter Matthiessen, *The Snow Leopard*

As soon as Jurek Kukuczka arrived in Kathmandu, he got on the radio to Andrzej Zawada's team on Cho Oyu, anxious to know if they had already climbed the mountain. 'Polish Cho Oyu expedition,' he said. 'Polish Cho Oyu expedition. Come in, please.'

'Come in. I hear you,' a voice replied. And then he heard what he had been hoping for. 'Catch a plane immediately. We are waiting for you. Over.'

Jurek went straight out and bought a ticket for Lukla, the gateway to Everest and within striking distance of Cho Oyu. Then he fumed for two days as flights were cancelled. On the third day, the aircraft lifted off. Having landed in Lukla, he tracked down a porter who agreed to walk the first three stages of the trek to Cho Oyu base camp in one day. Jurek's feet were still numb and oozing pus but they walked three more stages on day two. On the third day, the porter finally said 'enough', and refused to take another step. As if on cue, a runner appeared from the Polish team, hoisted Jurek's pack on to his back, and marched back up the trail.

As he trudged onward, Jurek recalled his meeting with Andrzej Zawada and the Cho Oyu team in Kathmandu before they had departed for the mountain. When he had explained his ambitious scheme to climb Dhaulagiri first, before sprinting over to Cho Oyu to join them and hopefully slip in a summit bid, more than one member of the Polish–Canadian Cho Oyu team had protested that it wasn't fair. They would have done all the hard work of opening and equipping the route; Jurek would be landing just in time to summit. They had been counting on his help on the mountain, not to watch him simply clip into their fixed lines, sleep in their camps and tag the top. His late arrival would be a burden on the team, they had claimed; after all, it was a *winter* expedition. They regarded Jurek's request as self-serving in the extreme. Of course, they all knew about his race with Messner, and they understood Cho Oyu would bring him closer to his goal. But fair was fair, and this wasn't.

When the vote was taken it had been an even split. Everyone had looked at Andrzej. He was the leader, the schemer, the politician and visionary. He stared back at his 'Zawada Boys'. Each one of them had worked hard to be on this expedition. They had painted smokestacks to earn funds for the trip, left their wives and children with the full knowledge they might not return. But Jurek was special, and if anyone could pull off two 8,000ers in one winter, it would be him. A success like this would not only enhance Jurek's reputation, but also add value to the Cho Oyu climb, and to the Polish alpine community as a whole. It would raise the standard for winter climbing in the Himalaya, in addition to the new route they planned to tackle. Andrzej said yes.

At 2 p.m. on 9 February 1985, Jurek arrived at Cho Oyu base camp. His first question was about food. 'Do you have any *golonka* [pig's knuckles]?' Base camp was well supplied with this Polish speciality, so he sat down and enjoyed his best meal in weeks.

The sixth-highest mountain in the world, 8,188-metre Cho Oyu is twenty kilometres west of Everest at the head of the Gokyo valley. Its southern flanks are immense, and it was here, at the foot of the south-east pillar, that base camp was located. The expedition was already in full swing; the boys had been working hard on a new route up the pillar: camps were established and stocked with food, and a web of fixed lines laced the mountain.

Maciej Berbeka and Maciej Pawlikowski were at Camp 4, poised for the first summit push, with two more climbers at Camp 3 as backup and positioned for a second summit attempt. The tough, no-nonsense mountaineer Zyga Heinrich would form the third summit team with Jurek. When word came down that one of the Camp 3 climbers was retreating, the timetable shifted. Zyga and Jurek mobilised immediately: Jurek repacked, changed his socks and readied himself for an early-morning departure for Camp 1.

Next day they shot up to Camp 1, clipping into the fixed lines as they went, and continued the day after to Camp 2, where they would wait for the

Above: Maciej Pawlikowski and Maciej Berbeka after their first winter ascent of Cho Oyu. *Photo: Andrzej Zawada.*

Right: Polish Himalayan climber Zygmunt Heinrich, who, with Jerzy Kukuczka, was on the second summit team to climb Cho Oyu in winter. *Photo: Janusz Kurczab.*

two Maciejs to summit and begin their descent. Jurek and Zyga planned to skip Camp 3 and climb directly to Camp 4 at 7,200 metres, accelerating the pace of their ascent since they were both acclimatised, Zyga from his time on Cho Oyu and Jurek from his previous climb on Dhaulagiri.

While Jurek and Zyga waited expectantly in Camp 2, the atmosphere in base camp was jittery. Through their binoculars they could see two tiny dots creeping across the upper icefield. One disappeared, then the other. Andrzej Zawada grabbed the radio.

'Hello, do you hear me?' He heard only a crackling roar, the sound of the wind. 'Are you on top? Tell me if you are at the top. Over.'

A faint voice answered. 'I don't know. I don't know, but there is nowhere higher to go!' Maciej Berbeka and Maciej Pawlikowski were indeed on the summit, lying face down on the snow in fear of being blown off the mountain.

'We understand you. You are at the top. At the top.' Andrzej could not contain himself. 'Jesus! Ah! What joy! Such a climb, and in the winter!'

Their attempts to take pictures nearly ended in disaster. 'We instantly lost feeling in our hands,' Maciej Berbeka recalled, 'and even if we wanted to think about anything, the loss of sense of touch in hands and feet was progressing.'[1] They wasted little time before beginning the long descent.

Now it was Zyga and Jurek's turn. One thousand vertical metres lay before them. When they met the triumphant summiteers descending to base camp, Jurek admitted to a twinge of envy: not only had they nabbed the first winter ascent of Cho Oyu, this was the second time Maciej Berbeka had made the first winter ascent of an 8,000er, something Jurek had yet to do. What ambition!

Due to the immense height gain between camps 2 and 4, and the short winter day, Zyga and Jurek were at the most difficult section of the route as darkness fell. Then, while changing his batteries, Jurek dropped his headlamp. For the last 160 metres below Camp 4, he climbed by instinct, systematically driving each ice axe as firmly and efficiently as possible into the ice, listening for the familiar *thwunk* indicating a good placement. With both axes securely in place, he moved one cramponed foot up, slammed it into the ice, tested it, then moved the other foot, repeating this over and over, focused in the gloom on making each point of contact solid.

It was completely dark when Zyga fell, penduluming across the steep, icy face. As Zyga struggled to right himself, Jurek became dangerously cold waiting at the belay above him. It felt interminable as Zyga climbed slowly back across to the route, and then continued up. He finally reached Jurek but they had no idea where Camp 4 was and so hauled out their bivvy sheet, excavated a small hollow in the snow, sat on their packs, nestled together, and waited for morning. The temperature dropped and wind tore at their flimsy tarp as they shivered the night away. The dim light of dawn revealed a cruel sight: the tent was a mere sixty metres away. Crawling out of their bivouac, they staggered to the tent, where they collapsed in a heap and brewed some tea. Only a short rest, they thought. An hour at most, then continue up to the summit. An hour passed. Then another. They drifted off in the warmth of their sleeping bags. They drank more tea. The day passed, as did the night.

They woke early on the morning of 15 February, the last day of the permit. There was no discussion about which way to go but after several hours of plodding upwards, it was clear both Jurek and Zyga were moving too slowly. Zyga was probably not sufficiently acclimatised and Jurek was depleted from his Dhaulagiri climb. At 4 p.m. they were still nowhere near the summit. They stopped for a brief rest, leaning on their axes.

'What should we do?' Jurek asked. 'We might reach the summit before sunset, but we will certainly face a descent in the dark. And we might need to bivouac again.' It was an unusual question from Jurek; he rarely settled for anything less than the summit, regardless of the time, the weather or his level of exhaustion. Zyga was known as a careful climber, a conservative climber. Jurek half-expected the decision would be to descend so was genuinely shocked when Zyga rasped, 'We are too close to the summit … we go as long as we can.'

Jurek straightened up, turned around and continued plodding. The threat of another high-altitude bivouac loomed large, but he knew how to survive them. He'd had plenty of recent practice. But would Zyga?

At 5.30 p.m. they were on the top. When the sun slipped behind the ridge, the summit plateau became suffused in a warm purple glow. The temperature, however, was far from warm and plunged the moment the sun disappeared. 'I experienced a wonderful feeling,' Jurek said, 'as one step took me into another world. The steep walls and the knife-edged ridges vanished.'[2] After a few photos they began their descent in the gathering darkness.

Even Jurek couldn't have anticipated the level of suffering they faced in the ensuing days. Fatigue, frostbite, the altitude and cold all took their toll. Soon after leaving the summit, Jurek stepped off a steep sérac. When Zyga rappelled down to him they decided to stop before something even worse occurred. They spent the first night in a bivouac at 7,920 metres. The temperature at base camp was recorded at -33° Celsius.

With the light of dawn, they discovered they were only 200 metres from Camp 4, so crept over to the tent, exhausted and dehydrated. A full day passed while they drank and rested, and Jurek ministered to his bandaged and oozing feet. They barely made it to Camp 2 the next day, a distance which should have taken two or three hours. The descent was dragging on more slowly than was safe, but at least the depleted climbers were going down. The following day they planned to reach Camp 1 or, with luck, base camp. But though they were much lower on the mountain, and should have been recovering slightly due to the lower altitude, they couldn't push through their exhaustion. They crawled out of the tent much later than planned, then trudged on, slower and slower. Would it never end? When they reached the glacier on which Camp 1 was located, they spied tiny dots approaching them: their teammates coming up from base camp to help them down. Shortly before midnight on 19 February, they finally reached the safety of base camp.

The team had been waiting impatiently and was eager to leave, so they broke camp the following morning and headed down the trail. Jurek could now barely stand upright. His feet had deteriorated to a frightening state, but as he stumbled along his mind was racing. The two winter climbs placed him in a good position in his contest with Messner. Now he was determined to up the ante; he would do all of his six remaining 8,000ers either by a new route or in winter. 'This game was worth the candle,' he thought. 'It was big stakes.'[3] Each evening, the expedition doctor removed his soiled bandages, injected him with antibiotics, cut away dead bits of flesh, and then applied fresh bandages. Each morning, he began again, limping along.

Andrzej Zawada had gambled and won. As a leader occasionally criticised for his obsession with winter and the suffering it entailed, this climb proved Polish mountaineers could climb an 8,000er in winter by a new route, that they could do it with no casualties, and that two 8,000ers could be climbed in one winter by one man. It also proved something less tangible: that his climbers could rally their efforts not just for their personal ambition but for the entire team. Or in this case, for one man: Jurek.

When Jurek Kukuczka returned to Poland, he faced considerable criticism from the Polish climbing community. Despite admiration for what he had pulled off – two 8,000ers in winter, back to back – the fact remained he had climbed Cho Oyu on the shoulders of a team he hadn't supported. He hadn't fixed any lines. He hadn't placed any camps. He had parachuted in to a fully equipped mountain and climbed it. A summit on a silver platter, some said. He ignored the critics' voices and began planning his next ascent. It was hard to imagine enduring another 8,000-metre bivouac with his damaged feet, but Jurek had no time to rest. Messner wasn't resting.

While Jurek had been in Nepal, his second son Wojtek had lived the first months of his life. Celina had stopped working outside the home in order to raise their two young children. Essentially a single mother during this time, she relied heavily on her parents and Jurek's parents for support. While praising Jurek as a father, she had to clarify, 'When he was here, that is.' When they were together, the subject of Jurek's expedition life rarely arose in conversation. Celina often learnt about his plans from offhand remarks by his friends or from newspaper articles, including his plan to climb all fourteen of the 8,000-metre peaks. His life was divided into two separate worlds: climbing and family.

It was an approach Ewa Berbeka described in her marriage to Maciej as well. Home was home and climbing was climbing. The compartment-alisation seemed to work, at least for the climbers. Celina admitted she occasionally hoped that Jurek might give up mountaineering to be with the family, but she doubted this was possible. The longevity of their marriage was in great part due to Celina's acceptance of Jurek's double existence. The unconditional love from both Celina and Ewa is reminiscent of the late Wendy Bonington, wife of British alpinist Sir Chris Bonington, who once said: 'Love to me is the whole plant ... once we put conditions on something, that is cutting off one branch of growth. There are very often things about another person that you cannot understand, but to me that does not change whether you love them or not.'[4]

Maciej Berbeka's triumphant return to Poland was unmarred by the criticism Jurek faced. Ewa treasured his homecomings, but his son Stanisław described them in a slightly different light: 'Every time he came back from the mountains, he showed us slides and pictures and talked about the expedition.' Then he added, 'But in fact he never completely opened up in these stories, he didn't talk about his inner experiences or dangerous situations. I guess he kept it all to himself and experienced it deep inside. I think that, even though the mountains were always a part of our home and family, they were somehow reserved for Dad. And we agreed to that.'

They all understood his return would be temporary, that he would rest awhile, and that he would soon be planning the next expedition. That's the way it was for Polish Himalayan climbers in the 1980s: at least half the year in the Himalaya, three or four months at a time. But even though Maciej had chosen this life, every departure was hard. 'Goodbyes are very difficult,' he said. 'I dislike them a lot. I guess nobody likes this kind of farewell. You never know what an expedition might bring and how it is going to end.'[5] In 1985, on Cho Oyu, it ended well.

Not so in the winter of 1989–90, when a seven-member Korean expedition and a Belgian team led by Alain Hubert came to blows on the mountain. The Belgians claimed that as they began removing their fixed lines at the end of their attempt, they were attacked by three climbers wielding fists and sticks. Korean leader Lee Ho-Sang denied any Koreans were involved, but admitted a Belgian climber had received a serious head wound while his neck had a rope around it and his arms were tied behind his back. The Belgians fled and the Koreans reached 7,800 metres before giving up. In addition to the assault, Sherpa Ang Lhakpa fell to his death during the course of the expedition. Elizabeth Hawley, Nepal's legendary chronicler of Himalayan climbing, reported that Ang Lhakpa was one of five Sherpas to die on winter expeditions that year.

Three years later, on 10 February 1993, Swiss climber Marianne Chapuisat reached the top of Cho Oyu, becoming the first woman to summit an 8,000-metre peak in winter. Chapuisat was part of an international team that had no climbing Sherpas and used no supplemental oxygen. For Marianne, climbing Cho Oyu in winter was as unlikely as going to the moon. Only twenty-four, her previous high point was 6,959-metre Aconcagua. An 8,000er in winter was clearly *not* the next logical step. But love ignores logic, so when she fell in love with the Argentinian climber Miguel Sánchez, she accepted his invitation to Cho Oyu. Sánchez was on the summit with her, along with Spaniard Luis Arbues. Two days earlier, four of their teammates, including expedition leader Manuel González, had also summited.

More than twenty-five years later, Chapuisat was still thrilled at her ascent. 'Those last metres along the summit plateau are still etched in my mind as if it were only yesterday: the feelings are intact and strong, a kind of euphoria of living, an intense happiness.'[6] A modest woman, she credited her Cho Oyu summit to beginner's luck. She climbed Gasherbrums I and II and Nanga Parbat in the years to come, but Cho Oyu in winter remained the crowning event of her climbing career. It would take twenty-five years before another woman summited an 8,000er in winter, despite many dramatic attempts.

5

KANGCHENJUNGA

How Much is Too Much?

Death is always on the way, but the fact that you don't know when
it will arrive seems to take away from the finiteness of life.
Paul Bowles, *The Sheltering Sky*

The cost of climbing can be extremely high. For Australian nurse Cherie
Bremer-Kamp, it was unacceptably high: all of her fingers, all of her toes,
and the life of her husband, American mountaineer Dr Chris Chandler.
They had already made an attempt on Kangchenjunga West in the spring of
1981, but their climb had ended after an avalanche buried their equipment.
Determined to try again, they applied for another permit. When they learnt
the next available slot was a winter permit, they accepted.

On 15 January 1985, their forty-ninth day on the mountain, things went
terribly wrong. The summit seemed tantalisingly close in the clear thin air,
but they were deceived; it was still more than 600 metres away. The couple,
together with a high-altitude worker called Mangal Singh Tamang, had
spent the previous night in a snow cave, severely dehydrated and cold. The
temperature outside was -50° Celsius. Chris was in the cave melting ice on
their butane stove; Cherie was outside the cave, preparing for the climb. She
could hear that the stove had gone out and, knowing Chris was now
breathing deadly fumes, called out a warning to him. But Chandler's
situation was much more serious than gas fumes. He was fumbling with his
clothing and unable to attach his crampons.

'I can't see anything. I'm blind,' he exclaimed. She knew at once he was
suffering from cerebral oedema and that his only chance was descent.

'My heart froze and my fingers turned into claws,' Cherie recalled.

'My body must have gotten a sudden surge of adrenaline, and the blood vessels to my hands and feet tightened up as if a clamp had come down on a garden hose.'[1] Her fingers turned numb, white and hard as marble. She banged them together, but felt nothing. In his confused state, Chris laughed and wriggled as she tried to dress him with her fumbling hands. She and Mangal managed to tie him in to the middle of the rope and started their retreat. Chris stumbled and lurched, toppling over at times. Hours later, as darkness gathered, they stopped, dug a small platform on the snow slope and lay down in their sleeping bags, spooning Chris to warm him. When he slipped off the platform, he panicked and tried to run, but his sleeping bag tripped him and he fell backward on the slope.

'Will somebody help me?' he begged. Cherie tried to resuscitate him, but it was too late. Her husband was dead.

'I didn't know what to do with Chris,' she said. 'The traditional climber's burial, placing the body in a crevasse, repulsed me. Pushing the body over a cliff was equally disgusting.'[2] Instead, she propped him up on their little platform, his pack and his ice axe beside him. 'I would like to think that he remains there, frozen forever above this holy place.'

And so ended the first attempt at climbing Kangchenjunga, third-highest mountain in the world, in winter.

In late January 1986, twelve months after Cherie Bremer-Kamp left her dead husband sitting in the snow, a Polish team also gunning for the first winter ascent of Kangchenjunga returned to Kathmandu, subdued and tired. They had succeeded, but the cost had once again been too high.

Andrzej Machnik, a mountaineer from Gliwice who had been on both the Manaslu and Dhaulagiri winter climbs, was leader of the team. Andrzej's strategy was to assemble a group of fourteen high-altitude climbers who knew each other well, ensuring a smooth operation on what would undoubtedly be a long and difficult climb.

One of his first picks was Przemysław Piasecki, a climber from Poznań. Przemek, as friends called him, brought previous experience of Kangchenjunga. The 8,586-metre peak is a complex massif located on the border between Sikkim and Nepal. With five distinct summits, four of them over 8,000 metres, the mountain is a sprawling affair. Przemek had summited one of its higher summits, Yalung Kang, in 1984, and was familiar with the approach route, the safest places for camps, and the route through the lower and upper icefalls. His knowledge would save them precious time.

First they had to get there. Back in August 1985, they had packed eight tons of equipment and food on to a sturdy Jelcz truck, driven it north to the port of Gdynia and on to a ship bound for Mumbai, then known as Bombay: plenty of time to arrive well ahead of the expedition. But when the team arrived in Delhi at the end of October, they learnt that their supplies were still at sea, steaming towards India. Nobody knew when the ship might arrive: two weeks, three weeks, even six. As Przemek recalled, 'We were facing defeat at the very outset.' Three of the climbers scurried to Mumbai to be on hand when the ship arrived, while the rest of the team headed for Kathmandu: anything to escape expensive Delhi.

Another nasty surprise was waiting for them in Kathmandu. Inviting foreign climbers on expeditions had been an important feature of how the Poles financed their trips. The Kangchenjunga team had done the same, but mountaineers joining from the USA, UK and Brazil arrived with only 60% of the agreed funds. While they waited for news from Mumbai, they scoured the outdoor shops in Kathmandu where they borrowed, bought and rented used equipment. When the ship finally docked, the three waiting climbers sped north but it would be another two weeks before the team, their food and equipment were all in one place. Every passing day reduced their chances on the mountain.

One of the strongest climbers on the team was Andrzej Czok, the powerhouse who had not only summited Dhaulagiri with Jurek Kukuczka the previous winter but had survived two open-air bivouacs above 8,000 metres with him. Andrzej was one of the few Polish alpinists who could keep up with Jurek and match his endurance. But it wasn't clear if he would rope up with his old partner this year, since Jurek, who was also on the team, was once again planning to arrive late.

Jurek's race with Messner was reaching its climax, so a number of Polish teams were allowing him the privilege of joining their expeditions at the last, crucial phase rather than expend his energy and time preparing fixed lines and camps. He had done the same on Lhotse that autumn, arriving late from a successful summer Nanga Parbat expedition. Now he and Krzysztof Wielicki were joining the Kangchenjunga team late, after resting with their families in Poland following their attempt on Lhotse. Jurek and Celina had two young boys, and Krzysztof and his wife Jolanta, a son and two daughters.

The leave-takings were getting so difficult that Jolanta admitted Krzysztof had taken to leaving for expeditions during the night so as not to upset the children. Jurek had negotiated their late arrival with Andrzej Machnik, similar to the deal he had struck the previous year for Cho Oyu. Przemek assumed Jurek would be climbing with Krzysztof, since they would be equally acclimatised from Lhotse. It's unclear how Andrzej Czok felt about this arrangement, since he had been Jurek's preferred partner in the past.

As on Cho Oyu, some were annoyed at Jurek and Krzysztof's late arrival. Artur Hajzer, the youngest member of the team, observed: 'Wielicki and Kukuczka weren't exactly warmly regarded in base camp. They were treated more as the star players who were coming to shoot the goal, whereas the rest of the climbers had to play defence, guard the net and protect the expedition against an avalanche of problems.'[3] Krzysztof later admitted he could feel the tension. 'Yes, there is a grain of truth in that,' he said. 'That's just how it was … I didn't feel great about it. We wanted to improve that, and got to work right away, putting in the higher camps.'[4]

Few on the team could imagine the illustrious future of the ambitious Artur Hajzer. But on Kangchenjunga he was still inexperienced, and Bogusław Probulski, the man assigned to be his partner, was not pleased about the pairing. In fact, in the early morning hours of 5 January, Bogusław actually slipped out of camp, leaving a note that he was going to solo the peak. He was turned back below Camp 1 in the middle of the lower icefall, where part of the ice wall had collapsed, taking the fixed lines with it. As Przemek later commented: 'He was extremely lucky that he wasn't there a few hours earlier or he would have ended up under that heap of ice.'

Krzysztof recalled the organisational philosophy of the expedition was somewhat haphazard, but admitted, at the time, it didn't matter to him. 'Jurek and I were in such a rush, that only getting to the top mattered. The question of whom we were going with was secondary. We knew that we would be following the peak and not the leader.'[5] At least he was honest.

By 10 December, advanced base camp (ABC) was ready for occupancy. Within ten days, fixed lines were in place on the lower icefall and the steepest part of the upper glacier, and tents were set up at Camp 2 at 6,700 metres. While the lead climbers opened the route and equipped it for the rest of the team, porters carried loads of equipment, food and fuel up to ABC. By the time Jurek and Krzysztof arrived on 19 December, after hitching rides across Tibet on anything that moved, including a tractor, the lower half of the mountain was laced with fixed lines and equipped with well-stocked camps.

Then the weather changed. Heavy snowfall and hurricane-force winds ripped tents off the glacier and locked the climbers in base camp until 30 December. The following day, Jurek, Krzysztof, Andrzej and Przemek started up, intent on setting up Camp 3 at 7,250 metres. In addition to establishing Camp 3, they planned to cache bivouac equipment at around 7,750 metres, which would eventually be Camp 4. Andrzej and Przemek dropped their load at the high point and descended to Camp 3, but Jurek and Krzysztof opted to set up their tent and spent the night.

Jurek was disappointed that he and Krzysztof weren't moving as quickly as they had hoped at this altitude. They had counted on their residual acclimatisation from Lhotse, but the weeks of rest back in Poland had reduced much of their advantage. While frustrated with his own performance, Jurek noted that Andrzej Czok was moving even slower, battling a cough that worsened the higher he climbed. Coughing at high altitude isn't unusual, but Andrzej's cough seemed to be wearing him down.

During their first night in Camp 4, Jurek and Krzysztof considered making a rogue dash for the summit. Forget about setting up two tents at Camp 4. Forget about moving back down the mountain to rest. Forget about supplying Camp 4 with food. Simply go for it. But when the weather broke the next day, they descended all the way to ABC. It was much later when Przemek learnt of their intention, and later still when Krzysztof admitted to the lunacy of the plan. 'To be honest, I don't know where such an idiotic optimism came from. To be at Camp 3 and 4 for the first time, and wanting to go to the summit? Looking back, it was a bad idea.'[6]

On 7 January, the four lead climbers left ABC at dawn, planning to continue to the summit as a team. They kept together at a similar pace as far as Camp 2, where they checked in with ABC.

'How is everyone feeling?' asked Robert Janik, the expedition doctor. Andrzej's coughing was clearly audible in the background.

'Everyone is fine,' Andrzej responded.

'I think you should consider descending,' Robert suggested. 'Your cough is worsening. It won't improve if you go higher.'

'No, I'm feeling okay,' Andrzej replied. 'I'll continue to Camp 4 tomorrow.'

Przemek tried to put Andrzej's cough into perspective. 'We were all coughing. The night temperature in ABC was -20° Celsius or lower. In Camp 2 the reading on the thermometer dropped below its scale: well below -40° Celsius. The wind was reinforcing the cold and freezing our throats. Breathing the ice-cold air was causing irritation of the upper respiratory tract, even mild inflammation. At times, during the evening in ABC, one might have thought this was a consumptives' sanatorium and not an alpinists' camp.'

They continued up. No longer roped together, each climber moved at his own pace, scattered across the slope below Camp 4. Jurek and Krzysztof arrived first, Przemek about half an hour later, carrying the second tent. He immediately started hacking at the icy slope in order to create a platform. Andrzej arrived an hour and a half later. 'He was exhausted,' Przemek said. They crawled inside the tent, which was so small they were forced to lie head to toe. Andrzej rested with his head at the back of the tent, while Przemek's was at the entrance, more convenient for lighting the stove and melting ice for water. It sounds simple enough, but the tedious process of melting ice was fraught with danger. A tiny lapse of concentration or a sudden movement could spill a tin of water on to a sleeping bag: a disaster in these temperatures. While Przemek cooked, Andrzej's cough intensified.

Jurek and Krzysztof were in the other tent, doing exactly the same: melting ice, preparing drinks, and resting. They could both hear that Andrzej was suffering. 'He was not the Andrzej I knew, always in excellent condition and the best, the most reliable ox as far as mountain work was concerned,' Jurek said. 'Now he was only making progress by sheer willpower and he never stopped coughing.'[7]

After resting, rehydrating with warm tea, and taking a diuretic prescribed by the expedition doctor, Andrzej felt somewhat better. Well enough to dismiss the suggestion of a retreat while talking to ABC during a radio call. All that separated them from the summit was 800 metres of moderate terrain. 'However, I soon lost any remaining hope when listening to my partner's cough and shallow breathing later that evening,' Przemek recalled. 'I knew already he would need to start descending in the morning and he wouldn't be able to do so on his own. This was the end of my dream of climbing Kangchenjunga.'

Since the tents were only a few metres apart, Jurek later admitted it was hard to fall asleep because of all the coughing. He eventually called over to ask what their plans were. 'I'm feeling really rough. I think I'll be going down,'

Andrzej said. 'Fine,' said Przemek. 'In that case we'll go down together.' Jurek answered, 'Okay, so we'll try and go for the summit.'[8]

Shortly before dawn, Jurek and Krzysztof began climbing, taking the only radio with them. Andrzej and Przemek were slower to leave the tent since Andrzej was weak from his wretched cough. Przemek helped him attach his crampons and emptied the contents of Andrzej's pack into his. They started down around 8 a.m., moving quickly at first, using the fixed lines below Camp 4. 'I was descending in front of him in the direct line of a potential fall,' Przemek explained. Then Andrzej began lagging, stopping every few steps to catch his breath. Halfway to Camp 3, Andrzej sat down, unable to move. Przemek slammed his ice axe deep into the wind-hardened snow and secured Andrzej to the makeshift anchor. 'I promised to come back with help,' he said. Although he could see Camp 3 in the distance, he couldn't call for help because he had no radio.

The four climbers at Camp 3 had been watching as Andrzej and Przemek descended. Sensing something was wrong, they had already started up before Przemek reached camp. They first tried to carry Andrzej down but it proved so difficult and dangerous, they eventually placed him in a sleeping bag, bound it with a rope, and slid him down to Camp 3. Ludwik Wilczyński, a climber and classical musician from the Kraków area, offered to scoot down to Camp 1 and bring an oxygen bottle up to Camp 3 for Andrzej. When Przemek radioed ABC, they were shocked at the news. They had heard nothing on the radio the entire day and were surprised that the team of four was now two teams of two going in opposite directions, with one person in trouble.

Andrzej was now so weak he could no longer talk. When he coughed, those helping him heard a crackling sound in his lungs, a likely symptom of pulmonary oedema. After placing him in a tent, still wrapped in his sleeping bag, Przemek slipped two folded backpacks under his head and shoulders, hoping it would ease his laboured breathing. Coached by the expedition doctor, Przemek nursed Andrzej with strong rehydrating drugs. 'Over a number of hours, I was either emptying his urine container or melting ice to provide him with water, sip by sip, so he could avoid extreme dehydration,' Przemek recalled. 'Those were long hours. I was growing anxious about Andrzej's fate and fighting my own extreme fatigue. Many hours of long descent, constant concentration and control over my partner's every move, exhausted me completely.' Their descent, which would normally take an hour and a half, had taken six hours.

During those hours, Jurek and Krzysztof had been moving in the opposite direction, trudging upward in the thin, cold air. After only a few hundred metres they lost feeling in their legs. At 10 a.m. the sun finally appeared, warming them slightly. Krzysztof sat down on the snow, took off his boots, and rubbed his feet furiously. He had bought the boots in Kathmandu, leftovers from a French winter Everest expedition. They were supposedly cutting-edge – a new prototype – but unfortunately were one size too small.

Each of the climbers moved alone, unroped and at his own pace. The climbing was easy, so there was no need to belay. They turned inward in that oxygen-deprived zone, as though the cold was entering more than just their flesh. Krzysztof tagged the summit first. He waited about half an hour – he couldn't be sure how long – and then started down. Jurek met him near the summit where they exchanged not one word: mechanical robots doing their job. After a few photos, Jurek also turned down. It seems like strange behaviour, this indifference to each other, but they were well past the stage of 'normalcy'. Krzysztof later reflected in conversation with Jurek: 'I'm not sure how it came about. I waited on the summit for you about half an hour. Just when I saw you approaching, I got up and started down. As if I could not have waited those extra few minutes.'[9] On further reflection, he added, 'Obviously it was freezing cold. It was windy. Maybe what I thought was, okay, Jurek's here. I can go down. But still, it's odd that we shouldn't congratulate ourselves at the top and take a photo together.'[10]

While still on the summit, Jurek realised he should radio base camp to tell them the news. But there was some confusion with the radio batteries and he later reported he couldn't find them; he had moved them in an attempt to keep them warm, but where? Getting down seemed more important than searching for batteries, so he gave up and started descending. When they arrived at Camp 4, they crawled into their sleeping bags, melted ice for tea, and only then, radioed ABC. The response was strangely muted because by now, much lower down the mountain, Andrzej was gravely ill.

The issue of radio communication, or lack thereof, arises repeatedly on winter climbs of 8,000-metre peaks. No doubt the extreme conditions, extreme altitude and extreme exhaustion all contribute to this inability to stay in touch with each other. But there are other theories as well: impatience with the constant checking in, with the poor performance of teammates, and an overpowering need for some individuals to succeed at any cost. Whatever the reason, in this case the lack of radio contact meant Jurek and

Krzysztof were unaware of how serious Andrzej's condition was, and Przemek's lack of a radio meant he couldn't mobilise a rescue sooner.

Down in Camp 3, Przemek continued monitoring Andrzej, who was in and out of sleep, his eyes glazed, his breathing interrupted by fits of coughing. At one point he stopped coughing long enough to drift off. Finally, there was stillness in the tent. When the silence became prolonged, Przemek understood what had happened. 'I called Krzysztof Pankiewicz for help. He tried resuscitation. In vain. It was 10.30 p.m. on 11 December.'

Przemek fell into a state of shock. The concentration he had marshalled for the long descent, the nocturnal vigil over his friend, all came crashing down in waves of exhaustion and feelings of helplessness. He was so distraught by morning that his teammates had to accompany him down the mountain. Przemek switched into automatic mode: clip into the fixed rope, plunge his legs into the deep snow, switch to the next fixed rope, again and again. The hours passed. His body did what was required but his mind reeled with one question, over and over: *why?*

Andrzej Machnik, leader of the expedition, declared it finished. He directed Jurek and Krzysztof to strip Camp 4 and head down. But what were they to do with Andrzej Czok's body: bring him down off the mountain or bury him in a crevasse? They chose the crevasse. Since he was already in his sleeping bag, it was simply a matter of binding his body with ropes, sliding him over to a crevasse about fifty metres from Camp 3, and lowering him in. The ceremony was brief and muted. The team was in shock. Andrzej Czok the indestructible. Czok the survivor. Czok the Ice Warrior – no longer.

The climbers dismantled Camp 3 and fled to ABC. Krzysztof and Jurek left the mountain the following day. They felt their job was done, but some on the team felt otherwise.

Przemek wasn't convinced they had done their share, and he wasn't impressed with their behaviour at base camp. 'I still have a sense of distaste when reflecting on the situation after Wielicki and Kukuczka's return from the summit,' he reflected. 'Not only did they both not participate at all in expedition preparations, they showed up when the hardest sections of the route were already protected with fixed ropes, and they also didn't feel the need to participate in the last phase of the expedition, even in a symbolic way.'

Krzysztof later tried to justify their actions. 'It's true we wanted to leave early because it was our second expedition in a row. We figured, maybe not

Krzysztof Wielicki and Jerzy Kukuczka after their first winter ascent of Kangchenjunga, 11 January 1986. *Photo: Krzysztof Wielicki Archive.*

in the best way, that we had done our share. So, others could look after taking down base camp and all the organisational stuff.'[11]

Things got worse. The expedition's financial situation was still a mess and there were unpaid debts to be settled, but Krzysztof and Jurek didn't appear interested in the final accounts and only wanted to be reimbursed for their own expenses. When Andrzej Machnik refused, they left. Przemek speculated their premature departure might not have been completely due to finances. 'It might be that, in a way, they were running away from remorse,' he said. 'After all, Andrzej Czok should have been able to count on more interest from Jurek Kukuczka, his long-time partner. I started to suspect Kukuczka was using his partners as a mere means to an end.'

One more Polish first winter ascent of an 8,000er, one more 8,000er for Jurek, and one more death.

When the team arrived back in Kathmandu, there was no sense of celebration within the sombre group. In the months and years to come, Przemek often reflected on what had happened. Was there anything that could have been done to change the tragic sequence of events? 'I came to the conclusion nothing could change the outcome,' he said. 'It was Andrzej

[Czok] who decided to continue, against Robert Janik's advice to descend to base camp.'

His conclusion had substance. The final assessment of a climber's physical condition is often based solely on his partner's judgement, particularly with high-altitude climbing in winter. Bundled in clothing, even inside the tent almost nothing is exposed. All you can see are a frozen nose, cracked lips and eyes reddened from the wind. Sometimes that's enough to make an accurate assessment but more often it's not. And it's equally difficult to refute statements from a strong personality like Andrzej Czok. He was known for his strength and determination, his stamina. Surely, he would know his own body and its limitations. But the first symptoms of altitude sickness are not so obvious and can be confused with other factors. 'I am persuaded Czok wasn't aware of the danger,' Przemek said. 'His condition got worse extremely fast. Too fast to fight it with willpower. Even the availability of oxygen bottles in Camp 3 wouldn't have helped without rapid descent to base camp. Such a rapid descent was impossible.'

There was no shortage of opinions about the expedition and its tragic end. Andrzej Zawada weighed in, stating that Andrzej had lost his life because of his ambition. Przemek thought this was too harsh. Ludwik Wilczyński felt that in order to fully understand Andrzej's death, you had to consider the last months of his life. While climbing Dhaulagiri the previous winter and surviving two open-air bivouacs above 8,000 metres, he had suffered severe frostbite in his hands and feet. The treatment and rehabilitation had lasted well into September 1985. During this time, he wasn't as active as usual and gained almost ten kilos. 'He was simply not prepared for the Kangchenjunga expedition,' Ludwik said. 'And yet, he was still young and ambitious.'

The two had talked on the approach march, where Andrzej had assured Ludwik that the three-week trek would whip him into shape. Ludwik admitted that Andrzej had lost the excess weight but doubted his fitness had returned to its previous level. On the mountain itself, Ludwik felt Andrzej was carrying loads that were too heavy, doing too much work, too much up and down. 'I think he was exploited,' Ludwik said. Not only that but disappointed as well. Ludwik felt sure Andrzej had anticipated climbing with his old partner, Jurek. But when Jurek arrived late to the expedition with Krzysztof, there was no talk of partnering with Andrzej. 'It was a disappointment for him,' Ludwik said. 'We saw it.' He added it was also obvious he was sick. 'It was only thanks to his physical hardness and exceptional ability to force himself to extreme effort,' that Andrzej got as high as Camp 4.

Anna Okopińska, one of Poland's best female high-altitude mountaineers of that generation, considered Andrzej Czok to have been one of the 'truest men of the mountains' and was greatly moved by the tragedy on Kangchenjunga. 'His death showed how attentive and sensitive one has to be to the problems of colleagues in the difficult conditions of Himalayan winters,' she explained. 'If somebody who is extremely strong suddenly weakens, this is a signal which cannot be ignored.'

Years later, Krzysztof reflected on his awareness of Andrzej's deterioration. 'Maybe I should have been more sensitive to his condition in the early phases of the approach ... Even asking him how he felt that night when we were leaving for the summit. But those thoughts only come in the aftermath.' At the time, nobody was thinking about a tragedy, or that his life was in danger. But Krzysztof later wondered if the signs were clearer than they cared to admit. 'His pace was much slower going up to Camp 4 but we probably thought he had a heavier pack or was having a bad day ... Unfortunately, pulmonary oedema progresses very quickly ... It's easy to take a cough not too seriously. Czok was already coughing when we were in base and it was with him the entire expedition.'[12]

As usual in Poland after a tragedy in the mountains, there was an inquiry. In this case, two: the PZA and the Gliwice Mountain Club. They sent surveys with questions to the climbers, who mostly felt it to be an exercise in finger-pointing. In response to the inquiry, which suggested a possible rivalry within the team, Krzysztof wrote an impassioned letter: 'My dear people ... You actually believe that the cause of altitude sickness, in this case pulmonary oedema, was a result of rivalry between Kukuczka, Przemek, Andrzej and myself?'[13] Krzysztof felt the accusation was incomprehensible. 'It was then, and it remains so today,' he stated. 'I completely didn't feel rivalry and I don't know whose idea that was.'[14]

Ludwik continues to be troubled by his memories. 'I loved Andrzej for his mildness, his love for his family and for his ambition, which in the end brought him to perdition.' Displaying classic signs of survivor's guilt, he added, 'It was horrible ... I felt partially responsible for the harm to Andrzej's family. I couldn't believe we were unable to help him.'

Although Ludwik believed he would never climb again after the tragedy on Kangchenjunga, he did, the following year, on Manaslu. Przemek had the climb of his life later the same year, when he made the first ascent of the 'Magic Line' on K2 with Peter Božik and Wojciech Wróż. When Wojciech fell on descent, Przemek lost his second partner within a year. Jurek completed three more climbs in just over a year, with a summer ascent of a new route on K2, an autumn ascent of a new route on Manaslu with Artur Hajzer, and a first winter ascent of Annapurna, also with Artur. Jurek, too, lost another partner, when Tadek Piotrowski fell to his death on descent from K2, having bivouacked two nights above 8,000 metres.

Overexposure to premature and sudden loss of life gradually emboldened those who survived to ignore their own mortality rather than surrender to the trauma. The survivors pushed themselves harder and longer on increasingly difficult and dangerous routes. The harder they pushed, the better they became, but the cost was tragically high. Poland's winter dominance in the high mountains was beginning to look more like war.

6

ANNAPURNA

Carpe Diem

Returning home, I breathe easier. My life appraised
from the vantage of Himalayan slopes.
Anatoli Boukreev, *Above the Clouds*

Annapurna, at 8,091 metres, is the world's tenth-highest mountain and was the first of the 8,000ers to be climbed, by the French in 1950. It is the highest point of the Annapurna Massif, which is indeed massive, with one peak over 8,000 metres, six peaks over 7,000 metres and four peaks over 6,000 metres.[1] By 1986, there had been several impressive ascents of this Himalayan giant, but nobody had climbed it in winter.[2]

Poland's most ambitious mountaineer of the day, Jurek Kukuczka, began showing interest. He had already climbed Kangchenjunga, K2 and Manaslu that year, so was almost permanently acclimatised. Why not add one more? He had recently lost his race with Reinhold Messner, who climbed Lhotse, the last of his 8,000ers, on 16 October, but Jurek's quest to climb all of the 8,000ers either by a new route or in winter was still unprecedented. Annapurna in winter would be a fine addition to his collection.

Climbing was one thing, but organising was something entirely different. Jurek wasn't fond of the process and didn't have much experience since most of his Himalayan excursions had been arranged by other people. But Annapurna in winter was his idea so it was his responsibility to get a permit, select the team and raise money. He chose his Manaslu partner Artur Hajzer and his Kangchenjunga partner Krzysztof Wielicki, as well as Rysiek Warecki and Dr Michał Tokarzewski. Money was a tougher problem and so, against his better judgement – and prejudice – he added a woman to the mix to attract funding: the famous Wanda Rutkiewicz, who secured a film commission from Austrian television, bringing badly needed cash to the expedition.

Jurek wasn't the only one disinclined to have Wanda on the team. She had a formidable reputation: Poland's most prolific female high-altitude climber, with several 8,000ers in her pocket, including the first Polish ascent of Everest and the first female ascent of K2. She planned to be the first woman to climb all of the 8,000ers, and she wanted to do it quickly. But Polish men, mountaineers in particular, found Wanda 'difficult'. When Jurek and his wife Celina discussed the idea of women on expeditions, he had declared categorically that mountaineering in the Himalaya was not for women. Celina disagreed. She understood that the heavy packs and endless trail-breaking would be arduous for a small-framed woman but she knew it was possible. Wanda was proof of that.

The other men on the team weren't overly worried. Jurek had invited her, they reasoned, so Jurek could climb with her. They invented all kinds of reasons why they didn't want to: she was too slow; she bivouacked too often; and she always brought too much 'stuff'. And on Annapurna, they noticed her fitness was lacking. She was still very motivated, but she was slower than before. 'She was about to turn forty-four but since she was such a well-known climber, none of the men on the Annapurna expedition,

especially the ones younger than her, were brave enough to tell her this fact,' Jurek stated.[3]

They were on the north side of the mountain: the easiest side, but also the darkest side. And in winter it was desperately dark. 'The North Face of Annapurna is as ugly as night,' Krzysztof Wielicki wrote. 'It is potentially the ugliest wall of all the 8,000-metre peaks.'[4] To make up for the lack of light, they savoured the good food,

Polish Himalayan climber Wanda Rutkiewicz on Annapurna during the winter 1987 expedition.
Photo: Artur Hajzer.

in particular, Austrian *speck* (ham), courtesy of Rysiek. But at base camp, *speck* was mysteriously scarce. The climbers' disappointment was tempered by the amusing sounds emerging from Jurek and Wanda's tent, strange, smacking sounds. Their imaginations ran wild. 'We thought, oh boy, Celina will be jealous,' Artur said. In fact, Celina *was* slightly concerned before the start of the expedition. She knew Wanda and Jurek would be sharing a tent and, while she admired Wanda, even idolised her, she later admitted she wasn't blind to her feminine charm. As it turned out, her worries were unfounded; when the expedition ended and they were packing up base camp, Artur discovered a pile of *speck* wrappers hidden under Jurek and Wanda's tent. The suspicious noises had been more gastronomical than amorous.

The climb was curious in several ways. The team arrived at the base of the mountain on 18 January 1987, quite late for a winter attempt, and instead of setting up a proper base camp, they started up the mountain immediately. As a result, Camp 3 was in place before base camp was fully established. This was partly due to the acclimatisation Jurek and Artur had retained from their autumn ascent of Manaslu. Since their Annapurna permit expired on 15 February, they felt pressured to begin.

Wanda wasn't well: she had a sore throat and was fevered, typical for her at the beginning of an expedition. She usually improved during the course of a climb but opted out of the first load-carrying trip up the mountain. Jurek, Krzysztof and Artur were busy packing and negotiating what to include. Artur recalled that, as usual, he wanted to take more equipment and, as usual, Jurek wanted to take more food. Jurek's appetite seemed to improve the higher he climbed, unlike most people, whose appetites die at altitude. Artur later recounted a conversation he overheard between Wanda and Rysiek in the mess tent.

'I know these sons of bitches. They're going to try to get to the top now,' Rysiek said.

'Do you really think so?' Wanda asked, obviously surprised.

'Well, what would they be waiting for?'

When Artur entered the tent, Wanda asked him directly, 'Is it true you are going to try and go to the top right away?'

Artur didn't know how to respond to this seemingly simple question. In theory they were still equipping the camps and acclimatising, so the answer would be no. But in reality, it might be possible for him and Jurek to make an early summit bid because they were moving quickly, they were fit and healthy, and they were still acclimatised from Manaslu. In this case, the answer would have to be 'maybe'. Unsure of what to say, he deferred to Jurek. 'I simply follow the leader,' he said. 'If the leader stops, I stop. If the leader goes, I go. If the leader backs down, I back down. I'm not the one to make the decision.'

Wanda smelled a lie and stomped out of the tent in search of Jurek. He admitted that, if there was a chance to go to the summit now, why would they wait? It seemed obvious. Wanda was angry and hurt. She wasn't ready yet. The expedition was moving too quickly. 'If, as you say, there is a chance you'll go all the way to the summit, what will happen to me?' she asked. 'You know I can't try for the summit right now. I think you should designate someone to stay behind and be my partner on a later summit attempt.'

Wanda's demand made no difference: Jurek, Krzysztof and Artur were going up and that was that. She now felt pressured to join them, despite her questionable health. Jurek and she would share one tent, Artur and Krzysztof the other. It seemed the rope teams had evolved. Artur, who had hoped to climb with Jurek, was now paired with Krzysztof. He knew that Krzysztof, though not as psychologically tough as Jurek, was in even better physical condition and was exceptionally fast. Jurek, on the other hand, was more driven, with unbelievable stamina. Either of them would make a formidable partner. 'To put it bluntly, switching partners can be compared to getting out of a Toyota diesel into a gasoline Mazda,' he said. He was merely thankful he wasn't matched up with Wanda.

At 6,800 metres, they excavated a ledge on the icy slope and set up their tents, planning to stay one night to acclimatise before descending to base camp to rest before a serious summit attempt. Jurek was reclined in his and Wanda's tent, sipping tea, feeling healthy, fit and ambitious, and scheming madly. Krzysztof and Artur were preparing for bed in the other tent when suddenly Jurek called out a challenge: 'I'm going up tomorrow! Who'll come with me?'

There was a small delay while everyone collected their thoughts. Wanda knew she needed to go down before climbing higher. Krzysztof wasn't completely acclimatised either, but he was fast, and he trusted his speed. He could probably go higher and get down safely. But he didn't want a repeat of his horrible experience on Makalu in 1986 when he had outpaced his good friend Marcel Rüedi, who had later died of exhaustion on the mountain. He was still weighing the pros and cons of Jurek's invitation when, from the other side of the tent, Artur shouted as loud as he could, 'Me-ee-ee!'

The young one, the upstart, the brash and cocky Artur, had seized the day. Krzysztof wasn't overly concerned at first because this was not a summit attempt. He assumed that they were still acclimatising, and that a true summit bid would happen in good time. In retrospect, he realised how clever Jurek was in his choice of words: he didn't ask who wanted to go with him to the *summit*, but rather who wanted to go *up*, meaning simply *higher*. 'That was his tactical play because if he had said anything about the summit, then Wanda would definitely be upset because she was, at that moment, his partner,' Krzysztof explained.[5]

The following day, 1 February, Krzysztof and Wanda descended, fully intending to rest, rehydrate and head back up in a couple of days for a summit attempt. Wanda was still battling her throat infection and her fever, but she was confident it was only a matter of time before she recovered and was strong enough to climb the mountain.

Jurek and Artur started up. Each of them admitted fleeting feelings of guilt for their actions: not about deceiving Wanda, but for squeezing Krzysztof out of the play. 'Had I dumped Krzysiek?' Jurek asked himself. 'I consoled myself with the assurance that he really was not adequately acclimatised.'[6] Artur was worried Krzysztof might hold it against him. Krzysztof, who was a much bigger player in the Polish Himalayan community than Artur, had an edgy reputation. Some called him harsh, bossy, expecting others to perform at the same level as him. Having Krzysztof as an enemy would not be a smart move for young Artur. Yet here he was, heading up the mountain with Jurek on what was most certainly a summit bid. At that moment, it felt worth the risk.

They stopped at 7,400 metres as the weather began to worsen. Neither of them was moving quickly, despite their residual acclimatisation and their drive. Jurek suggested spending one more day to wait out the bad weather and to rest before the final push. It was a strange tactic, since 'resting' at that sort of altitude is a misnomer and there was no indication of any improvement in the weather. Yet, his intuition proved right. At 4 p.m. on 3 February, sixteen days after arriving in base camp, Jurek and Artur reached the top of Annapurna.

Their achievement was remarkable not only because of the speed with which they climbed it, but also because of the stroke of luck that brought them back to their highest camp. As usual, they were descending in the dark, floundering around in a storm, trying to remember the route in reverse.

At 10 p.m., Jurek stumbled over something that felt softer than the slope: it was their tent.

When the pair trudged into base camp the following day, Jurek was waving his arms, belting out a popular Polish song at the top of his voice: 'I love you, life.' His joy was infectious, but Krzysztof and Wanda still had a job to do. They tried one more time, but climbed only as high as Camp 4 before retreating. Wanda was suffering from her lingering infection; her willingness to give it another try was a sign of her dogged determination, but probably not her best judgement.

Jurek speculated that Krzysztof could probably have made a solo sprint to the top, had he not chosen to climb with Wanda. Krzysztof rejected this. 'I never even considered it because I thought the mission was accomplished. After all, it was all about Jurek getting to the top: the initiator of this expedition. For me it wasn't the end of the road but for him, in a certain sense, yes.' Then he added an important, niggling observation: 'But this was the first successful expedition on which I hadn't got to the summit.'[7] Although disappointed, Krzysztof was determined to learn from this failure. 'The difficult experiences make you stronger,' he said. 'If you get kicked in the butt, you know what to expect in true extreme situations ... My generation really got kicked in the butt, which made us harder in body and spirit and we reaped the benefits later.'[8]

The climb was a breakthrough in Himalayan winter mountaineering. Previous winter ascents in the high mountains had used expedition-style approaches, with an army of climbers, plenty of fixed lines, and well-stocked camps. Long periods at base camp, two to three months, was the norm. On Annapurna, Jurek and Artur had sprinted to the top in little over two weeks, with a haphazard assortment of camps and only four active climbers. It wasn't quite alpine style, but it was close: a signal for the future.

The final summit team was determined by a combination of luck (both good and bad), scheming, lingering survivor guilt (in the case of Krzysztof), illness and blinding ambition. The machinations of the four major actors in the play revealed their entangled relationships: as friends, as teammates, even as competitors. The addition of Wanda to the mix increased the complexity, as the men struggled with their misogynistic attitudes, couched as teasing. But the mountain, after seven previous attempts, had finally been climbed in winter. Poland's Ice Warriors ruled.

If anyone deserved a winter ascent of Annapurna, then it was the Japanese. Over and over they'd tried: in 1980, 1983 and 1984, from the south side, from the north. Less than a year after the Poles summited, a Japanese team climbed Annapurna's notoriously difficult south face on 20 December 1987. Noboru Yamada, Yasuhira Saito, Teruo Saegusa and Toshiyuki Kobayashi reached the summit; it was Noboru Yamada's seventh 8,000er. But the expedition ended in tragedy when Toshiyuki Kobayashi fell to his death at around 7,900 metres and Yasuhira Saito did the same just metres above Camp 4 at 7,400 metres. Their tragic falls were likely caused by exhaustion.

The Japanese weren't the only ones vying for Annapurna's summit in winter. In the years that followed, more than a dozen teams launched themselves up the mountain in the cruellest season. Teams from South Korea, Bulgaria, Canada, Yugoslavia, the USA, Italy, Norway and Sweden all took their turn, and from most angles: north face, south face, north-east buttress. None of this dented Annapurna's reputation as a deadly mountain. In 1994, the Korean alpinist Jun Suk-Byun had the misfortune to die in a fatal fall on hard-crusted snow, not on the mountain itself but on day two of the trek back to Pokhara.

In the winter of 1997, Italian alpinist Simone Moro led a small team of three to try the south face. Born in 1967 in Bergamo, Italy, Simone had started climbing when he was thirteen. Rock climbing, alpinism and, finally, high-altitude climbing became his life passion. His mother described him as a quiet and solitary boy: 'My son wasn't so gregarious ... He had little to share because he didn't have a favourite pop star or soccer player. He had Messner.'[9] A compact man who trains relentlessly, Simone is easily recognised by his weather-beaten complexion, his thatch of unruly hair, his fierce gaze behind trademark horn-rimmed spectacles and, most of all, his oversized grin. The smile is sometimes overlooked because Simone is usually talking, like any good Italian adding expression, with his eyes, his hands and his arms: a consummate communicator. He's as passionate about his friendships as he is about alpinism, and one of his best friends was the legendary Kazakh high-altitude climber Anatoli Boukreev.

On 2 December 1997, Simone, Anatoli and filmmaker Dimitri Sobolev flew by helicopter to Annapurna's southern base camp at 4,095 metres. Their objective was the mountain's south face, but snow kept falling and the avalanche hazard kept increasing. When the new snow reached four metres in depth, they knew they had to change plans, opting instead for a line up the steep east face of Annapurna Fang (7,647 metres) to a series of notches between the Fang and Annapurna II. From the notches, they planned to traverse the ridge up and over the Fang, before continuing to the main summit. It was a longer route than originally planned, but a safer one, they believed.

Wading through snow that often reached his belly, Anatoli plugged away in front, breaking trail. He might have been unstoppable but he grew frustrated at shouldering the hardest work. That evening in the tent, there was a tense discussion about fairness. 'Anatoli started talking about the day's events, with the clear intention of highlighting his disappointment in the behaviour of Dimitri and myself,' Simone recalled. 'After a few minutes a harsh discussion erupted between the two Russians in their native language. Halfway through the discussion Anatoli started speaking in English. He obviously wanted me to understand what was being said ... "Dima, this is not like Everest in 1996! It was easy then, there were many of us and we also had oxygen. Here we are on our own, isolated and it is very difficult."

"What do you mean?" Dimitri replied.

"That it is totally different here."[10]

While Anatoli's remarks had been directed at Dimitri, Simone understood he was also being chastised. And yet, when Anatoli finished cooking (after his long day of trail-breaking), he first handed the pot of piping-hot soup to Simone. After taking some, Simone handed it to Dimitri, who eventually passed it back to Anatoli. 'That gesture was one of the many things that had struck me about Anatoli,' Simone later reflected. 'He was probably the only man and mountaineer to let his companions eat first, even though he was always the one to cook.'[11] The soup consumed, they wiped the pot with a couple of squares of toilet paper, and the 'dishes were done'.

Their next camp was at 5,500 metres. Dimitri cooked the soup that night, while Anatoli and Simone navigated a route through the bergschrund above their camp and began climbing the steepening wall that led directly to the ridge at 6,300 metres. After finishing the soup, Anatoli, with a sly grin on his sun-blasted face, produced a small flask of vodka. He looked at Simone and said, '*Ciu ciut*? A little bit. Do you want some?' Simone knew any answer other than 'Yes, of course' was unacceptable. 'That dinner lasted forever and like three friends at a bar we stayed up late laughing and shouting "*ciu ciut*",' Simone recalled.[12]

The following morning, Christmas Day, Simone led a technical section and then continued to move slowly towards the ridge while Anatoli unspooled coils of rope down below. When he was about sixty metres from the ridge, Simone heard Anatoli yelling that he was out of rope. He stopped to set up an anchor so Anatoli and Dimitri could follow. Stomping out a small platform and placing two ice screws, he secured the rope and began the long wait while the others climbed up to him. This was as far as Dimitri was planning to climb; he would continue to film from below as Anatoli and Simone climbed through the overhanging cornice that towered over them to reach the ridge. Then he would descend to base camp alone. Simone decided to film them climbing up to him, removing his gloves to better operate the camera.

Suddenly, he heard a great rumbling roar. In seconds, blocks of rock and ice shrouded in spindrift were rushing towards him. He screamed, and in a strange, almost trance-like state, saw Anatoli begin to move out of the way of the falling debris. 'Still to this day I remember his eyes,' Simone recalled. 'I don't know how, given the hundreds of metres that separated us, but I remember their expression as though he were in front of me. It's difficult to express what those blue eyes said to me … [they contained] a mixture of fear with a strong resolve to survive.'[13]

Simone was then slammed against the slope, gripping the rope like a vice. His efforts were useless. 'I wasn't able to resist the fury of this mass for even a second and I fell rapidly, grasping the rope between my hands as it burned and lacerated my fingers almost through to the bone. The series of flights, slides and ricochets seemed like they would never end. All I could do was go along with the movement of the avalanche, often tumbling at breakneck speed and losing orientation.'[14]

After almost 800 metres, Simone finally stopped, half-buried by the avalanche. His face had been hit: he could see nothing out of one eye. His hands were stripped of skin, his clothing was in shreds and he had lost all his equipment bar his crampons. He staggered about on the avalanche debris, screaming, 'Dimitri, Anatoli!' No response. Miraculously, he had landed fifty metres from Camp 1. He stumbled over to the tent but couldn't open its iced-up zipper with his injured hands. He slammed his cramponed boot against the edge of the tent and grasped the zip with his teeth, opening it enough to dive through the door. Inside, he found extra clothing and mitts to cover his hands and stem the bleeding. He still faced a 1,500-metre descent through a crevasse-riddled glacier to reach base camp and initiate a rescue for Anatoli and Dimitri. 'In that precise moment I found myself having to turn my back on the place where my friends were buried, perhaps still alive. But where?' he later wrote.[15] He yelled at himself, bullying himself to keep going. 'Get up, you coward!' he shouted. 'Get up! This is the moment to show me you've got the balls! Count to ten and then get up and go on, okay?'

'"1-2-3-4 ... 10," and my legs straightened up, I took ten steps and then threw myself to the ground. "Well done, well done! I knew you could get up. You can do it; you can do it. Come on, another ten and then up again. 1-2-3-4 ... 10," and another ten steps and down again. "That's how to do it. That's it!"'[16]

Six hours later Simone arrived at base camp. His cook left immediately to trek more than ten hours through deep snow to the nearest village where a helicopter was summoned to whisk Simone away. Three days later, he was back, flying over the avalanche, searching for any sign of life: a piece of clothing, a glint of metal from an ice axe, anything at all. There was no trace.

A few days before the accident, Anatoli had called his girlfriend from Pokhara. Linda Wylie remembered that he was in good spirits. 'After talking about schedules and business, my children and animals, we said goodbye but both of us held the line. There was a long silence and he asked again, "Linda, how are you?"

"Think about Annapurna, Anatoli, I am afraid of this mountain. Have you had dreams?"

"No, no dreams," he said, then wistfully adding, "I have been so much in the mountains this year, inshallah, we will rest in the spring."'[17]

Even though Simone survived the Christmas Day avalanche on Annapurna, he never fully recovered from Anatoli's death. 'When Anatoli died, it rocked my life to its core,' he said. He had loved Anatoli as a brother, not only as a climbing partner. 'This was a Russian with a heart as big as the mountains he climbed.'[18] And with Anatoli and Dimitri's deaths, two more tragedies were added to the high cost of winter at 8,000 metres.

7

LHOTSE

Climbing in a Corset

Being alone strips you naked, it makes you understand who you are,
what is your value, the things that matter in life.
Hansjörg Auer

Having tasted success in winter for the first time in 1973 on Noshaq, the
second-highest peak in the Hindu Kush, Andrzej Zawada turned his attention
to the Himalaya. He reasoned (correctly, as it turned out) that if you could
climb to 7,492 metres in winter, why not 8,000? When the Polish Mountaineering Association (PZA) turned Zawada down repeatedly for Everest, his
preferred objective, he settled for the 1974–75 winter season on Lhotse, Everest's
neighbour and at 8,516 metres the world's fourth-highest mountain. Although
more correctly an 'autumn' expedition, since his team arrived at the mountain
in late October, the actual climbing took place in December, so it was
certainly 'wintry'. And back in 1974, it was also considered somewhat radical.

Zawada brought some of Poland's strongest climbers, among them
Zyga Heinrich and Voytek Kurtyka from Kraków, Bogdan Jankowski
from Wrocław, Tadek Piotrowski from Szczecin and Ryszard Szafirski from
Zakopane. He took a film crew along as well, including Jerzy Surdel
from Kraków and Stanisław Latałło from Warsaw. Also from Warsaw came
a rising young star in Polish alpinism, Anna Okopińska. Andrzej had seen
the impact a team of Japanese women had made climbing Manaslu and
thought his team might also benefit from taking a woman. Two women were
in contention, Anna and Wanda Rutkiewicz, Poland's most famous female
climber. The decision of which one to take came down to a ballot of the
relevant committee. Anna won, by a vote of five to one.

Polish team gathers in Warsaw before leaving for the 1974 autumn/winter expedition to Lhotse. Andrzej Zawada, expedition leader, is on the left. *Photo: J. Barcz.*

The Poles established base camp at 5,300 metres on 21 October and having threaded a route through the labyrinth of crevasses and leaning séracs in the Khumbu Icefall, set up Camp 1 on 26 October on the far-right side of the Western Cwm. Taking full advantage of a fine weather pattern, Camp 2 was in place by 1 November and Camp 3, on the Lhotse face at 7,100 metres, on 7 November. Three camps in twelve days and a height gain of almost two kilometres. Impressive.

Anna appreciated her unique position on the team, recalling, 'It was a great honour to take part in a national expedition with the best Polish climbers.' She sensed some of the older men were unaware of her experience and were initially uncomfortable with her being there. 'I suspect they were afraid that the participation of a woman would depreciate their success,' she said. But she proved herself soon enough, acclimatising well, helping prepare the route through the Icefall and up on the Lhotse face. 'By working together, my antagonists changed their mind about me and the atmosphere on the expedition became excellent. Everything worked fine.'

Until it didn't.

The weather shifted and the ferocious Himalayan winter tore through their camps. 'We now had to face a severe test of endurance,' Andrzej explained.[1]

The Icefall was constantly changing, with séracs toppling over, ice bridges collapsing, and wind drifting the snow so that the architecture of the route shifted hourly. Camp 1 was destroyed by wind and needed to be relocated to the bottom of a gaping crevasse. Camp 2 had to be moved to escape the violent winds roaring down the Western Cwm. It had taken only twelve days to establish the first three camps. Camp 4, the launching point for their summit attempt, took another thirty-four days to get in place. As the climbers weakened and began to fall ill, they retreated to base camp to recover. But they weren't finished with Lhotse.

It was late in the day on 11 December when Poland's leading rock climber, Voytek Kurtyka, and two others, Kazimierz Rusiecki and Jan Stryczyński, began chopping out a small platform at 7,800 metres on Lhotse's icy wall. They hacked at the bullet-hard ice with their ice axes but couldn't excavate a platform large enough to erect the tent. Instead, they hung it from a tent pole like a bivouac sack and huddled under it throughout the cold, windy night. Such was Camp 4. Exhausted from the sleepless hours, they descended the next morning.

The same day, Andrzej and Zyga started up on the first summit attempt. High on the mountain, they were encouraged by the quality of the ice, which allowed them to move confidently on their crampons rather than having to chop steps with their axes. 'We climbed slowly one step at a time, at the rate of about 100 metres an hour,' Andrzej recalled. 'We had to stop often to try and gulp in as much of the frosty air as we could with our mouths wide open. We reached the Nuptse ridge. The sun was on the horizon and suddenly from the South Col a freezing gale-force wind started to blow. It tore at our shoulders and caused us to lurch forward, losing our balance. I pushed my whole body against the slope and held on to the ice axe with all my strength.'[2]

When they reached the tent at Camp 4, they crawled inside, seeking some protection from the storm. But the wind ripped at the flimsy nylon and extinguished the flame of their butane stove so they gave up and dived into their sleeping bags, massaging their hands and fingers, which were showing alarming signs of frostbite: white as chalk and swollen as sausages. It was impossible to get warm so they finally donned oxygen masks and inhaled the life-giving gas from bottles they had carried up the mountain. The storm got worse. 'Then we heard an ear-splitting roar and, in a few minutes, we were in the centre of a hurricane,' Andrzej exclaimed. 'We clung to the rocks, worried we might be swept off together with the tent.'[3]

The night passed slowly. Worn out from their struggle, they came to the bitter realisation that they would have to descend. Within two days they were back at base camp.

On 15 December, Andrzej Zawada directed Tadek Piotrowski to go to Camp 3 with the two filmmakers, Jerzy Surdel and Stanisław Latałło. Anna had climbed with Stanisław several days on the mountain, and had assessed his abilities as marginal: 'He climbed efficiently … but the lack of experience on ice and the lack of self-confidence were visible … he asked me frequently which way to go. He also asked about technical details, such as belaying, jumars, knots. Moreover, he usually had terribly heavy luggage – plenty of film equipment in addition to expedition loads assigned to members.' From Anna's observations, Stanisław clearly needed to be accompanied by a more experienced member of the team.

Tadek, by far the most experienced of the trio, and the one Andrzej had asked to 'take care' of the filmmakers, reached Camp 3 well ahead of them. Jerzy arrived next, informing Tadek that Stanisław was moving slowly and would need a fixed rope for the steep section leading up to Camp 3. He went back out and fixed a line for Stanisław, who eventually arrived at the tent. Two days of bad weather then pinned them down at Camp 3 and when they realised the blizzard wasn't going to let up, they decided to brave the storm and descend to Camp 2. The howling wind created a ground blizzard, reducing visibility to a few metres. Tadek once again moved ahead of the others. 'They were coming down without a rope,' Andrzej explained, 'and they lost touch with each other. Piotrowski [Tadek] reached Camp 2 first, since he was coming down as leader.'[4] Jerzy was having problems with his crampons so he actually turned around and crawled back up to Camp 3 to repair them inside the tent, protected from the blizzard. When he reached the fixed line below Camp 3, he discovered Stanisław hanging from the rope, attached by his jumar, his pack weighed down with heavy filming equipment. Stanisław had apparently died of exposure and exhaustion. Jerzy could do nothing but descend to Camp 2.

The team was horrified at the tragedy and when the wind moderated slightly on 23 December, they climbed back up to Stanisław to bury his body in a crevasse. But Andrzej and Zyga did not descend; instead, they carried on up to Camp 4. The expedition was not yet over. That evening, Christmas Eve, Andrzej radioed down to base camp to 'wish everyone a happy Christmas.' It couldn't have been very happy, having just buried one of their friends.

Andrzej and Zyga snuggled into their sleeping bags and tucked in to their Christmas Eve dinner: ruby red borscht and a jar of jellied carp. Christmas morning seemed like a miracle because the wind had dropped, though conditions were still inhospitable at -46° Celsius. A clear sky lured them out of the tent, but not quickly enough since they took three hours to boil water and another two to successfully strap themselves in to the oxygen apparatus and connect to the frozen valves. It was already 11 a.m. when they began their summit bid. After two hours of climbing, the summit of Lhotse was clearly visible against the sky. Andrzej, who was a little ahead, looked at the altimeter: 8,250 metres. Only 260 metres to the top. Suddenly, he heard Zyga shout.

'Andrzej, we have to go down immediately.'

He drew his mask aside and shouted back, 'What's the matter?'

'Look what's happening down there in the Western Cwm! Come back!'

Andrzej looked down into the Cwm. 'A feeling of anger and despair took hold of me,' he later wrote. 'Cumulus clouds were rising swiftly towards us and a violent gale-force wind was swirling a blizzard of snow upwards in our direction. I dug my ice axe in the ground and gripped it firmly with both hands holding on for dear life. The icy wind hit my shoulders and snow covered my face completely.'[5] Slowly and carefully, the two retraced their steps, thankful for the oxygen masks that shielded their faces from the direct force of the raging blizzard. When they reached Camp 4, they realised there was a good chance that, if they stopped, they could be cut off from the lower part of the mountain. If they ran out of bottled oxygen, they knew they would freeze. So, they gathered whatever strength still remained and carried on down to Camp 3. 'I will never forget that bitter struggle we had in order to keep alive,' Andrzej recalled. 'The hardest thing of all was to overcome our increasing indifference … The only thing we wanted was to rest, to stop moving, to lie down and to sleep.'[6]

The two reached Camp 3 safely that night and carried on to base camp in the following days. Instead of revelling in relief at having survived, Andrzej remained obsessed with the summit. He sent a request to Kathmandu for permission to extend the expedition into January, convinced they had enough food and energy and determination to finish the job. Kathmandu turned them down. Their deadline was 31 December and there would be no more discussion.

The Poles had been defeated. Not only did they fail, but they had lost a team member on the mountain, a tragedy for which Andrzej, as leader, was responsible. He had to explain and justify the loss to the mountaineering authorities. Anna felt sure that, from the moment Stanisław was found dead on the fixed rope, the expedition was over. The last attempt was simply optics. Andrzej later called the failure 'the biggest disappointment of my life because we got so close to the top.'[7]

Nevertheless, the team *had* climbed above 8,000 metres, setting an altitude record in winter and setting the stage for the future of winter climbing in the Himalaya. This gave Andrzej the confidence to stretch the boundaries of what was considered possible.

———————

Fourteen more years passed before anyone reached the summit of Lhotse in winter. Fourteen years in which a lot changed in the world of high-altitude winter climbing. Poland's Ice Warriors had proven, six times over, that they could manage the sub-zero temperatures, the howling high-altitude winds and the cruelty of short days and long dark nights. Zakopane native Maciej Berbeka had made first winter ascents of two 8,000ers and come close on a third. His quiet, easygoing character was a welcome addition to the winter teams, and his dogged determination kept him going in the worst conditions imaginable. Jurek Kukuczka had proven three times over that he could handle everything winter could throw at him.

Krzysztof Wielicki was one of the Ice Warriors, too. He and Leszek Cichy had made the first winter ascent of Everest in 1980. He and Jurek had been first up Kangchenjunga in winter, and he had tried hard on Annapurna. In addition to his winter trips, Krzysztof had climbed Broad Peak in a blistering twenty-two hours and ten minutes, forged a new route on Manaslu, made an alpine-style ascent of Makalu, and made two serious attempts at the forbidding south face of Lhotse. He struck an impressive appearance, with his drooping handlebar moustache and his deeply lidded eyes shadowed by heavy brows. Soft-spoken, his words often contained wry moments of humour. His compact frame was all sinew and bone; he moved quickly, lightly, like a sparrow.

Krzysztof was in high demand in the mountains, spending almost as much time in the Himalaya as in Poland with his family. He was fully aware of the consequences of his chosen lifestyle, even though he had no plans to change it. 'If you want to climb, there is a cost,' he said. 'Usually the cost is the family. I have to say sorry, sorry, sorry. They suffer at home and we suffer on the mountain.' He seemed to take extra perverse satisfaction in that suffering. 'To experience pleasure when you have everything against you, you must have some kind of warrior philosophy,' Krzysztof explained. 'It is more appealing. It is more exciting.'

When a Belgian team secured winter permits for both Everest and Lhotse in 1988, it's no surprise Krzysztof was asked to join them, and not only Krzysztof. Leszek Cichy and Andrzej Zawada were also invited to round out the winter roster. The Belgians were strategic: they knew who the Ice Warriors were and wanted a few on their team. It was Andrzej who had wrangled the invitations; he knew the Belgians wanted to climb Everest in winter and had offered the trio's expertise in return for a double permit, one that included Lhotse. Still stinging from his Lhotse defeat all those years ago, this would be a second chance.

There was one small problem. Krzysztof was still suffering from a climbing accident four months earlier on Bhagirathi in India's Garhwal region. The doctor's diagnosis was unequivocal: lung trauma with compression of the eighth thoracic vertebra. The patient would need to be immobilised to prevent further spinal cord trauma. No more mountaineering for Krzysztof. Yet, when Krzysztof received his invitation for Lhotse that winter, he said yes, and promptly wedged himself into a special corset to stiffen his injured spine.

When the team arrived at the mountain on 10 November, Krzysztof noticed almost immediately the difference between a typical Polish effort and the Belgian and Korean expeditions then at base camp. With their unlimited budgets, each team had hired an army of strong and experienced Sherpas to equip the Icefall with dozens of ladders. But when Sherpa Lhakpa Dorje was tragically killed during the Belgian team's summit bid on Everest, their expedition quickly lost steam. As they prepared to leave, only one of them, Ingrid Baeyens, decided to stay and try Lhotse with the three Poles.

So they were now a team of four. The departing Belgians offered the remaining Sherpas some of their equipment and leftover food but during this redistribution a few of the Sherpas became swept up in the generosity of the moment and climbed up to Camp 2 to take down tents and strip them of all food and equipment. It was by chance that Krzysztof realised what was happening. He emerged from his tent early in the morning to relieve himself, only to spy the Sherpas leaving base camp for the Icefall. Krzysztof couldn't catch them but when he reached Camp 2, as he expected, they were in the process of dismantling the tents. They argued. It even turned physical when Krzysztof had to tear certain pieces of equipment from their hands. 'Fortunately, we were able to defend some of the most essential items,' he recalled.[8]

Still wearing his corset, Krzysztof was coping well with his broken back. 'You can definitely walk with a corset,' he said and joked how, 'Because of it I was even a bit warmer.'[9] Even so, he still struggled carrying a heavy pack and descending steep ice, both of which would be required on Lhotse. More problems arose. Ingrid was fighting an upper airway infection, Leszek was on antibiotics to fight an infection and Andrzej was showing early signs he was next in line for the bothersome bug. In spite of his back, Krzysztof felt healthy and fit. When the weather forecast improved, he threw out the idea of a solo attempt. They agreed. It was, he said, a completely unpremeditated plan. 'But sometimes a situation arises and you have to decide ad hoc,' he explained. 'I felt good and the weather was good because it was sunny. Obviously on the upper parts of the mountain it was a bit windy, but it wasn't the typical hurricane.'[10]

And so Krzysztof began climbing Lhotse alone. He moved confidently up the mountain but was disappointed to discover his camera had disappeared from Camp 3. He attributed it to the Sherpas 'clearing the camps', but wasn't sure. Now he would be without a camera to document his movements and hopefully his summit. These were the days before climbers were expected to *prove* their summits but he still wished he had that camera. 'In those days we didn't take selfies,' Krzysztof explained. 'We would take photos of our partner or our pack. Without this ability, I decided to use my eyesight, which is a great register, and memorise the details of the topography of the terrain, which would allow me to then answer questions about whether I had gone to the summit or not.'[11]

His hoped-for summit day didn't begin well. He had taken sleeping pills at Camp 4 the night before and overslept. But once he started moving, he climbed quickly over the hard snow and occasional patches of ice. With an ice axe in each hand he swung with confidence into the firm snow, placing his crampons with care, developing a high-altitude rhythm that wasn't fast, but steady. His mind grew more powerful, muscular even, propelling his body upwards. 'Finally, I was able to step up from the last ledge and reach the summit, where there are two snow domes, the bigger one on the left and

Top: Climbers on the Polish 1979-80 winter Everest expedition in base camp, listening for messages from their families and friends back home.
Photo: Ryszard Szafirski.

Left: Krzysztof Wielicki on the summit of Everest, first winter ascent. *Photo: Leszek Cichy.*

Above: Krzysztof Wielicki and Leszek Cichy in Everest base camp, two days after having made the first winter ascent, 17 February 1980.
Photo: Bogdan Jankowski.

MANASLU (OPPOSITE)

Top left: Climbing on Manaslu,
winter 1983-84. *Photo: Lech Korniszewski.*

Top right: Mountain burial of Stanisław Jaworski, who
was killed while descending a fixed line from Camp 1
during the Polish winter expedition to Manaslu.
Photo: Lech Korniszewski.

Bottom left: Maciej Berbeka topping out on the
summit of Manaslu, 12 January 1984, the first winter
ascent of the mountain. *Photo: Ryszard Gajewski.*

Bottom right: French alpinist Élisabeth Revol on
her 2017 solo attempt to climb Manaslu in winter.
Photo: Elisabeth Revol.

DHAULAGIRI

Top: Polish climbers training for winter climbing
in the Tatras. *Photo: Alek Lwow Archive.*

Right: Andrzej Czok and Jerzy Kukuczka starting their
summit attempt on Dhaulagiri in winter.
Photo: Adam Bilczewski.

CHO OYU

Top: New route and first winter ascent of Cho Oyu by the Polish team, 12 February 1985.
Photo: Andrzej Zawada; topo: Janusz Kurczab.

Above left: Maciej Berbeka on the summit of Cho Oyu, the first winter ascent. *Photo: Maciej Pawlikowski.*

Above right: Marianne Chapuisat and Miguel Sánchez on the summit of Cho Oyu on 10 February 1993, signalling the first ascent of an 8,000er in winter by a woman. The photo was staged, as Marianne described: 'It was "un clin d'oeil" to Messner ... I had one of his books with exactly that picture of the top of Cho Oyu with Kammerlander (5 May 1983). So, we tried to take the same photo with Everest and Lhotse behind.' *Photo: Marianne Chapuisat Archive.*

KANGCHENJUNGA

Top: Advanced base camp, Polish 1985-86 winter expedition to Kangchenjunga.
Photo: Przemysław Piasecki.

Above: Andrzej Czok, member of the Polish 1985-86 winter Kangchenjunga expedition.
Photo: Krzysztof Wielicki Archive.

Above right: Andrzej Czok and Przemysław Piasecki, on their way to Camp 2 during the Polish 1985-86 winter Kangchenjunga expedition.
Photo: Krzysztof Wielicki Archive.

Right: Artur Hajzer preparing Andrzej Czok's body for a mountain burial on Kangchenjunga during the Polish winter expedition. *Photo: Krzysztof Wielicki Archive.*

ANNAPURNA

Top left: Polish Himalayan climber Artur Hajzer at Annapurna base camp on the winter 1986–87 expedition. *Photo: Artur Hajzer Archive.*

Top right: Krzysztof Wielicki and Wanda Rutkiewicz on Annapurna in winter 1987. *Photo: Artur Hajzer.*

Bottom left: Anatoli Boukreev, member of the 1997-98 winter expedition to Annapurna. He and Dimitri Sobolev were killed by an avalanche on Christmas Day. *Photo: Anatoli Boukreev Archive.*

Bottom right: Jerzy Kukuczka on the summit of Annapurna, 3 February 1987. He and Artur Hajzer had just made the first winter ascent of the mountain. *Photo: Artur Hajzer.*

LHOTSE

Above: Polish Himalayan climber Andrzej Zawada, leader of the 1974 autumn/winter expedition to Lhotse. *Photo: Bogdan Jankowski.*

Right: Marek Kowalczyk and Anna Okopińska in the Khumbu Icefall during the Polish 1974 autumn/winter expedition to Lhotse. *Photo: Mirek Wiśniewski.*

Below: Ingrid Baeyens and Krzysztof Wielicki at base camp during the joint Belgian–Polish winter expedition to Lhotse in 1988. *Photo: Krzysztof Wielicki Archive.*

SHISHAPANGMA

Below: Christmas at Shishapangma base camp during the first winter attempt by a Polish–Italian team in 2004. *Photo: Piotr Morawski.*

Bottom: Simone Moro on the summit of Shishapangma, having made the first winter ascent with Piotr Morawski on 14 January 2005. *Photo: Piotr Morawski.*

smaller on the right. I climbed between them but didn't risk standing on either of these domes because of cornices.'[12]

Having memorised the scene, gathered a few small rocks from the couloir leading to the snow-covered summit, and planted a Polish flag, Krzysztof savoured a freeze-frame moment of total fulfilment, when all his expectations had been met and the world was perfect. But it was only a moment. Because of his late start, he had reached the top just a couple of hours before dusk and now needed to descend swiftly, focused on one thing: the tent at Camp 3. It was now that Krzysztof began to suffer. His corset had performed well on the ascent, but, as he recalled, 'It was only during the descent that the firmness of the slope caught up to me because when you descend, you must kick your steps more forcefully,' he explained. 'I started to feel a burning sensation around the fracture, as if someone were poking me with a hot rod.'[13]

He would manage ten to fifteen steps, then plant his ice axe firmly into the snow and lean on it. During those rests he often lost consciousness. 'It's an incredible feeling,' he said. 'You fall asleep and the pain slowly goes away. You surrender to that pleasant feeling, which lulls you to thinking it's all good and the suffering is finished. It is warm and soft. It's probably similar to what people feel as they are dying from hypothermia.'[14] Each time he snapped out of his reverie he felt a moment of panic, since the only thing attaching him to the slope was his ice axe. He would tighten his grip, relieved not to be sliding down into the abyss. Then he would start the painful ordeal all over again. Ten more steps, searing pain, a short rest on the axe, this one longer, ten minutes or more and sleep – oh, beautiful sleep.

Leszek, Krzysztof's summit partner on Everest in 1980, was watching his tortured descent, puzzled by the slow pace. Concerned, he suited up and started climbing towards Camp 3 to help him. 'When I saw someone coming up, it motivated me,' Krzysztof admitted. 'Physically it made no difference, but the psychological effect was amazing.'[15] By the time Krzysztof reached the tent at Camp 3, Leszek was there, making tea. Krzysztof later joked he had been hoping it was Ingrid, but Leszek was a fine consolation prize. He crawled into his sleeping bag and accepted a cup of tea.

'Here, drink this. It will warm you up,' Leszek said. But holding the cup was almost impossible because he was shaking so badly from the early stages of hypothermia.

'I can't drink it. I'm spilling it.'

'Try again. You need to drink.' Eventually, the shaking stopped and he drifted off to sleep under Leszek's watchful eye. It was New Year's Eve.

Later, when news of Krzysztof's ascent of Lhotse appeared in a Polish newspaper, his doctor learnt his advice had been ignored. Disgusted, he declared Krzysztof 'stupid'. In retrospect, Krzysztof was inclined to agree.

Years later, Italian alpinist Simone Moro, by then a leading high-altitude winter specialist, criticised Krzysztof's Lhotse climb, and several more of the earlier winter ascents, averring they didn't qualify since the expeditions had been working on the mountain outside the strict calendar definition of winter: 21 December to 21 March. In the case of Lhotse, it was because the expedition had reached base camp in November. Krzysztof was quick to defend his climb, pointing out it would be hard to argue his summit day of 31 December wasn't winter.

Simone insisted that to qualify as a true winter ascent, no activity on the mountain could begin before 21 December. This disqualified the first winter ascents of Manaslu, Dhaulagiri, Lhotse and Kangchenjunga (all of them Polish). He classified these climbs as 'trips carried out not fully in the winter season'. But Simone was also aware of the contextual importance of when the climbs were done – in the 1980s – and was diplomatic enough to acknowledge that the 'rules' he currently followed were guidelines for the 'modern' era of winter mountaineering in the highest mountains. Strict adherence to these dates was similar to judgements of climbing in 'cleaner' style – alpine style, rather than siege style with its fixed lines, Sherpa support and prepared camps – that earlier expeditions had used routinely.

Krzysztof, reflecting on this criticism, explained that although he respected Simone's commitment to winter ascents done with smaller teams in alpine style, a lot had changed over the years to allow this evolution in style. One of those changes was communication. Reliable contact with the outside world and stunningly accurate weather forecasts made it possible to calibrate the precise moment to act on a mountain to a specific day or even hours within a day, revolutionising the logistics of high-altitude climbing, particularly in winter. When Andrzej Zawada first started leading Himalayan expeditions in winter, he would take fourteen climbers, not because he needed all of them for the summit teams, but for rotations on the mountain, constantly hoping for good weather with at least two people positioned at a high camp. The approach might have seemed almost random, but it was the only way to have people in roughly the right place for a dash to the summit during a weather window. And in winter, those windows are short. When the accuracy of the forecasts improved, it became possible to remain in base camp in relative comfort while waiting for a window. This strategy meant far fewer climbers were needed.

'Simone was born later, and doesn't feel that difference, so he measures the routes done thirty years ago and today's on the same scale,' Krzysztof said. 'It's without a doubt a mistake of ahistorical thinking,' and then added, 'You can't entirely rule out that he is doing this for media purposes. Someone like Reinhold Messner is better able to make that comparison because he thinks synthetically and is historically prepared.'[16] An understanding of mountaineering history requires a contextual approach that takes into account the era in which climbs were done, the equipment and technology available and most importantly, the lack of knowledge about the climbing itself. Every one of those early winter ascents posed a huge question mark. Could they be done? Nobody knew. They were the real essence of adventure: journeys into the unknown.

For Andrzej Zawada, there was no doubt about the validity of the Lhotse climb, but rather the completion of a circle which he had begun back in 1974. His team had failed to reach the summit of Lhotse, but in 1988, the job was done. And he was there to help make it happen.

Six more teams attempted Lhotse in winter in the coming years, including two solo attempts on the notoriously difficult, almost unimaginably steep south face. French soloist Marc Batard reached 7,000 metres in late November 1989 before turning back, and Christophe Profit, also French, reached 7,300 metres in late December before retreating. To call their objective ambitious would be an understatement. Many had died trying to climb the south face in spring or autumn, including the seemingly invincible Jurek Kukuczka in 1989. Jurek's tragic, fatal fall from high on the face stunned the mountaineering community and forced many high-altitude climbers to re-evaluate their own sense of immortality in the mountains.

The teams most likely to succeed on this formidable face were the teams from Asia using a siege approach. In 2001 the Japanese Alpine Club's Tokai Section, led by Osamu Tanabe, one of Japan's leading high-altitude specialists, reached 7,600 metres before retreating on 22 December. In 2003 they were back, once more led by Osamu. He described the great threat on the face from rockfall: 'shrieking stone-bullets out of the blue at any time, despite incessant watch to avoid possible risks.'[17] By 5 December, they had surpassed the high point of their previous attempt and set up Camp 3 at 7,850 metres, from where they hoped to mount their summit bid. The temperature was -35° Celsius. But as so many before them had discovered, while the lower part of the south face was challenging and terribly dangerous, the real difficulties start near 8,000 metres: technical, steep and loose rock, with mind-bending exposure and crippling altitude. 'The crux of the wall actually started from there,' Osamu wrote, 'a fact yet unknown to us.'[18] They reached an astonishing 8,250 metres before turning back.

The Japanese weren't about to give up on the magnificent south face. In the winter of 2006 they were back, along with a Korean team trying the same line. They joined forces, alternating leads to push the route and fix ropes up the mountain. The morning hours were bitterly cold as they worked in shade. By noon each day the sun would swing around, bringing some badly-needed warmth to their freezing limbs but unleashing lethal volleys of stonefall and menacing waves of spindrift. Even worse were the seventy-kilometre-per-hour winds that knocked climbers off their feet and sent rocks high above them spinning into the air and triggering avalanches. Korean alpinist Ahn Chi-Young described it as a 'climbing hell'.

On 27 December, Takahiro Yamaguchi, Sherpa Pemba Chhoti and Osamu reached the top of the south face and the summit ridge of Lhotse. They were at 8,475 metres and it was now 3.35 p.m. 'At last we had accomplished the complete winter ascent of the Lhotse south face. It was a moment when I was deeply touched and my dream came true.'[19]

Although they weren't on the summit, it was pointless to continue. They would need to ascend and descend tricky technical terrain for at least another 200 metres along the ridge to gain the last forty-one metres of elevation, an almost impossible task. Similar to other impressive face climbs in the high mountains, which hadn't actually reached a summit but only the top of the face, this one was claimed by Osamu as a success. Historian Elizabeth Hawley refused to endorse it as a winter ascent of Lhotse, and British historian Lindsay Griffin agreed, writing, 'After previous attempts in the Nepalese winter seasons of 2001 and 2003, a Japanese expedition led by Osamu Tanabe has made the first winter ascent of the 8,516-metre Lhotse's immense south face, though the successful party was forced to retreat from a point on the summit ridge just forty-one metres below the top due to the lateness of the hour.'[20]

Eight expeditions to Lhotse in winter, some very near misses, an impressive ascent of the dangerous south face, but only one summit – by a slight Polish alpinist, without supplemental oxygen, alone, and in a corset.

8

SHISHAPANGMA

The Italian

History is not what happened, but what survives the
shipwrecks of judgement and chance.
Maria Popova, *Figuring*

After Krzysztof Wielicki's ascent of Lhotse in 1988, sixteen long winters passed before another 8,000-metre peak was climbed in the coldest season. This was not from lack of effort. Dozens of teams from around the world travelled to the Himalaya and the Karakoram in search of the kind of suffering only possible in the highest mountains in winter. Some wanted a first winter ascent, others a new route in winter, perhaps a winter ascent in alpine style, or a solo winter ascent. Top climbers from France and Italy, Poland and Japan, Korea and Spain, all took their chances in the thin cold air and the debilitating winds. Many chose to climb in winter because of the solitude, for as Himalayan climbing increased in popularity, due in part to the commercialisation of the sport, summers were getting crowded. Winter offered quiet isolation.

Although Everest and Annapurna were inundated with winter attempts during these years, Shishapangma, lowest of the 8,000ers at 8,027 metres, did not attract much interest. One possible deterrent was access, through Tibet, as well as the costly, necessary permits – from China. The mountain's topography also discouraged winter specialists. Even in summer, many climbers turn back after summiting the 8,008-metre Central Summit, since those extra nineteen metres of elevation to the Main Summit require two additional hours of slogging across a high plateau. Bad enough in summer, the screaming high-altitude winds of winter could prove impossible on this summit plateau. By coincidence, when two expeditions finally decided to attempt Shishapangma in winter, they chose the same year.

Shishapangma is the sole 8,000er located completely within Tibet. Only after its first ascent by a Chinese and Tibetan team in 1964 did the Chinese begin issuing permits to foreign teams. The sprawling massif is considered the easiest of the 8,000ers to climb via a route on the north-west face. A much steeper profile of the mountain faces south, and it was this side that caught the interest of Italian alpinist Simone Moro. Most importantly, it would be in the sun.

Simone already knew something about winter, from his tragic attempt on Annapurna in 1997, when Anatoli Boukreev and Dimitri Sobolev had both died in an avalanche. But he also knew the greatest winter expertise rested with the Poles, that few could surpass their ability to endure inhumane conditions for months at a time. So, he jumped at the chance to join an expedition that included four of them: Piotr Morawski, Darek Załuski, Jacek Jawien and Jan Szulc. Darek Załuski had the most experience at high altitude in winter. Born in 1959, Darek bridged the original Ice Warriors generation with younger Polish climbers, most of whom weren't overly keen on winter. Lean and lanky, Darek had climbed and filmed with Andrzej Zawada on Nanga Parbat, and with Krzysztof Wielicki on Makalu, K2, and again on Nanga Parbat, all in winter. He had also summited Gasherbrum II, Cho Oyu and Lhotse in summer. Darek felt comfortable up high. Seventeen years younger, Piotr Morawski was already exhibiting the skills and attitude that would propel him to the top of six 8,000ers in his short but meteoric career. Simone happily found himself paired with Piotr.

Arriving in Tibet, they learnt for the first time that two British alpinists had been on the mountain since November. Victor Saunders and Andy Parkin reached 6,500 metres before turning back, and by mid-December were already on their way home. Simone, a stickler for details, particularly when it came to the definition of 'winter', didn't hesitate to pass judgement: 'we have some difficulties to consider that expedition a winter climb. If nothing changed in the world, winter starts the 21st [of] December.'[1]

Working in teams of two, they took turns fixing lines on the south face: Camp 1, Camp 2, and finally Camp 3 at 7,100 metres. Above Camp 1, the mountain remained consistently steep. The icy ledge at Camp 2 was so narrow that one third of each tent hung suspended over the void. True, the other two-thirds rested on terra firma, but the climbers dared not unclip from their anchors in what was almost a hanging bivvy. Camp 3 was equally precarious and cold, -40° Celsius, but it provided the perfect launching pad for Simone and Piotr's first summit bid. Above Camp 3, a couloir narrowed to a funnel of wind-polished ice, crumbling rock and compact snow. Switching leads up this, Piotr was out in front and out of sight when Simone's handheld radio burst into life.

'Simone, come up! I'm finally out of the couloir, in the sun, on the ridge. It's gorgeous up here!'

Relieved, Simone answered, 'Okay, I'm on my way!'[2]

The view was indeed splendid, but the open expanse in front of them was exposed to the jet stream. They still had 500 metres to go in winds of 150 kilometres per hour and temperatures down to -52° Celsius. Piotr and Simone struggled along, braced against the wind. At 7,750 metres Simone looked at his watch: 3.30 p.m. and 270 metres to the top. Piotr saw him checking the time but said nothing.

'It'll be dark in an hour and a half,' Simone told him.

Piotr, the less experienced of the two, responded with a question. 'What are we going to do?' Simone looked up at the summit.

He looked back at Piotr, who pleaded, 'I'd really like to get up there, now that we've done all of this.' Yet the voice of reason and experience prevailed.

'We have to go back, right away,' Simone said. 'We have the whole couloir to descend and we'll have to do it in the dark as it is.'[3]

They embraced, congratulated each other on their high point, and started the long and delicate descent, guided by the tiny bobbing orbs of light from their headlamps and arriving back at their tent in full darkness. Piotr descended to base the following day and Darek climbed up to attempt the summit with Simone. That attempt also failed when a storm moved in. Although the expedition was now over, they had come tantalisingly close.

One year later, the same team returned to Shishapangma. Once again, Simone was the only non-Pole involved. Darek felt that having a world-famous 'foreigner' on the team was a good thing. 'When Simone started winter mountaineering, it became a bit more accepted,' he said, citing the tendency for Poles to downplay their accomplishments simply because they were Polish. Simone was fully aware of his position as a 'foreigner', writing, 'To tell you the truth winter ascents on 8,000-metre peaks are still waiting for a non-Polish climber to write this little page of vertical history.'[4] Simone wanted to write that page.

The team planned to acclimatise on a trek in Nepal, then slowly move into Tibet to the bottom of the south face, and start climbing after 21 December to satisfy the conventions of a true winter ascent. While still in Nepal, they learnt that elite French alpinist Jean-Christophe Lafaille was also planning a winter ascent of the mountain – solo.

JC, as he was known, was an all-round tour de force. An internationally qualified mountain guide, a top-level rock climber, and a high-altitude mountaineer who had proven himself repeatedly, most notably on Annapurna in 1992 when he managed what mountaineers around the world considered an extraordinary and improbable self-rescue off the south face, alone, and with a broken arm. The diminutive – little more than five feet tall – JC was no slouch. The Polish–Italian team had reason to worry if they wanted to snag the first winter ascent.

They also knew JC was planning to arrive at the mountain in late November and make his solo dash in early December. Once again, Simone weighed in on the definition of winter. 'If winter starts 21 December, I refuse to arrive in base camp before that date,' he explained. 'And it's not just a question of numbers. Up until the first two weeks of December, weather conditions are perfect, in fact.' He clarified that, if you arrive in early December, all of the setting up of camps and fixing lines can be done in optimal conditions. 'After that, everything gets complicated, almost hellish: snow slows everything down, intense cold which freezes the hands and feet, wind which makes the base camp setup an adventure unto itself,' he explained. 'So, this matter of 21 December is not a case of neurotic perfectionism. Rather, it's an actual fact which must be respected and accepted.'[5] His Polish partners agreed, so rather than rush to the mountain to compete with JC, they stuck with their plan.

As did JC. He arrived at base camp on 14 November, acclimatised until 8 December, and left next day to start the ascent. He was standing on the summit on 11 December at 11.30 a.m. 'Despite my elation, I had to concentrate on the cold that lived in my feet and my entire body, and on the descent that awaited me,' he recalled.[6] The formerly perfect weather broke down and the mountains became enveloped in dark heavy clouds. It snowed and blew and snowed some more, testing JC on his descent. He down-climbed, rappelled and plunged the thousands of metres to base camp, arriving on 12 December. 'My project ended as it had begun, in infinite solitude,' he said.[7]

As remarkable as it was, few regarded his climb to be a winter ascent, although his wife Katia did. This aroused the ire of Krzysztof Wielicki, who wrote to the *American Alpine Journal* refuting the claim. His observations were much the same as Simone's; at the end of his comments, he concluded, 'Therefore, I think that Lafaille had rather excellent fall conditions rather than real winter ones.'[8] Facts are facts. Winter is winter.

Simone and the three Poles reached base camp on 23 December and like the year before started working in rotating teams of two: Darek and Jacek, Simone and Piotr. Up they went again, setting up ABC, Camp 1 at 6,500 metres, Camp 2 at 7,000 metres. By this time the mountain was in the severe grip of winter, and strong winds only amplified the bitterness of those frigid days. The saving grace was the sun, but the higher they climbed, the stronger the wind. Struggling under the weight of ungainly packs crammed with ropes to fix on the steep upper slopes, they had to concentrate on their balance every step of the way. One hundred metres at a time, scraping on rock steps with their crampons, slamming their axes into patches of ice, their cumbersome down suits impeding their movements, their bulky goggles limiting their vision, their heaving lungs gasping in the thin air. Simone was filming Piotr when he heard a cry. 'Simone, come up! We're finally on the riiiidge!'[9]

For the second time, the two were atop the summit ridge of Shishapangma. But this time they had a tent. Having learnt their lesson from the previous year, they had planned this year to camp on the ridge at 7,350 metres to shorten the distance and time it would take to climb to the summit. But the wind! After only partially unfurling the tent, Piotr crawled inside to prevent it from being blown to oblivion. Simone tossed in his pack to provide more ballast. They secured it as best they could and settled in for the night, planning to descend the following day and rest at base camp before a final summit bid.

Neither Simone nor Piotr could sleep. The tent fabric snapped and crackled from the relentless wind. In the middle of the night, Simone, frustrated at his insomnia, sat up, reluctantly withdrew one hand from his warm sleeping bag and opened the tent zip a few centimetres to peer out into the night. The star-studded sky shimmered and the wind, although still steady, seemed to have moderated to something more tolerable.

Polish Himalayan climber Piotr Morawski, who made the first winter ascent of Shishapangma on 14 January 2005 with Simone Moro. *Photo: Darek Załuski.*

'Piotr, you sleeping?'

'No, what is it?'

'There's a starry sky and the wind is strong but doesn't seem to be getting worse … what if we try for the summit tomorrow? What do you think?'

'I was thinking that myself,' Piotr answered. 'I wasn't sleeping, partly because I had this idea buzzing around in my head.'[10]

Now sitting upright in their bags, humming with excitement, they hatched their plan. They would leave at 6 a.m., taking nothing but their cameras and a video recorder. No packs to weigh them down. Since they were not fully acclimatised, they would need to hustle if they hoped to tag the summit and get back to their tent by dark. After setting a firm turn-around time of 2.30 p.m. and promising each other to honour it, they slid back into their bags and set the alarm.

Next morning, they started up the ridge at 6 a.m., taking turns breaking trail. The frigid air burned their straining lungs as they gained altitude. Their rests lengthened as they hunched over their axes fighting for breath; the number of steps before the next one decreased. They looked up the gently rising ridge and spied a hump. Was that the summit? Encouraged, they climbed it, only to see the ridge continuing. At noon the wind picked up, became gusty, raking the ridge, blowing plumes of snow across its sculpted white cornices. They adapted their rhythm, now resting during the strongest gusts and moving during the lulls. 'We took the last series of steps with heads bowed, not looking up,' Simone recalled. 'We wanted to relish the sight hitting us all at once.'[11]

At 1.15 p.m. on 14 January, Piotr and Simone clung to each other on the summit of Shishapangma in temperatures of -52° Celsius and wind gusts of 115 kilometres per hour. 'What joy something so apparently useless, so dangerous, and so stupid can give,' Simone recalled. 'Surrounding us was an infinity of mountains, powerful and silent. Marks that will disappear with the first gust of wind, cries that will be lost in thin air, stories that will never change the world. It seems to be so absurd to climb these peaks and so insane to do it during winter. Instead I felt terribly alive, logical, a direct protagonist of my life with that magical ascent. From a dead man I had become alive, from a slave I was free, just like the alpinism which had trapped me and from which I had managed to escape.'[12] Despite the intense cold, they stayed fifteen minutes, photographing, filming – drinking in the immensity of the view.

Before leaving they tried to radio base camp but the signal was too weak, so they headed down, practically sprinting. When they reached the tent, they dived in and began melting snow immediately, their first drops of liquid since leaving many hours earlier. The radio crackled to life: it was Darek.

'How did it go today? What did you do?' Darek asked.

'All good today, we went to the summit,' Piotr cheekily responded.

'And this is how you tell us?!' Darek shouted. 'You're awesome, congratulations, that's great! Terrific, terrific!'[13]

Darek and Jacek had planned their summit attempt for the following day, so Simone and Piotr met them at around 6,700 metres: two climbers going up, hopeful for a summit, the other two exhausted and heading down. They could all see that the weather was worsening. Snow and sleet and even more wind. The summit soon disappeared, shrouded in cloud.

That night, Darek and Jacek had to fight for their lives when a violent storm broke over their tent at 7,350 metres. It was like a physical assault. They were sure their tent would be ripped from its moorings and blown off the ridge. So sure, they wore their boots and all their clothing inside their sleeping bags, ready to leap into action should the tent start to slide. All night they fought with the cold, with their fears. By morning they were so exhausted from the ordeal there was no question what direction they would take: down. With zero visibility in the raging, high-altitude storm, they inched down the mountain, relying on the fixed lines to guide them back.

The expedition was over. Darek and Jacek had survived one of the worst high-altitude storms of their lives, while Piotr and Simone had made the first winter ascent of Shishapangma.

During the preceding seventeen years, there had been few winter attempts of 8,000ers – in part because so many of the Polish Ice Warriors had died in the mountains. After seventeen years of failures, this successful climb of Shishapangma reignited interest in the art of suffering. It didn't hurt that there was a famous Italian alpinist on board, one who could express himself well, who was embraced by the media. Simone later reflected on the importance of the climb: 'Alpinism is an art form, like painting or music. Just as there are those who portray fantastic landscapes on canvas and write extraordinary scores, there are also those who attempt to venture into different territory – the territory of innovation, a more complicated and perhaps less readily understood form of art … each form has its dignity.'[14]

Simone's partner, Piotr Morawski, continued with the art of alpinism, making five more ascents of 8,000-metre peaks. But like so many others, his career ended in tragedy, when he died in a crevasse on Dhaulagiri, on 8 April 2009, aged thirty-two.

With his success on Shishapangma, Simone had found his niche: winter. Polish mountaineers had mixed reactions to his success. Some, like Darek, were pleased a non-Pole had succeeded on a winter climb of an 8,000er. In some strange way, it burnished their previous first winter ascents – all seven of them – with a sheen of respectability. There were others who thought Simone's ascent was a one-off. And anyway, he had been with a Pole. They weren't expecting more from Simone's direction.

History would prove them wrong.

9

MAKALU

Two Against the Wind

Climb if you will, but remember that courage and strength are nought without prudence, and that a momentary negligence may destroy the happiness of a lifetime. Do nothing in haste; look well to each step; and from the beginning think what may be the end.

Edward Whymper, *Scrambles Amongst the Alps*

Having dispensed with his corset, Krzysztof Wielicki came up with an interesting plan. Emboldened by his lonely winter ascent of Lhotse in 1988, and a subsequent summer solo ascent of Dhaulagiri, Krzysztof wondered if a solo winter ascent of the spectacular and difficult west pillar of Makalu might also be possible. 'It was a time when I dreamed bigger than I should have … surely I was on a roll,' he later said, laughing. 'Things were going well and I thought I could take it one step further. Especially since I really liked this pillar. It's beautiful in profile when seen from the south face of Lhotse.'[1] Indeed, the striking pillar slices this majestic peak in two, dividing Makalu's west face from its south-west face. But in winter? Alone?

Makalu, on the border between Nepal and Tibet, is, at 8,485 metres, the fifth-tallest mountain in the world, a steep and stunningly beautiful four-sided pyramid. It had been attracting Ice Warriors ever since the first winter ascent of nearby Everest. Many of those warriors were women. The first attempt came in the winter of 1980–81 with an international team led by Italian alpinists Renato and Goretta Casarotto. They were defeated primarily by strong winds. A British team led by Linda and Ron Rutland tried a year later but retreated from 7,315 metres, also defeated by winds that reached 160 kilometres per hour.

French alpinist Ivan Ghirardini tried a solo ascent of the difficult west buttress the same year, but 200-kilometre-per-hour winds and temperatures that routinely plunged to -50° Celsius beat him back as well. A strong Japanese team reached 7,520 metres in 1985 before high winds destroyed their camps, forcing them to flee for their lives. Famed Italian mountaineer Reinhold Messner was next, making a winter attempt with Hans Kammerlander, his regular partner of that period, in 1985–86. Even these two Himalayan superstars were defeated by the wind.

An even stronger Japanese team tried an alpine-style winter ascent in 1986. Legendary climbers Noboru Yamada and Yasuhira Saito opted for an 'early winter' approach, reaching their high point of 7,500 metres on 9 December before the wind overpowered them too. A mostly Polish team also reached the 7,500-metre mark, in January 1988, but Makalu's by now notorious winds of 100 kilometres per hour pushed them back.

Wind. Wind. Wind. Would the winds of Makalu ever let up?

Two years later, Krzysztof Wielicki assembled a four-person team with his good friend and former teammate Ingrid Baeyens, from Belgium; one of Poland's leading female high-altitude mountaineers, Anna Czerwińska; and Ryszard Pawlowski. Ryszard's resilience had been honed in Silesian coalmines, then on the towering smokestacks of Katowice, and finally in the Himalaya. Krzysztof's first obstacle was money. The communist regime in Poland had recently collapsed and traditional sources of government funding for expeditions had shrunk to a trickle. Thank goodness for Ingrid, who brought hard currency from Belgium.

Although he had his own agenda – the west pillar – Krzysztof acclimatised with the team in order to set the stage for their ascent of the north-west ridge. Although everyone got along well, Ingrid didn't speak Polish and was often isolated. They would meet in the mess tent each night for dinner but the conversation usually stalled. Before long, they would be back in their individual tents. 'Not much atmosphere,' Krzysztof recalled.[2] They managed a bit of cheer on Christmas Eve when they hung mandarin oranges from the ceiling in an effort to create an upside-down Christmas tree. It looked 'festive', in a winter expedition, base camp kind of way.

On Krzysztof's first try up the west pillar, the wind swept him off at 5,800 metres. On the second attempt, he crept higher, his bivouac crammed into a crevasse at 6,600 metres. The next day, carrying everything with him, including a tent, the possibilities for a bivouac site appeared even slimmer. He ended up overnighting in a shallow rock scoop at 7,300 metres. When he tried to erect his little bivvy tent, the wind snatched it and slammed it against

Christmas Eve at Makalu base camp on the 1990-91 Polish-Belgian winter expedition. *Left to right:* Anna Czerwińska, Ingrid Baeyens, Ryszard Pawlowski, Krzysztof Wielicki. *Photo: Krzysztof Wielicki Archive.*

the rocks, smashing the tent poles. Now he was without a tent, only a bivvy sack. 'But with the perspective of time I think it was good the tent broke,' he later reflected. 'It's hard to say how things would have ended if I had gotten to the difficult summit dome ... God, I think, gave me a bit of a warning and taught me a lesson.'[3] He still had almost 1,200 metres to the summit, and the terrain was steep and technical. If he carried on up and ran out of time, he would need to continue over the top and down the other side. On Lhotse he had also climbed alone up the last 1,200 metres, but with the assurance of a tent waiting for him below. Here, there would be no tent, merely a stash of food and equipment on the far side of the mountain. He retreated, and the expedition ended.

Krzysztof returned to Makalu in the winter of 2000–01, leading a group of Poles from the Ice Warriors generation – *his* generation, some would say. Fifty years of age at the time, Krzysztof was fully aware that both he and his team were aging for such an ambitious project. But life had changed in post-communist Poland. People had jobs, careers. 'The younger climbers in the 1990s had to stay behind and look after their families and businesses, so long expeditions weren't a good fit for them,' Krzysztof explained.[4] His Makalu team was 'old school'; when someone called these guys for an expedition, regardless of the season, no matter how long, they simply packed up and went. They were part of the immense brotherhood of Polish Himalayan climbing. One of these was Darek Załuski from Warsaw. Although younger than the others by about eight years, Darek had already amassed an astonishing amount of winter experience. He was a workhorse who, despite a deceptively thin frame, could haul loads, fix lines, set up camps and suffer with the best. Darek would eventually participate in nine winter expeditions to the highest mountains on the planet, so Makalu with Krzysztof was nothing out of the ordinary.

The team lacked focus from the beginning, moving from the west pillar to the Japanese route to the normal route. They wasted precious time and effort in the process, and the mountain and the Makalu wind wore them down. Almost twenty years later, Darek described that wind: 'From base camp we had this huge mountain above us, and imagine that there is this sound. I was sure this strange noise was a river, but it was from the wind up high. It was pushing down on us the entire time – like Mordor. All the time. No break from this sound.'

It was much worse higher on the mountain. As the team grew weary, their motivation eroded and, after forty days, they wanted to go home. Krzysztof was surprised. Three-month-long winter expeditions were the norm for these guys. What happened here? He finally attributed their foot-dragging to their advancing age, their longer recovery time from stints at high camps, and the horrible, annoying, relentless wind. 'I quickly made peace with our failure and came to the conclusion that after two failed attempts on this peak, we should leave it for others,' he later said.[5]

Possibly because he had twice failed on Makalu, or because it had been too long since a purely Polish team had succeeded on an 8,000er in winter, Krzysztof launched his famous 'Winter Manifesto' the following year. He was well qualified to write this call to action. He had been one of the first two to climb an 8,000er in winter when he and Leszek Cichy climbed Everest in 1980. He adored Andrzej Zawada, the founder of high-altitude winter climbing, and had never lost sight of Andrzej's dream. But now in his early fifties, Krzysztof knew the continuation of this winter legacy must rely on younger climbers.

He called upon 'young, angry and ambitious' Polish alpinists to finish the remaining peaks. 'Let the nickname "Ice Warrior", given us by Englishmen, be inscribed in the history of Himalayan climbing forever.' He offered Poland's youth a direct challenge:

According to the old rule, you should do what you do best. We were successful in high mountain winter explorations. After all, half of fourteen 8,000-metre peaks were climbed by Poles, within just eight years (1980–88) to boot. Six unconquered peaks are waiting for us … We have done one half of the job. Now it's your turn to finish it: you the young, angry and ambitious. We are giving you eight years, the same time as we needed. It's fair enough, is it not? If you could pull it off, would it not be great? Can you imagine that? All 8,000-metre peaks conquered for the first time in winter, all by Poles. There is a chance for success. It is a game worth devoting time, money and effort. Now is the time to make decisions … You can count on my generation, on our help, even our active participation. The choice is yours! … Let's join Europe, with our head held high and with self-esteem. There is little time left![6]

Jean-Christophe 'JC' Lafaille could not have known how little time he had left when he went to Makalu in 2005–06. The forty-year-old French alpinist, known for his quiet, unassuming and gentle disposition, was attempting a winter solo ascent of the mountain when he vanished on 27 January 2006. 'He was a little guy but phenomenally strong, very, very fast and absolutely gifted,' said American alpinist Ed Viesturs, one of his former rope mates. 'He was technically the most talented all-round climber in the world. He could climb anything.'[7]

On his last night, after six weeks on the mountain, JC pitched his tiny red tent at 7,600 metres. He woke at 5 a.m., heated some water, ate a little and packed. Outside the tent it was dark, -30° Celsius, with a light wind. The summit of Makalu was still ten hours of hard and dangerous climbing away, even with his almost supernatural speed. He would need to climb steep icy slopes, across crevasse-strewn glaciers and up rock steps, wheezing in the thin air at an altitude not far below where passenger jets cruise. Before setting off for the summit he called his wife, Katia, on his satellite phone. He told her he hadn't slept much due to the altitude and cold, but that he felt strong. He said he would check in during the day and keep her updated on his progress. It was his last call.

On 4 February, a search team consisting of Katia, her brother and Veikka Gustafsson, a Finnish alpinist who had climbed with JC and knew the route, arrived at Makalu. They flew by the peak in a helicopter and spied his little tent. But nothing more. No pack. No clothing. No JC. They left some supplies at base camp, on the remote chance he managed somehow to return alive, but Veikka doubted that would happen. He knew the route was riddled with treacherous, hidden crevasses; he had fallen into three of them on his ascent of the peak ten years earlier, but had been roped up with two others and consequently survived. JC was alone. There would be no one to pull him out of a slot. Veikka was convinced this was how JC lost his life, on that long, lonely climb. One of the truly great Himalayan alpinists was gone. Another widow left to mourn, a fatherless son and daughter.

But who was this widow? Many people had strong impressions of Katia Lafaille. Yann Geizendanner, Chamonix's official weather forecaster, described her as JC's manager, his sponsor supplier, his media guru. He described the couple as a team: the climber and the support. Katia enabled JC to accomplish incredible feats in the mountains. 'Katia wanted him to focus on training, to not be distracted or worried by the groupies, the criticism, the jealousy,' Yann explained. 'She was the only one to whom he would really listen. Alone, Katia would have done nothing; alone, JC would have been a good alpinist. But together they became a legend.'[8]

Katia understood JC's passion for the mountains. She was also a climber, and she knew he needed the beauty and purity of the mountains more than anything. Some people accused Katia of trying to mould JC into a collector of 8,000ers, similar to Reinhold Messner, Ed Viesturs and Krzysztof Wielicki. She defended herself, saying he was climbing them anyway, so why not do it properly? Make a career out of it.

In her own way, Katia was with JC on Makalu. They spoke to each other frequently on the satellite phone. She knew from the tone of his voice how he was feeling, how strong he was at any moment. She advised him while he climbed, even coached him, sometimes motivating him but, other times, encouraging him to retreat. Theirs was an unusually close relationship, one based on a full understanding of the risks. Still, it was hard. 'I thought about what it would be like if he was killed many times, of course, but I never imagined the void, the emptiness,' Katia said six weeks after his death. 'The emptiness is terrible. We had so much ahead of us.'[9]

Makalu, which seemed unassailable in winter, continued to attract women. Goretta and Linda, Ingrid and Anna, even Katia. In 2007, more women arrived to try their hand. The Italian–Slovenian team of Nives Meroi and her husband, Romano Benet, arrived with another Italian, Luca Vuerich. Both Nives and Romano were well on their way to collecting all fourteen of the 8,000ers, and were serious contenders for the first winter ascent. They weren't alone. Four Kazakh army mountaineers, including the unstoppable Denis Urubko and his equally resilient partner, Serguey Samoilov, were there as well.

Born in 1973 in Nevinnomyssk, Russia, Denis soon moved with his family to the mountainous island of Sakhalin because of his severe childhood asthma. He learnt to climb while attending high school in Vladivostok, Siberia, and discovered a natural affinity for the sport. 'I came into the world of mountaineering the way a drop of water rolls into the only spot intended for it.'[10] Soon after the Soviet Union collapsed in 1991, he moved to Almaty, the capital of the newly independent Republic of Kazakhstan, and joined the Kazakh military. Trained under the military as a climber to the 'point of self-obliteration', Denis's career as an alpinist was underway. By the time he found himself on Makalu in the winter of 2007–08, Denis had already proven himself on ten 8,000ers, all without supplemental oxygen. But Makalu wasn't giving up easily.

Denis sent regular reports to the Russian climbing media, tracking his struggle with the 200-kilometre-per-hour winds. At times, it seemed they would drive him crazy. Then, on 24 January, they temporarily weakened.

'Good morning! The sun rises above Makalu ... Eugeny, Serguey and I will start on the summit bid tomorrow ... I shaved, I put on clean clothes and am ready for the fight.'

The calm air was short-lived. They reached 7,400 metres where the wind roared like a fast-moving train, picking them up and throwing them down. They had no choice but to flee.

3 February. 'We are in crisis – have been virtually blown off by the wind. Have you ever seen a flying Samoilov? That's a heart-breaking show. We've got some frostbite. But we're alive. Thought we had a chance. Tomorrow we'll begin our way to home.'[11]

It was a rare admission of defeat from the strongest Himalayan climber active in the high mountains at that time. Denis Urubko wasn't used to retreating. Karl Gabl, the Innsbruck meteorologist who had been advising the team, confirmed that wind speeds on Makalu averaged 135 kilometres per hour and temperatures -35° Celsius. The jet stream had picked them up like insects, tossing them about, slamming them down on to the wind-hardened snow.

Another winter season on Makalu. Another battle lost to the wind.

Denis was not yet finished with Makalu, however. One day his phone rang. It was Simone Moro.

'Denis, how are you?'

'Good, my friend. What's up?'

'Makalu. Do you want to go back to Makalu? I am planning a winter expedition for 2008–09 and I think you should come with me.'

'Good idea, Simone. Who else on the team?'

'Just the two of us. Fast and light.'

Denis said yes. He had a score to settle, plus he liked climbing with Simone. He enjoyed his 'hot-chilly' character, and he respected him. 'We have confidence in each other's technical experience, professionalism and endurance,' he explained. 'Plus, we know each other's capabilities. And we are sure that one will not leave the other, no matter what. We'll crawl if we have to, but not leave without attempting a rescue.'[12]

Makalu wasn't actually Simone's first choice that winter. He had hoped to return to Broad Peak in the Karakoram for his third try in winter, but when he learnt a Polish team would be there, he changed his plans. No need to create a real-time competition in such a dangerous sport. And besides, on Makalu he could tie in with Denis again. He valued their brotherhood of the rope dearly. 'He and I truly have a special connection, unparalleled,' he said. 'Together we're better. I'd love it if our climbing partnership were remembered as the union of two personalities who were able to perfectly mesh in ability, character, and imagination to pursue a common dream. Sharing success is important. It's a cornerstone of life and coexistence.'[13]

And with that elevated level of mutual trust, they decided to attempt this behemoth in winter as a twosome, alpine style, and as fast as possible. A day after unloading their precious cargo at base camp, they made a short acclimatisation jaunt up one of Makalu's long ridges, immediately above camp. Having reached 5,300 metres, they returned, feeling strong, though buffeted as usual by the Makalu winds. They planned to start moving their gear up the mountain the following day, and return to base camp. The weather was stupendous: clear, sunny, and without wind. The absence of wind was almost unsettling. Simone's mind was racing. 'Denis, I think we should change our plan. The weather is perfect. Instead of a gear drop, let's pack for three or four days of climbing and just go up. What do you think?'

'Incredible. I was thinking the same thing,' Denis replied, with a wide grin. The synchronicity in their partnership was catching fire.

They climbed to 5,400 metres and camped. Since the following morning was also perfect they continued up to 5,650 metres and established their advanced base camp (ABC), unfortunately atop a latrine left behind by a summer expedition. Holding their noses, they decided to stay. The third consecutive stellar day saw them reach 6,100 metres, where they set up Camp 1. When Simone called Karl Gabl on the sat phone, their meteorologist promised one more day of good weather.

Twenty-first-century high-altitude climbers all relied on Karl's forecasts. In addition to standard global weather models, he could access data from balloon-based instruments launched from nearby locations in Srinagar, India and Tibet, as well as by coalition forces in Kandahar and Kabul, Afghanistan. These self-destructing balloons rise to 30,000 metres, transmitting an exact profile of atmospheric temperature, humidity and air pressure, along with wind direction and speed. Karl analysed this data to formulate accurate forecasts of both temperature and wind speed. For each day of an expedition, he created a folder with countless columns of numbers. Based on these figures, he could see what was happening at 8,000 metres.

With Karl's promise of yet another good day, the temptation was overwhelming to carry on, to make a summit bid. But both Simone and Denis knew their bodies, and they knew the routine of high-altitude climbing. Inadequate acclimatisation is a sure ticket to disaster. Still, the summit beckoned. They packed up their gear, strapped on their crampons, tied in and headed up.

At 6,400 metres, a series of crevasses crisscrossed the glacier, forcing them to zigzag with a tight rope between them. The snow was hard and they were fit: they moved confidently, heart rates quickening as their breathing became shallower. When they reached the usual location of Camp 2 at 6,750 metres, they still felt good. 'We hope to become not too greedy of this metres that we are doing now so easy,' Simone said. 'The weather sooner or later will change, so it's better to have fun.'[14] They decided to keep going, just a little farther, only stopping for the night at 6,913 metres.

Digging and scraping, they excavated a level platform for the tent, set it up and dived in. Rehydrating was now an urgent necessity, since they had essentially raced up the mountain in only five days. They boiled water and drank tea until nausea forced them to stop. Next up was tortellini in a soupy broth, topped by a hefty chunk of parmesan and a square of rich dark chocolate. Satiated, they slept: in Simone's case, badly. The 1,800-metre gain in five days didn't agree with him. Although the following morning his eyes were swollen with oedema, they drank some more, ate a bit of food and continued up.

The plan was to reach at least 7,000 metres to memorise the route in case of whiteout conditions on descent, as well as search for old fixed ropes for their summit bid. Simone slogged on, dry-heaving and gasping. Denis climbed like a machine. At 7,050 metres they turned around, stripping their camp on the way down, burying a cache of gear in the snow and marking it with wands. Part of their strategy was not to leave any tents on the mountain. They knew the fierce Makalu winds would likely rip them off. This meant heavier packs and they would need to pitch the tent each night as they moved up, but this way they were guaranteed shelter. They left nothing to chance, since they knew from Karl that 150-kilometre-per-hour winds were in the forecast for the next few days. Still retching, Simone lost altitude as quickly as he could, following Denis back down the mountain.

ABC was a welcome sight, even if it *was* on top of a latrine. The temperature was so cold the odour barely penetrated the walls of the tent. They gorged. Simone, being Italian, was master of the menu; he wasn't going to live without plenty of delicious food. Their high-altitude sprint was rewarded with spaghetti and tomato sauce and, of course, more parmesan. The next night's menu featured a roast chicken, dripping in fat. Although the weather had changed, they didn't care: they were safely in camp, eating like champions. 'The wind had picked up and from that day on, its sound was the background noise of our expedition. That constant, powerful rumble coming from Makalu's ridge was a clue to the force of the gusts at higher altitude,' Simone recalled.[15] It brought to mind Darek's description a few years earlier. Like Mordor.

The storm continued to rage. A call to Karl Gabl confirmed there was no point in moving up the mountain. They would simply be blown off. The days passed. They chatted with the Nepali crew living in camp with them. Simone spoke with his daughter Martina on Skype, showing her his life at ABC. They wrote their blogs and listened to music. They read.

Finally, they had the chance to move a little. They climbed back up to Camp 2, reaching it at noon, dug up their cache, and set up their little camp. That night they suffered. The intensity of the cold was easy to forget down in ABC. They continued up the following morning without their packs, intent on going higher than their previous effort. In a couloir at 7,100 metres, they began to find fragments of fixed ropes, hacking them free from the snow and ice with their axes. The wind came in gusts, knocking them off balance, both physically and mentally. They stopped at 7,300 metres and turned around, racing down the mountain, seeking thicker air, warmer air, stiller air. Within a few hours they were back in the safety of ABC.

They waited for days on end as winds roared through their camp, dislodging heavy stones, ripping guywires, shearing ropes. It was truly frightening. Karl Gabl continued to describe them as hurricane-force winds. But he had some good news as well.

'I see a three-day window of pretty good weather, but with increasing wind,' he said. 'Tomorrow it'll be forty kilometres per hour; the day after, seventy; the third day, ninety. Then the jet stream will come through again, the hurricane, whatever you want to call it.'

'Wow, great, thanks Karl!'

'Simone, wait. Promise me you'll go back to Camp 1 in three days' time. Promise me that. Listen, if you stay up on the mountain in that wind, you'll die.'

'Okay, Karl. I promise. I'll still call you every day, even from the higher camps, so you can confirm the weather and update me on any developments.'

'Sounds good, Simone, ciao and good luck.'[16]

Their weather window had arrived, if you can call ninety-kilometre-per-hour winds a 'window'. With their third partner, Karl, on standby, Denis and Simone planned to leave the next day, aiming for the Makalu La at 7,400 metres. They packed their climbing and camera gear, a bit of food, a gas cartridge, their high-altitude suits, some extra clothing and a two-person ultra-light tent. At 10.30 a.m. they started up. The clock was ticking. They had seventy-two hours.

By this stage, both men were well acclimatised and still extremely fit. They reached 6,900 metres in less than four hours and set up the tent. That night's menu was tortellini with parmesan, salami, cheese, crackers and tea. Their appetites were holding up, a sign their bodies had adjusted well.

Next morning they left at 7.25 a.m., the earliest they could face the bitter cold. Clad in their high-altitude suits, balaclavas, down mittens and special wool socks, they soloed through sections with fixed ropes, then roped up when the fixed lines ended. Rather than belaying, they simul-climbed, moving together. A slip by either would likely have been fatal. The wind churned, threatening to pick them up and toss them down but they made it safely to the Makalu La, which was bathed in sun, offering a bit of psychological warmth. Another 1,100 metres to go. Although they had planned to camp at the Makalu La, it was early and they were still feeling strong and motivated, so they continued to 7,700 metres, where they stopped and set up the ultra-light tent. Less than 800 metres to go.

The temperature inside the tent was -40° Celsius that night. They slept in their down suits and boot liners inside their sleeping bags. They cooked. Talked. Took pictures. Planned. 'Temperature felt as if we were in the space,' Denis recalled. 'During all night we felt freezing fingers and toes by pain ... A simple breath became as a torture ... It became necessary to cross all rings of hell for the beginning of [the] final route summit push.'[17] They set the alarm for 3 a.m. but when they unzipped the tent, they were met with gusts of snow-laden wind. It appeared the weather was starting to break down. They bent into the wind, strapped on their crampons, and tied in to their twenty-five metres of seven-millimetre rope.

'The cold took our breath away,' Simone said. 'Warming our frozen muscles took a tremendous effort but we eventually got into a rhythm: twenty or twenty-five steps followed by a rest to catch our breath. We repeated this sequence over and over again, like robots.'[18] With ski goggles to protect their eyes, balaclavas on their faces and puffy high-altitude suits encasing their bodies, they resembled space travellers, astronauts, other-worldly beings. The wind shrieked, tearing at them, knocking them off balance, filling their ears with a monstrous roar. They didn't speak, but gestured to each other occasionally, moving together like a single organism. At 8,000 metres they stopped for a short rest.

'How's it going, Simone?' Denis asked, their first verbal communication in hours.

'Good, I'm good. It's fucking cold and this wind is hell, but I'm good, I'm still strong.'

'Perfect. Me too. We're at 8,000 metres and it's only mid-morning. We're doing well.'[19]

There was no more discussion. It was now clear that Denis and Simone were bound for the summit. Still roped together, they alternated leads, moving in fits and starts as they wrestled with the gusts of wind. They reached the north-west ridge at 8,200 metres. It was hard as stone. And later, it *was* stone, with rocky pillars that needed bypassing. At the base of a buttress, the snow changed quality: fresh, unconsolidated, unsupportive.

Their progress slowed as they slipped backwards with each step. Simone grabbed a fragment of old fixed rope poking out of the snow. Eighty metres left. The ridge was sharp now, so they moved carefully, one at a time, belaying each other, anchored to an old piton left by some previous team. It was hard to know if it would hold a fall; this was merely 'social belaying'. If your partner falls, you will likely fall as well. Denis was now out front. He stopped, signalling Simone to join him. The last five-metre traverse to the summit was knife-edged, exposed, its cornice unravelling like a scroll. In the screaming wind, Denis and Simone now stopped to discuss, almost argue over who should lead these last five metres and who should film. Finally, Denis convinced Simone to go first and at 1.53 p.m. on 9 February 2009, he was on the narrow top.

Summit moments are private affairs. Some experience elation. Some feel gratitude. Almost all are overwhelmed with exhaustion and an innate reflex to descend. Quickly. The compulsion to survive takes over. Simone's reflections on the summit of Makalu were unusual. As he fell to his knees, he swung his ice axe with all of his might into the snow-capped summit. 'I channelled everything into that motion, all my effort, joy, energy, rage,' he said. 'That swing was for all the people over the years who'd done nothing but hassle me about why I share, why I talk, why I write, why I climb, why I fly, why, why, why …'[20] Even on top of this splendid mountain, this lonely summit, with his friend nearby, Simone could not block out the white noise of the naysayers, the competitors, the media, the detractors.

After a few moments he climbed down to Denis and they swapped places. Now it was Denis's turn. Ever the disciplined, military-trained athlete, his time up top was brief. He lifted his arms and smiled, and was immediately back with his partner. 'Okay, Simone, let's get down. You first.'[21]

They reached their tent in the last lingering moments of daylight, crawled inside and looked at each other. They had done it. The following day was a nightmare of snow and wind and cold as they inched down the mountain, kicking steps in the ice, grabbing bits of fixed line where they could, planting their ice axes carefully. When they reached their little tent at Camp 2, they loaded everything into their overflowing packs and kept going. Now they were lower, the wind was slightly less annoying and the temperature not so frigid. At 6,200 metres, they met their cooks Jagat and Mingma, who had climbed up to them with tea and cookies.

ABC was as smelly as before, but oh, such a sweet smell. Sweet comfort.

Sweet safety. 'It was a real battle – like a test of our friendship,' Denis reflected. 'When I looked back at Makalu's top, I understood that nothing is impossible. We can do everything we wish. We need to follow our aims.'[22]

Twenty-nine years had passed since the first winter attempt on Makalu. Thirteen other teams had tried it. Denis and Simone climbed it in superb style, fast and light, nineteen days after their arrival at base camp. They used neither supplemental oxygen nor high-altitude Sherpas, and they left nothing on the mountain. Even their footprints were gone in an instant.

And now the Karakoram was waiting.

10

GASHERBRUM II

Avalanche

'Something felt a little sinister,' Cory Richards said, recalling his moments on
the summit of Gasherbrum II. 'It was almost like the mountain was pissed that
we climbed it. Then everything went to hell.' A rope of fear uncoiled in his
stomach, and he shouted: 'We have to get the fuck out of here!'

Winter in Pakistan's Karakoram range is not to be taken lightly. Farther
north and west than the Himalaya, temperatures are commonly 10° Celsius
colder. The mountains are in the direct path of the jet stream roaring in from
the north. Winds are, on average, forty kilometres per hour stronger than in
the Himalaya, information that is of interest primarily to pilots and climbers.
No surprise then that before any of the Karakoram 8,000ers was climbed in
winter, all but one of the Himalayan peaks were done. The exception was
Nanga Parbat, which, at the far western extension of the Himalaya and with
a notoriously low base camp, has a climate more like the Karakoram than
peaks farther east.

Even Ice Warrior Artur Hajzer expressed his doubts about the Karakoram.
'Maybe it is impossible to climb an 8,000-metre peak in the Karakoram in
winter.' He offered some advice for anyone considering it. 'Unless you are in
Denis Urubko's shape, don't even try. Agree and accept that you could die.
Train your mind, accept high risk, and climb against weather forecasts.'[1]
Was he joking? Tossing out an invitation? At least one Italian alpinist saw it
as a direct challenge. 'Impossible? No way.'[2]

Gasherbrum II is part of the Gasherbrum group of six peaks encircling the South Gasherbrum Glacier. Second highest in the group at 8,034 metres, it is an angular piece of geometric perfection. The summit pyramid is guarded by towering ice walls, fields of tumbling séracs, labyrinths of gaping crevasses, and one long, bony spine of rock leading upwards.

Simone Moro, now with first winter ascents of two 8,000-metre peaks, chose Gasherbrum II as his objective for the winter of 2010–11 for several reasons. There were five 8,000ers still unclimbed in winter: K2, Gasherbrum II, Gasherbrum I, Broad Peak and Nanga Parbat. He knew of expeditions going to all except Gasherbrum II and K2. As K2 is much higher and notoriously difficult, he eliminated it as an option: Gasherbrum II might offer a remote chance of success.

As a member of the North Face athletic team, Simone is in the enviable position of being a well-supported professional alpinist. The North Face, along with his other sponsors and supporters, allows him to launch several expeditions each year. His only limitation is his body, and the number of hours in the day. For Simone, even these aren't major hurdles since, if there aren't enough daylight hours to maintain his training schedule, he trains at night. His philosophy is simple: 'For every hour of training not executed, an extra hour is given to your rival.'[3]

Inviting Denis Urubko to Gasherbrum II was a foregone conclusion. Having climbed Cho Oyu the year before, Denis had summited all the 8,000-metre peaks, including Makalu in winter, and had extensive winter experience in the Pamirs. He was a hard-as-nails climber. The two had shared a rope many times already, in the Himalaya, the Karakoram, the Pamirs and the Tien Shan, in both winter and summer. They had learnt how to mesh their individual abilities, characters and strengths into a formidable team. Together, they forged a seemingly unbreakable bond.

Simone's second invitation was to American climber and photographer Cory Richards. Born in 1981, Cory was eight years younger than Denis and fourteen years behind Simone, had climbed only one 8,000er – Lhotse, in summer, with supplemental oxygen – and had made two winter ascents of 6,000-metre peaks in Nepal. He had spent several winters in the Canadian Rockies, honing his ice-climbing skills and his photography craft with some no-nonsense locals: Will Gadd, Barry Blanchard, Steve Swenson and Raphael Slawinski. Cory was a good climber, but in his own words, 'not a great climber'. He had gained a reputation in the Rockies for trying too hard on climbs that were too difficult for him, and was affectionately dubbed 'Little Whipper Bitch', by Blanchard for the occasional unexpected 'flight'.

Cory didn't mind the teasing. His winter routine in the Rockies was simple and focused, a welcome respite from his earlier years of chaos. His childhood had been troubled, to put it mildly. The second child of Utah skiers, he grew up in Salt Lake City. He was so moody that his mother brought him to a child psychologist when he was just a year old. By the time he was in sixth grade, a doctor had diagnosed him with severe depression and prescribed Prozac. Not content with pharmaceutical drugs, Cory was soon dropping acid. After a disastrous stay at a juvenile psych facility, he ran away from home, climbing and skiing, ricocheting from friends' homes to park benches to drug dealers to relatives. Rebellion seemed to be his guiding principle.

When he finally dragged himself home at the age of seventeen, it was back to the psych ward, this time with marginally better results. Surprisingly, to Cory, he discovered he had a creative side, an eye for composition, colour, balance and texture, all of which he could apply to his experiments with a camera. He soon found work as an assistant to fashion photographer Bill Cannon, and when two of his photos were accepted by *Climbing* magazine, he realised his work must be good. So good that when Simone Moro wanted a third person for Gasherbrum II, someone who could not only climb but also document the expedition with still and moving images, he turned to Cory.

When Simone announced his team, there was a flood of criticism. Cory Richards? For Gasherbrum II in winter? Without supplemental oxygen? What was he thinking? Simone ignored the naysayers, trusting that Cory could do the climb, that he could manage the added responsibility of seeing the perfect shots, get himself into position to take those perfect shots, and then actually take them.

Cory understood the significance of the invitation. 'Simone and Denis were icons in the climbing world … Mountaineers choose their climbing partners with extreme care … These two legendary climbers asking me to join their expedition was sort of like an ordination into a priesthood.'[4] But he was also aware of the doubters. 'It wasn't tremendously bothersome to me,' he said, reflecting on the sceptics a few years later. 'I still have a big enough ego that I just sort of said "fuck you, watch me".'

Simone felt sure that Cory and Denis would get along, a prerequisite for a small team of three. But earning Denis's trust would not be easy. Naturally sceptical, somewhat defensive and always on guard for signs of weakness, Denis could be difficult. It didn't help that Cory was American. As Simone explained, 'Denis suffers from a kind of "Soviet syndrome": he can't hug or kiss Americans.'[5] Even though kissing and hugging wasn't actually required, establishing some level of trust was.

And so, the trio was formed: a taciturn, military-hardened Russian whose smouldering features and searing stare could penetrate stone; a flamboyant and animated Italian with a wide-open smile and an insatiable need to communicate; and a wild-haired American, tall and fair, with the saddest eyes.

They arrived in Islamabad shortly after Christmas, 2010. After several days of meetings with the Pakistan Alpine Club and packing and repacking their supplies, they flew to Skardu in early January. They planned to travel by jeep from Skardu towards Askole, and then climb Kosar Gang, a 6,400-metre peak where they could acclimatise. As they neared the strained border between India and Pakistan, jumpy Pakistani security forces hovered around them, inquiring about their plans, testing the veracity of their stories. While walking in to base camp, Simone could feel the stress leaving his body. It's easy to imagine the sigh of relief from the man who delivered dozens of lectures every year, travelled the globe for his sponsors, appeared at film festivals on a regular basis, and had recently qualified as a helicopter pilot, as he shouldered his pack and simply placed one foot in front of the other.

Four days later, at 5,800 metres on Kosar Gang, Cory could no longer feel his feet. Simone called a retreat, despite a withering look from Denis, who was *not* cold, was *not* tired, and could see the summit a short distance away. It was not a promising start to the team-building exercise.

On 10 January, they boarded a military helicopter in Skardu and headed for Gasherbrum II base camp at 5,000 metres. It is a wildly beautiful place, surrounded by towering Karakoram spires. Improbably, they had neighbours: Pakistani soldiers living in a nearby military camp. Subsisting in dirty, malodorous, plastic igloos, they were serving six months at a time in this high-altitude ghetto, guarding the border with India in a standoff that has gone on for decades.

After a welcome night of hospitality, courtesy of the troops, Simone, Denis and Cory set up their base camp, ideally sheltered from the wind in a gully between the glacier and a group of ice towers. It was a reasonably comfortable camp, with individual tents for each man and a generator humming away outside the cook tent, providing warmth and light and a telecommunications hub.

Simone was painfully aware of the climbing purists who disapproved of his use of satellite technology and communication with the outside world. He scoffed at their sanctimonious attitude. 'These people would have exploration done silently, sufferingly, heroically, almost theatrically, while the story goes untold,' he ranted. 'Their butts are safe and warm as they write and speak. They're annoying, blathering on and lecturing on blogs and various forums.'[6] He fully intended to stay in touch with his family, with his sponsors, and most importantly, with Karl Gabl, the weather forecaster from Innsbruck who would provide them with accurate forecasts. An added – and unexpected – bonus was the interaction with the soldiers, who would, from time to time, wander over to check their emails and call their families.

Two days later, the trio set off to explore the crevasse-riddled Baltoro Glacier that defends the approach to Gasherbrum II. They signposted a meandering route through the crevasse field with bamboo wands topped with bright red flags, established a fixed line through the steepest section of séracs, and at 5,500 metres they dropped a cache of supplies. Ahead of them lay a flat section of glacier that looked relatively benign but was in fact a labyrinth of slots, obscured by a thin layer of snow. It was becoming clear there would be no straightforward travel on any single part of this mountain; the dangers were ever present, lurking.

The next foray up the glacier was just Simone and Denis, since Cory felt ill and opted to rest in base camp. A few years later, Cory reflected, 'If I'm blatantly honest, I think I was more scared than anything else. But rather than explaining that to either of those guys at the time, I simply said I'm not feeling well. I'm going to stay down.' As Simone and Denis pushed farther up the glacier, ploughing through soft and bottomless snow, waist-deep in places, they stole a moment from their labour to look up: they were encircled by the magnificent peaks of the Gasherbrum massif. Now at 5,700 metres, they set up their little yellow tent amidst a sea of gaping holes in the glacier.

With the light of the following morning, they discovered a welcome swathe of hardened snow, avalanche debris that provided a firm base for much faster travel. Still planting bamboo wands every fifty to a hundred metres, they reached a large sérac at 6,000 metres on top of which they erected their tent. This would be Camp 1. 'To reach Camp 1 in summertime takes not more than five hours,' Denis said. 'With pleasure.' Meaning it was ordinarily fun. 'In January 2011 we spend two days. Without any pleasure.'[7]

On 20 January, Simone and Denis returned to base camp where Cory had been getting to know the soldiers in the Pakistani encampment. In a highly unusual display of trust, they had allowed him to photograph their life in the military camp. This fortuitous turn of events resulted in a series of exceptional images that eventually led to a career with *National Geographic*. But there was an immediate risk for Cory, since he was now less acclimatised than his teammates. Simone contacted Karl Gabl for a weather forecast and radioed other winter expeditions in the region. 'Karl Gabl was our fourth rope partner on Gasherbrum II,' Simone explained. Like the climbers on the mountain, Karl spoke the language within a language – the code – of high-altitude climbing.

After a couple of days' rest, they were back on the glacier, this time as a threesome. Denis wryly noted that his highly socialised partner was in good form: 'Simone was full of energy and heroism after online talking around the world.'[8] They reached Camp 1, which had taken two days the first time, in half a day. From here, they could see a snow cone at the base of a steep couloir leading up to the shoulder of Gasherbrum II. While climbing this section, Simone spotted a piece of red rope embedded under five centimetres of ice. Feeling sure it could be useful as a fixed rope, both for the ascent and, more importantly, for the descent, he freed it. Bright red, it might provide a valuable clue in bad visibility.

They slept that night in a temporary camp at the base of a blade of ice and snow known as the 'Banana Ridge', a feature of the mountain they would come to know well. Their tent was so small the three climbers had to insert themselves carefully, aware that only a thin layer of nylon protected them from the elements. They had a ritual. Two would wait patiently while the first person removed his boots and his down suit, unstuffed his sleeping bag, slipped in and edged as far to the side of the tent as possible. Repeat for climber number two. The unlucky third would remain in his down suit, tending to the stove, melting snow and cooking until, finally, he too could remove his high-altitude boots, his steaming socks and down clothing, and burrow into his bag.

Their spirits were high. Still and moving images from the interior of the tent reveal a jovial crew, laughing and joking, since everything is relative, even the cold. Denis jested with his friend, Anna Piunova, back in Moscow, about the temperature. 'How much is in your apartment? Plus 25? And on the street? Minus 16? The difference is 41°. In my tent it is -20°. But on mountain it was -40°. It's 20° difference only … So, for you it is much more difficult probably. :)'[9]

Cory was still feeling his way with Denis, occasionally resulting in amusing exchanges. 'My opening relationship with Denis was humorous because he obviously didn't trust me,' he explained. 'To the point of discussing me in the tent with Simone. In front of me. In English!' All I could do was laugh, and say, 'Hey, guys, I'm here!'

Moving up the Banana Ridge required care since the ice was as hard as marble. Reach up and swing one axe, swing it again, one more time and the pick connects firmly with the ice, swing with the second axe, making sure it has penetrated the ice deeply enough to hold, move one foot up and stab hard with the front points, kick again to be sure, shift the weight, get in balance, leave the security of the last stance with the second foot, kick hard with the front points. Success: half a metre gained.

Carrying heavy packs, calf muscles screaming, it took an entire day to climb 250 metres of ice. At the top of the Banana Ridge they were rewarded with a generously wide platform for Camp 2. That night they celebrated with goulash and polenta. Simone hadn't compromised his requirement for high-quality food on an expedition: no freeze-dried packets of tasteless poison. He preferred tortellini, salami, prosciutto, cheese, chocolate, candies, wafers and jam. But the goulash was something special. He had gone with his brother-in-law, only two days before the expedition, to a favourite butcher's in Anterivo, a South Tyrolean village of just 250. The owner, Mr Mattivi, had 'cheeks as rosy as his flavourful steaks, the nose of a grappa lover, and last but not least, the winking eye of a Romeo.'[10] From that rosy-cheeked butcher, Simone had purchased three kilos of locally raised and slaughtered meat for the goulash. His wife, Barbara, had prepared the goulash and then packaged and frozen it so the merry trio could smack their lips at the top of the Banana Ridge on Gasherbrum II.

Next day they retraced their steps to base camp for a rest. Tuning into the outside world on 26 January, they learnt the Polish team on Broad Peak had run into extremely cold temperatures and severe winds. They were surprised, since Broad Peak was practically next door, yet the weather on Gasherbrum II, even though it was cold and windy, was bearable. It showed how weather patterns are site-specific, particularly in the mountains, where one side of a valley can be relatively calm and the other battered by hurricane-force winds.

Those same winds soon arrived at their camp, pummelling the tents, forcing them to brace the poles to prevent them from bending or snapping. 'Fear was overriding the entire climb,' Cory recalled. 'I have no problem talking about these fears.' After three days of battling the wind, they called Karl for some news.

'Hi, Karl, what's the scoop?'

'I only see one break in the weather, Simone. A thirty-hour window, I repeat, thirty hours, three days from now! Before and after that, the weather will be like it is now. Actually, it looks as though after that, it will get worse.'

'Are there any other possible windows? Maybe further off?'

'You know I don't make forecasts more than five to seven days ahead. You can't trust them. Besides, the numbers aren't showing anything good.'[11]

The news wasn't great, but it was conclusive. If they wanted to climb Gasherbrum II, they would have to start in bad weather, climbing two days in a storm to reach Camp 2 at the beginning of the thirty-hour window. Thirty hours was all they would get. Thirty hours to reach the summit and get back to Camp 2. 'If you want to reach an 8,000er in winter, then you must not be like a tiger chasing its prey forever, you have to be a snow leopard,' Simone explained. 'The snow leopard waits until there is a good chance, then he hits.'

After a short discussion, they agreed on the snow-leopard approach.

They left base camp on 30 January in 'insane wind and cold'. Each time Cory operated his camera he was forced to remove his mitts and work in his gloves. Each time increased the risk of frostbite. They arrived at Camp 1 at 2 p.m. The gusty wind was cause for a restless night in the cramped tent, but next morning, they repeated the routine: tea, dress, pack, boots, crampons, break camp, climb. Ahead of them was a long stretch of crevasse-riddled glacier, the ramp, the couloir, the Banana Ridge and finally, the sharp ridge to Camp 2. Cory continued filming throughout this punishing day. If Denis had any lingering doubts about Cory's abilities and his commitment to the climb, they were dispelled in the process.

That night they called Karl for an update.

'We're at Camp 2,' Simone said. 'We're happy to be here, we're doing well, even though it was two days of hell, like you said.'

'Well done! I was waiting for your call. I can confirm the good weather

Winter ascent of Gasherbrum II. *Photo: Cory Richards.*

window starting early tomorrow morning. Listen, don't forget. There's only about thirty hours. Then a scary wind will blow through, with gusts up to 140 kilometres per hour.'[12]

The trio fine-tuned their strategy: they would head out next morning when the sun hit the tent. No earlier. It was simply too cold. They would aim for a final camp around 6,800 metres, leaving more than 1,200 metres for the summit day. It was an ambitious plan, especially as the last 1,200 metres were completely unknown to them.

With a wary eye on the sky, they climbed steadily next day, wading through deep snow, searching for bridges across crevasses, skirting leaning séracs, front-pointing on sections of black, wind-polished ice. The variety of climbing demanded complete focus and the hours flew by. Too quickly, it seemed. At 6,820 metres they came to a mounded sérac that provided barely enough space on which to erect their tent. One last call to Karl confirmed the weather would change abruptly around noon the following day. He begged them to not overstay their time on the mountain.

They woke at 1.30 a.m. on 2 February and were out of the tent by 3 a.m. In that pitch-black world, the frigid air hit them like a punch in the face. They switched on their headlamps and started up. Unfortunately there was nothing straightforward about the route. Gaping crevasses would appear without warning, hidden from view by the limited scope of their headlamps.

Rock ramparts slowed them even more, with technical sections requiring delicate care. Yet after a long diagonal climb above the rock rib, they sensed a slight lifting of the heavy darkness.

At 7,450 metres, a ray of sunlight crept above the skyline, bathing them in a band of golden light. Behind them the mountains lit up, first in shades of blue, then sliding into radiant orange: Chogolisa, Broad Peak, K2, the Gasherbrums, Masherbrum, like tent pegs holding up the sky, the entire Karakoram on fire with life-giving sun. The valley flickered in and out of shadows and the temperature leapt from -50° to -35° Celsius. They felt warm. Cory yelled to stop a moment. Ignoring the altitude, he rushed ahead of them up the slope, dropped to his knees, and took out his camera. 'Okay, carry on,' he called. Two creatures clad in bold, primary colours, lit up like beacons, emerged slowly above the infinite emptiness of the Karakoram.

The wind stiffened at 7,700 metres, nullifying the warming qualities of the sun. They still had 350 metres to go and four hours in which to do it. They carried on up the ridge, one axe swing at a time, one kick of the crampon after the other, one foot in Tibet, the other in Pakistan. When climbing isn't difficult, but rather monotonous and apparently endless, the mind wanders. Every climber handles these mind-numbing hours in different ways. Simone's thoughts and emotions ricocheted from memories of training sessions to feelings of rage to constant monitoring of the wind direction and the sky. Cory was operating on two channels: Cory the climber and Cory the photographer. The light was ethereal. He knew how fleeting those moments could be, so kept shooting, darting ahead, crouching, focusing his camera, shooting, darting ahead. The ridge went on forever. 'I felt different,' Denis recalled, 'from full despair till crazy rapture. "We won't climb ... there'll be ice ... That's 7,800 already! ... Waw, there's 200 vertical metres more ... I'll die here ... Don't be afraid, soldier! And how will we descend here? It's so dangerous! FIRE!"'[13]

Denis spied a length of old fixed rope. He stopped, clipped in, and suddenly realised it led directly to the summit, now clearly in sight. When the rope ended ten metres below the summit, he unclipped and continued slowly upward. Whirlwinds of sharp ice crystals lashed his face as he stepped on to the summit of Gasherbrum II, his hands lifted to the sun. 'And the thought appeared, like an incredible ice crystal, like a blue frozen lightning: "That's all. I'm here. FIRE!!!"'[14] Simone followed, collapsing on the summit in a fit of coughing and retching. Cory came last, moving steadily with his camera, recording the moments. The image of Simone, prone on the summit, head bowed down into the snow, Denis comforting him, arm around him, reveals the effort they had given. 11.35 a.m., 2 February 2011: first winter ascent of Gasherbrum II, alpine style.

Denis later admitted he had trouble appreciating the moment. 'I was not able to switch off my mind,' he recalled. 'Any additional minutes up there could be somebody's life.' Twenty-five minutes ahead of their self-imposed turnaround deadline, they prepared to descend. But not before Denis sent a cursory text to Lena Laletina at RussianClimb.com: 'Summit at 11.35. Going down, 7,800. Hope to reach tent before darkness.'

In Cory's summit footage, you can clearly see ominous clouds funnelling towards them. 'I was very much aware our acclimatisation was less than optimal and the weather was awful,' Cory said. He felt threatened, of what he wasn't sure. The feeling defined everything, causing his adrenal glands to pulse a steady stream. 'I wanted to get down. I tried to be pretty quick but they seemed calmer up there. I'm never calm on a summit.' He shouted to the others, 'We have to get the fuck out of here!'

Now engulfed by roiling clouds, as Karl had predicted, they started down. At 7,700 metres, they sheltered under an overhang while Simone called his wife, Barbara, on the satellite phone to give her the news. His second call was to Krzysztof Wielicki, the Polish Ice Warrior who was Simone's mentor. And the third was to base camp, informing them they were on the way down.

The storm was fully upon them now, with gusts of wind knocking them off balance. Thirteen hours had passed since they had tasted a morsel of food or a drop of liquid. The goal was Camp 3, but the terrain was steep and technical, requiring every bit of concentration, despite the distraction of the storm. At one point Simone lost all sense of how far they had come, or what distance remained to the tent.

'I can see a tent,' Denis shouted up.

'What?' screamed Simone.

'I can see a tent. For sure. But it's the wrong colour.'

'No problem,' Simone yelled back. 'It doesn't matter. Keep going.'

'Guys, it's yellow,' Cory cried. 'I can see it, too. It's yellow. It's our tent.'

Faces encrusted with masks of ice, they ripped off their crampons and piled inside. There was audible relief inside the tent as they congratulated each other on the summit, and the descent to Camp 3. Around 5 p.m., Simone began giving sat-phone interviews to the European press. Reinhold

Messner sent his congratulations. Despite their euphoria, tension remained as the storm raged, pummelling the tent with furious gusts. They took turns heating water, drinking as much as they could – rehydrating was a priority – swallowing a few bits of food to replenish the tens of thousands of calories they had burned. Their sleeping bags were useless now, stiff as ice coffins and offering little warmth. Denis lay awake, rehearsing again and again their escape route down to the living. 'All night it was a calculation in my mind,' he recalled, 'how to do, how to do … ' They remained in their down suits, waiting for dawn.

By 8 a.m. they had broken camp. Visibility was reduced to three or four metres and their goggles were iced up so badly they removed them, a terribly dangerous thing to do at altitude because of the risk of snow-blindness. Squinting and peering through the swirling mass of grey and white, they struggled to find the landmarks they had memorised. Almost miraculously, they stumbled upon the rope they had anchored in place on the way up. They rappelled down a steep sérac, crossed a crevasse and continued down, again rappelling the steepest bits. At last, Camp 2 came into sight. Now they knew exactly where they were. Down the Banana Ridge and the couloir to where the red rope awaited them. They were off Gasherbrum II. Victory. All that remained was the lengthy descent of the glacier between Gasherbrums I and II.

Red-flagged bamboo markers were meant to show the way, but the dense fog and blowing snow reduced their visibility to the point that the markers were too widely spaced. They wasted hours making one false start after another in their race down the glacier. They had planned to descend all the way to base camp, but by the time they reached the site of Camp 1, evening was approaching and they were exhausted. One more night of camping, and it would be done. One more night of huddling together, outside of their sleeping bags, hydrating, eating, shivering. Karl Gabl later admitted that, when he received Simone's call telling him of their decision to camp another night, he feared for their lives.

Next morning, the collapse in weather conditions struck them like a hammer. Fierce winds high on the mountains were scouring the upper ridges, dumping snow on slopes directly above the very glacier they needed to descend. Cory was worried: 'I've always had a healthy fear of avalanches. Partly because of my time in the Canadian Rockies and also because I grew up skiing. It was weird for me with these guys; was I being a pussy? Maybe that's what this kind of climbing is like.' Ploughing through drifts up to their hips, they crawled from one bamboo wand to the next, taking turns breaking trail but staying roped together: the only safe way to move through the crevasse field. Because of the deep snow, they were forced to spend an inordinate amount of time in a runout zone fully exposed to avalanches poised to rip out at any moment. In a cruel twist of fate, they had arrived at the most dangerous moment in the entire climb just as it was almost over. Like wild animals, they sensed the danger, but could not run from it. Sitting ducks. 'I had this bad feeling in my stomach,' Cory recalled. 'We were spending too much time under GV [Gasherbrum V]. It was one of those classic terrain traps. All of a sudden, I heard a big crack, and coming out of the cloud layer was – it's one of those things I couldn't exaggerate. It was so big. I knew innately – I think we all knew – we were going to die.'

A sérac had collapsed on a snow-loaded slope above them. A second boom confirmed their greatest fears: there is no sound on earth like the sound of an avalanche. The slope fractured, and tons of snow began surging toward them, slowly at first, then at a furious speed. There was no time to think, nothing to do, nowhere to go.

Cory tried moving his arms and legs as the avalanche roared over him, but he was soon spinning madly. 'It's hard to put into words the terror of that experience – being caught like prey in the teeth of a primordial monster, waiting for your spine to snap, your consciousness to wink out, the mountain to swallow you … I'd catch a blurred glimpse of blue sky, then dark, then blue, then dark, then black. My mouth and nose were packed with powder, and snow was stuffed into my down suit. The roar was replaced by a profound silence, and a heavy cold began seeping into my body.'[15] Cory's first thought was that he could breathe. His second was that he was the sole survivor: 'Fuck, I have to get out of this and descend alone, because those guys are dead.'

Simone was conscious when it ended. The ensuing seconds lasted forever. He was alive, but the others? Almost free of snow, he was frantic to find Cory and Denis. Visions of Anatoli and Dimitri on Annapurna drifted past. He pushed them aside. He spied Cory's orange suit and a portion of his head above the snow. He ripped off his pack and raced over, digging the snow away from Cory's face and upper body as fast as possible, before it hardened into a cement-like casing.

But where was Denis? He screamed his name and Denis shouted back. 'Okay, okay, Simone, I'm okay, take your time.' So he continued excavating Cory, finally freeing one arm, then the other. Although in shock, Cory instinctively opened the zip of his down suit, pulled out his camera, and started filming. While Simone ran over to Denis and began digging around his face, Cory filmed. Buried up to his chin, Denis somehow remained calm. 'It was not emotional,' he recalled. 'It was a computation of tasks.' Denis could do nothing until his arms were freed, but as soon as they were, he clawed at the snow along with Simone and ten minutes later, was free.

Panicking now, Cory yelled, 'Guys, get out, get going! Toward the valley! Fast. Now.'[16] He took off as fast as he could, but in the wrong direction. Denis yelled. Simone screamed. But Cory couldn't hear them and kept running until he dropped into a hidden crevasse. Thankfully, they were still roped together. Fifteen minutes later, he crawled out of the gaping hole, having used his ascension device and prusik sling to ascend the rope.

Ironically, the avalanche that nearly killed them now became their highway. The debris from the slide hardened almost immediately into a rigid surface over which they could sprint. Near the end of the glacier they stopped to rest, their adrenaline starting to ease, the fatigue settling in. Nearly blind with exhaustion, Denis looked up and shouted, 'Saeed Jan! Saeed Jaaaan!'

At 10.15 a.m. that morning, their cook Saeed Jan and his helper, Hassan Zhulan, had been huddled around the stove in the cook tent. A black crow hopped over and peered inside the door flap, which was slightly ajar. It lumbered into the tent, cocked its head, cawed loudly, stared a moment or two, and hopped out. A messenger, of sorts. Hassan jumped up from his seat, convinced something had happened to the climbers. They packed up some tea and food and headed towards the glacier.

When they met the climbers, they embraced, weeping in relief. Saeed Jan offered a bottle of cola he had begged from the soldiers, along with some tea and cookies. He took Simone's pack and Hassan shouldered Cory's. Denis declined the offer, some residue of strength or pride or training still coursing through his slight frame. Base camp sped towards them. Safety. Comfort. Home.

That night, neither Denis nor Simone could sleep. '[Simone] asks me, "Denis, why are you not sleeping?" I say, "Sorry, Simone, I don't know.

I wake up." And I ask Simone, "Why you don't sleep?" And Simone tells me, "I am getting pleasure from the life." And I tell him I am also getting pleasure from the life at that moment.'[17] Cory, meanwhile, slept soundly.

The aftermath of the climb differed for each of them. This was the third time Simone had made a first winter ascent of an 8,000-metre peak: Shishapangma in 2005 with Polish climber Piotr Morawski; Makalu in 2009 with Denis; and now Gasherbrum II. It was Denis's second winter victory, and he was approaching an astonishing twenty 8,000-metre summits. For both Simone and Denis, life carried on, with all of the usual lectures, festival appearances, blog updates and sponsor responsibilities. Denis and Simone both admitted that surviving the avalanche had been a miracle, but as Simone explained: 'I am not aware of great adventures that are not also kissed by a favourable star. We were simply no exception.'[18]

For Cory, the experience was radically different. The selfie he took immediately after digging out of the avalanche that nearly killed them went viral. It was on the cover of *National Geographic,* appeared on posters and billboards, and sped around the internet. The image that depicted suffering and fear and relief with such startling intensity became Cory's 'brand', following him around like a prowling cougar. On the plus side, it led to many lucrative assignments. But as he said, 'the story the picture suggests – of a heroic mountaineer who has just cheated death – has bothered me deeply.'[19] He explained that the perception of alpinism as a heroic activity didn't resonate for him. 'I've always thought an act of heroism requires some sort of higher purpose than just risking your life to see if you can make it to the top,' he explained.[20]

For Cory, climbing was less about heroism than it was about self-preservation. For a young man whose life had been focused on alcohol, drugs and escapism, it was his salvation, providing focus and healing. But his experience on Gasherbrum II did not make him healthy; it broke him. Like the avalanche that buried them, waves of panic would suddenly sweep over him. He would break out in a sweat, become enraged, irritated, confused. The chaos of his adolescence returned, only much more menacing. After landing in a psychological black hole, he sought help, finally learning he was suffering from PTSD. Therapy helped, but Cory couldn't escape the photo. 'It seems to follow me around like a ghost of some former self, reminding me of how fragile I really am. How fragile we all are.'[21]

Nevertheless, the significance of their climb remained: after a quarter of a century of trying, a team had finally succeeded on a Karakoram 8,000er – in winter. The expedition had taken only twenty-two days, and the summit push had occurred during a brief, thirty-hour window of good weather. Simone reflected on it in the *Alpine Journal*: 'This climb, and the style we did it in, belongs to the whole world climbing community; the message it sends is addressed to the next generation of climbers ... whose predecessors have continually pushed the boundaries in alpinism. The first winter ascent of an 8,000er in the history of Karakoram was not a race, nor a competition between nations or individuals. Nor was it a race to set a record, which sooner or later would have been achieved anyway. It represents rather a stage on the progression from a classic expedition style to a different one, more adapted to modern trends, techniques and a philosophy in climbing great mountains.'[22]

It's true that, on Gasherbrum II, the decisive factors were speed, tactics and a small team, one that included a very fine weather forecaster. Simone felt strongly that this strategy – alpine style, or at least a light and fast style – increased the chances of success on a winter expedition. Anna Okopińska, the Polish woman who was on the first winter attempt of an 8,000er back in 1974, agreed with Simone: 'I think that big, old-style expeditions are not a good idea nowadays. Small teams of very good and befriended climbers promise better hopes.'

As time passed, the three Gasherbrum II alpinists drifted apart. They still communicate with each other at the beginning of February each year, sending little notes, remembering their time together on the mountain, congratulating each other, small gestures meaning little. The 'small team of very good and befriended' climbers pursued their own dreams and objectives. Remarks made by Simone revealed the extent to which the bond between him and Denis was frayed. 'Unfortunately, our relationship has deteriorated. I think he has lost his direction.' He considered Denis's background: 'He has a Russian military mentality. It was important that I act, taking this into account, and it worked well. He is very strong and he has no fear. These are excellent qualities, but he has to be managed properly to prevent him taking stupid or fatal risks. We worked well together, but the leadership was always clear.'[23]

Cory, reflecting on the partnership, could not recall any obvious signs of 'management'. Instead, the youngest member of the trio speculated on more pragmatic reasons for the deterioration of the friendship: 'I think that what ends up happening, and this is from my own experience, is that you spend so many years in such stressful situations that, like a marriage, it kind of goes south; you get sick of each other's idiosyncrasies and nuances. It can be beautiful at first and then, when you grow apart, as we do in death, breakups, divorce, we create a mythology of the situation which helps to justify the situation. The problem is it becomes our outward story to the world and it can be hurtful and even untrue.' He added, 'I can't speak to their relationship, but Denis is his own fucking person and if people try to manage him, he fucking makes himself heard.'

Cory admitted he occasionally felt slightly irritated with Simone, who, he felt, took too much credit for 'making Cory's career' with the Gasherbrum climb. Cory felt it was a factor, but only *one* factor. But this was a minor irritant for Cory because, much more importantly, the Gasherbrum experience fundamentally changed his outlook on life. 'That avalanche was the biggest gift I've ever been given – professionally, personally, emotionally, physically,' he says. 'Because it pushed me into a place of such utter fucking darkness that I was either going to kill myself or I had to evolve … That's the beauty of any traumatic experience. It gives you the opportunity to grow.'[24]

Even more important than the avalanche and the trauma and the frayed friendships were the bonds that were forged in those most extreme of conditions. 'It was one of the most formative experiences of my life,' Cory said, 'and I am forever indebted to those guys in a way that it's sort of a love beyond words. They are both incredibly kind, generous, beautiful human beings, and collectively they are remarkable. It doesn't matter whatever happens in life, I will still hold that respect for them because they are incredible men and I shared some amazing time with them. We have that experience and I'm better for it.' Perhaps Anna was ultimately correct when she said small teams of friends 'promise better hopes.'

11

GASHERBRUM I

Lost Fathers

You are born alone. You die alone.
The value of the space in between is trust and love.
Louise Bourgeois, *Destruction of the Father / Reconstruction of the Father*

While Simone and his partners were on Gasherbrum II, another international team had arrived to attempt Gasherbrum I, the highest in the group at 8,080 metres. Sometimes called Hidden Peak, it was first climbed in 1958, but when border disputes between India and Pakistan erupted in 1965, the area was closed to expeditions for many years. The winter attempt included Canadian climber Louis Rousseau, Austrian alpinist Gerfried Göschl and Alex Txikon from the Basque Country: a small but exceptionally strong team. Louis is an ice-climbing specialist from Quebec, where the winter temperatures can be frigid. His capacity to endure cold was tested on most weekend outings from his home. 'My country is not a country, it's winter,' he once joked.[1] Gerfried already had seven 8,000ers in his pocket, including a summer ascent of Gasherbrum I. He and Louis had climbed Nanga Parbat together in summer: a proven rope team.

Both Louis and Gerfried were family men, somehow 'balancing' their passion for mountaineering with a rich home life. Gerfried's wife, Heike, explained how they managed. 'When we fell in love, he was a mountaineer, so I knew his fascination from the beginning … It was okay for me, because he was in the mountains only two months a year. The other time was great, we spent a lot of time together, we went climbing, hiking, later with the kids … Only the two months were terribly hard for me.'

Alex Txikon, the youngest of thirteen children, climbed his first mountain

The Göschl family: Heike, Helena, Hannah and Gerfried. *Photo: Göschl Family Archive.*

in the Basque Country at the age of three. By the time he joined forces with Louis and Gerfried, he had climbed seven 8,000ers and many other Himalayan giants in pursuit of his passion. With a mane of black hair and a swarthy complexion, Alex's arms were as thick as the logs he annihilated in log-chopping competitions back home. They each had their skills. Alex's strength was legendary, Gerfried's stamina was unmatched, and Louis was the technical guy: he could get them up the steep gullies of ice, as narrow as fingers, on this difficult face.

Theirs was a bare-bones expedition, unlike over on Gasherbrum II. With no money for helicopters, they took seven days to make the arduous trek from Askole to base camp at 5,100 metres where they had stashed equipment the previous autumn. When they arrived on 31 January 2011, nightly temperatures hovered between -20° and -30° Celsius. Their ambitious plan included making the first winter ascent of Gasherbrum I, via a partial new route that would link two existing routes.

They would spend more than fifty days trying.

The view of the south face of Gasherbrum I from base camp was nothing short of spectacular: consistently steep, with a complex network of rock pyramids, sweeping icefields and rock-scoured couloirs. During the first few days of the expedition they could actually see it. They began climbing on 10 February, loaded down with ropes and equipment to prepare the route.

The temperature was -25° Celsius, but instead of warming up through the course of the day, it grew colder the higher they climbed. At 5,800 metres they stopped, satisfied with their progress. When they returned a few days later, they excavated the lines they had fixed, now buried under wind-drifted snow. They reached their former high point and carried on up through the steepening ground.

Louis took the first lead: loose rock and seventy-degree ice. Alex and Gerfried belayed. 'Nothing is more miserable than belaying in the winter under such cold conditions,' Louis reflected. 'Leading is certainly riskier, but at least it keeps you warm.'[2] They climbed to 6,100 metres before returning to base camp, which they reached in the faint light of the moon. Twelve hours of effort.

The trio kept at it, inching up the mountain, one rope length at a time. The ice was so hard in places, marble-like, that they were unable to place ice screws for protection. The terrain didn't let up: relentlessly steep. After three full weeks of effort, of twelve- to fourteen-hour days, starting in the dark, ending in the dark, they reached the ridge at 6,300 metres.

Louis began dreaming of Albert Camus' words about King Sisyphus, the famous boulder-rolling character of Greek mythology. When Sisyphus rolled the boulder up, gravity would roll it back down again. Although Camus claimed, 'The struggle itself towards the heights is enough to fill a man's heart,' Louis wasn't sure. 'Camus certainly did not think about us when he wrote that! When you struggle towards the heights in -40° Celsius on an 8,000-metre peak, you need a little more to fill your heart.'[3]

They kept moving up but even when the fixed lines were in place their progress remained slow. Every move had to be calculated and sure. They climbed as high as 6,600 metres, but on 9 March they had to admit their objective was too difficult in winter. They simply could not penetrate the ice. They retreated to base camp, loaded down with all their gear. Exhausted now, they relaxed and recovered from their efforts, eating, resting, listening to music, analysing every detail of their attempt. After having climbed through weeks of foul weather, they thawed in the sun that had miraculously appeared.

The sunny weather demanded some action, so they called Karl Gabl, their weather forecaster. Karl had some good news: they had a window. What would they do with it? Their original route was too difficult, even in good weather, so they decided to try an alpine-style ascent of the mountain via the Japanese Couloir.

Gasherbrum I in winter. *Photo: Louis Rousseau.*

They left base camp on 13 March at 5 a.m., laden with four days of food and equipment. Their goal was to reach the Gasherbrum La, the col between Pakistan and China, from where they could approach the Japanese Couloir on the north-west side of the mountain. By 5 p.m. on 14 March, they topped out of the couloir and set up their tent at 7,050 metres. The summit looked so near they felt they could touch it. But the weather was changing and the wind was increasing. They struggled with the guylines of the tent, which flapped and snapped out of control. When they radioed Karl, he assured them the winds would drop during the night and they would have good conditions next day. Despite the bitter cold, they remained optimistic.

They began heating water at 2 a.m. The wind was still howling: eighty kilometres per hour at least. The summit was a thousand metres higher so they reasoned the wind would be stronger up there. Much stronger. So they waited. They drank more tea. And at 9 a.m., nothing had changed. Bitterly frustrated, they descended, arriving in base camp sometime during the night. They left the mountain on 21 March, the first day of spring.

As time healed their disappointment, Louis reflected that he harboured no regrets about their ambitious attempt. They had been young, naive, completely free of sponsors and unrealistic expectations from the outside world: most attention had been focused on the neighbouring peak, Gasherbrum II. They had gone to the mountain as amateurs and had enjoyed an adventure. And like Sisyphus, Louis eventually 'found some peace and happiness in the accomplishment of the task, rather than the goal.'[4]

Two teams headed to Gasherbrum I the following winter. One of them was led by Gerfried, who, on 12 January 2012, left his wife, Heike, and his two daughters, Helena and Hannah, for Gasherbrum I for the third time within a year. Heike wasn't surprised Gerfried was returning to the mountain to finish the job. 'It was logical,' she said. Once again he assembled an international team. He invited Louis but, as Louis explained, he had already spent six months in the Karakoram the previous year. If he expected to be part of, and enjoy, his family, he needed to spend time at home. But oh, how he longed to be there. 'I wish I was in the Karakoram every day, but more because I would love to help my friends on Gasherbrum I,' he said. 'Strange feeling actually!'[5]

Another reason for Louis's reluctance was the ambitious nature of the project. Gerfried wanted not only to finish the new route they had begun the previous year, but also make a complete traverse of the mountain. Louis understood the magnitude of the challenge and he worried. Was it too much?

Those who said yes to Gerfried included Alex, who would primarily be climbing with his own partner, Carlos Suarez. Polish winter specialist Darek Załuski was there, along with his partner Tamara Styś, as well as Cedric Hählen from Switzerland and the accomplished Pakistani professional mountaineer Nisar Hussain Sadpara. Cedric's portfolio included K2 and Kangchenjunga, and Nisar had climbed all five of the 8,000ers in his country. Darek brought the most winter experience to the group, and his partner Tamara, who had climbed Gasherbrum II in summer, and also been high on Gasherbrum I and K2, was there because she wanted to experience the Karakoram in winter. 'Winter climbing in high mountains is said to be Polish domain,' she said, 'so I wanted to check if it is actually so hard, and if somebody needs to be a bit crazy to try to reach the summit of an 8,000er in winter.'

Darek was still suffering from frostbite from his ascent (and filming) of K2 the previous summer. But Darek was old school; if there was a winter expedition to which he was invited, he said yes. Every time. Even with frostbite. 'It wasn't the first time for me to have frostbite,' he said. 'And there was no amputation – well, some flesh was gone, but no bone was gone.

It was uncomfortable – not painful.' So, minus a little flesh, he agreed and invited Tamara along: as it turned out, an inspired decision. He agreed to go as far as Camp 1 and film.

Nisar Hussain came from the village of Sadpara, south of Skardu. He was the eldest of seven siblings and, due to his father's chronic illness, had taken responsibility for his entire family. He began working hard labour, building roads as a teen, then graduated to 'low-altitude porter' and finally to 'high-altitude porter', much more lucrative but significantly more dangerous work. He had been four times on Gasherbrum II, three times on Gasherbrum I, and once on Broad Peak, Nanga Parbat and K2, becoming only the third Pakistani to climb all five of his country's 8,000ers.

A Polish expedition was also attempting Gasherbrum I that winter, via the Japanese Couloir. The team had a direct link to the original Ice Warriors because of their leader, Artur Hajzer. Artur had made the first winter ascent of Annapurna with the legendary Jurek Kukuczka, and had reignited the high-altitude winter climbing programme in Poland. The goal was for young Polish climbers to finish off the 8,000ers in winter, which the original Ice Warriors had started. 'For the moment,' he had said in 2009, 'Poland is in a position of being world leader in winter Himalayan climbing. But in the coming winter season there will be several expeditions, Russian, Austrian, Canadian, Kazakh, and Spanish, which is why the Poles, to not lose our primacy, should start acting immediately.' He then announced 'a multi-year sports programme that would identify and prepare team members, ready for such a goal.'[6]

In order to mount such an ambitious programme, he needed support from the government, as had existed in the time of communism. He and Krzysztof Wielicki formed a mini-delegation to approach the Polish ministry of sport with the plan. The atmosphere was heavy, Krzysztof recalled. A lot of serious faces. Dark suits. 'At that point, Artur took the lead and said, "Mr Minister, the Russians are beating us." This completely clarified the situation and the rest of the discussions proceeded in a relaxed atmosphere,' Krzysztof said, with a sly grin.[7] Shameless as it was, his approach worked. Artur was equally gifted at raising money, Krzysztof explained. 'Where it was needed, he would play the tune of the patriot, reminding people of old successful times of Wanda, Kukuczka and Zawada.'[8]

But in order to climb 8,000-metre peaks in winter, Artur desperately needed climbers. The old guard was gone; most of them had died in the mountains. The new generation wasn't interested in disappearing for months at a time to suffer in winter in the Karakoram. They climbed, and they climbed well, but their playground was on steep, technical terrain with a minimum of time commitment: big walls on 5,000- and 6,000-metre peaks. Oh, how the times had changed. 'When Zawada organised winter expedition to Everest,' Artur said, 'he contacted the Alpine Clubs in Poland and he received answers from seventy experienced Himalayan climbers. I have twenty-five, of which seven have different goals this year. And six of these I have put on a reserve list because they're not experienced enough. They haven't done enough climbs.'[9]

Artur needed to mobilise and train the younger generation of Polish alpinists to finish the winter programme, so he began by organising summer expeditions to increase their experience at altitude before progressing to winter. First were expeditions to Broad Peak and Nanga Parbat, neither of which succeeded. Many began to wonder why Artur had taken on this ambitious project. He had enjoyed a meteoric career back in the late 1980s but had given up high-altitude climbing after the death of his partner Jurek Kukuczka on the south face of Lhotse in 1989. He and Janusz Majer had gone on to create an outdoor clothing and equipment company that had succeeded, failed and reinvented itself as a viable business. He had started a family, had become comfortable: some even said 'fat'. Certainly, he had lost his youthful fitness. What he had retained was his sense of humour. When asked about his motivation for getting back into the high-altitude game, he answered, with an impish grin: 'It was a middle-aged crisis ... Fame, getting lots of women, did you know that your wife loves you more after one of these expeditions? She doesn't hassle you to take out the garbage and do chores. People let you go ahead in the line-up to the doctor. Your quality of life increases.'[10]

He readily joked about himself, but could easily shift the target to another: poking, prodding, sometimes insulting. People either enjoyed Artur's company, including his rough edges, or they steered clear of him. Artur's business partner at Alpinus, Janusz Majer, speculated that Artur had returned to the mountains for the simple reason that he was bored. 'For Artur, Alpinus was a chance to have a normal life. Capitalism was everyone's big chance,' Janusz said. 'He succeeded. But when the company reached its high point and then stagnated, he became bored. He needed something new – something to challenge him. It was then that he returned to the mountains.' Or maybe it was something deeper: the need to return to climbing, that tangible hub around which everything had rotated in those golden years in the mountains.

Artur was smart enough to know he wasn't twenty-five anymore. If he wanted to return to the high-altitude game, he would need to invest in his body. He hired a personal trainer, started running and lost weight. His ambitions didn't rest at base camp; he wanted to return as a full-fledged alpinist. He resisted the temptation to revert back to the 'old ways' of operating. Artur Małek, who would eventually play a major role in the winter programme, observed how, 'Some elders objected to using new technologies, Artur had no [such] objections ... That was the quintessence of Artur Hajzer: he was the mediator between the past and the present.'

One of Artur's choices for Gasherbrum I was forty-four-year-old Janusz Gołąb. Fair-haired, with piercing blue eyes, Janusz was one of those big-wall climbers who felt entirely at home on vertical or overhanging rock, whether it was in Greenland or Alaska, Poland or India. He was one of Poland's most accomplished technical climbers, but Gasherbrum I was his first time on an 8,000er. With him was twenty-eight-year-old Adam Bielecki, a colourful character, with his dreadlock ponytail, intense gaze and signature tri-colour hat hand-knitted by his mother. Adam was a psychologist but longed to be a high-altitude mountaineer. He knew about Artur's programme and was desperate to enrol. He had begged Artur to take him to Makalu on the 2011 Polish autumn expedition. He sent a letter, listing his best achievements: Pik Pobeda, Pik Lenin, youngest person to do a solo ascent of Khan Tengri, climbs of that nature. He highlighted his strengths, including his speed. 'I got up McKinley from the last camp twice in a 24-hour time period,' he explained. 'Matterhorn solo in under five hours.'[11] He promoted himself to Artur as an 'acclimatisation mutant' because of his ability to climb to 6,000 metres without acclimatising.

Artur read the letter and responded in typical Artur fashion: 'The ascent times you list don't knock me off my feet. Seriously, they are quite average. But it's a good base to work with ... At the moment the information you passed on to me doesn't qualify you for the Makalu expedition because I think if I were to fall into a crevasse you would not be able to get me out. I strongly encourage you to do some more work ... All the best, Artur.'[12] He couldn't have been clearer. Or more direct.

Adam swallowed his pride and began training, climbing the routes Artur had suggested, preparing himself to be the great climber he envisioned. Confident of his progress, he wrote to Artur once more, detailing the results of all his hard work. Artur relented, and Adam joined a group of young Polish alpinists who dubbed themselves 'Hajzer's pre-school'. He was given a spot on the autumn Makalu expedition after all, and proved himself by summiting: his first 8,000er. Artur had to admit Adam *did* climb fast. He *did* acclimatise quickly. He might even qualify for the winter programme. Thrilled at the opportunity, Adam later conceded that his alpine CV at that time was so small you could barely shine shoes with it.

Along with Adam and Janusz was Adam's older sister, Agnieszka, who came to manage base camp. Pakistani mountaineers Ali Sadpara and Shaheen Baig were employed as high-altitude porters and brought a wealth of experience, both being 8,000-metre summiters. Ali and Shaheen weren't there simply to carry loads; their role was to enlarge the team. When Polish teams first came to the high mountains back in the 1980s, they had come with an army of climbers. Lots of people to break trail, put in the fixed lines, set up camps, with energy left over to climb. Ali and Shaheen basically expanded the three-person team to five. Artur had invited Darek Załuski as well, much to Darek's delight. 'It was personal for me because he invited me to be his partner – two old guys with two young guys,' Darek recalled. 'It was the first time I felt this from Artur … For me it was important that he called me to be his partner. I was touched.' But Darek couldn't accept because he was already on Gerfried's international team.

Although the Polish and the international teams each had their own objectives on opposite sides of the mountain, they shared a base camp. They ate together, played chess together, shared weather forecasts together and dreamed together. In the end, they shared much more, including the ambition to be first. Darek agreed, noting a slight difference in character between the two leaders. 'I think that Gerfried would have been more likely to agree to a combined effort for the summit but Artur has the soul of a competitor. He wanted it for himself. For Poland.'[13] Alex wasn't so sure; he later claimed that Gerfried wanted to get to the summit a day earlier than the Polish team, and claim the first ascent.

The Polish team started up on 2 January. Conditions on the glacier above base camp proved difficult and dangerous: a mess of tilting séracs, gaping crevasses and sagging snow bridges. Getting from A to B usually required maddening detours around X, Y and Z. They had to rope up the entire time to avoid an unexpected plunge into a slot and, though they left wands to mark the route, the moving mass of ice would shift and groan, causing snow bridges to collapse, crevasses to expand or contract, and séracs to topple. What they had expected to be a relaxing glacier walk more resembled a nightmare. Humbled by the mountain, it took three days to finally reach the site of Camp 1 at 6,000 metres. 'We had done a fine, totally useless piece of work,' Adam announced, a bit disgruntled. 'Climbing in itself is a useless pursuit. It has no real meaning. My choice to pursue Himalayan climbing is my way of spending my life but I don't intend to convince anyone else that it's a fun way to spend your time.'[14]

Adam and his Pakistani partners descended to base camp the following day, while Artur and Janusz started up to Camp 1. Artur called Adam in the mid-afternoon. 'We can't find the way,' he said, in frustration. 'The tracks have completely disappeared and the wands have ended.'

At 4 p.m. Artur called again. 'We still can't find it. We aren't sure what direction to go.'

'Why don't you use the GPS device?' Adam suggested. 'It will be accurate.'

'I don't know how to use it. I can't make it work,' Artur admitted.

Winter days are short. At 5 p.m., as the sun was setting, the device indicated they were 'close' to Camp 1. They tried to zoom in but, in the plummeting temperatures, they didn't dare remove their mitts; they had resorted to using the tips of their ice axes to zoom – and it wasn't working. By 5.30 p.m. it was completely dark. They stopped moving. The GPS screen disappeared under a film of frost. Getting to Camp 1 had turned into a battle for survival.

'Climbing an 8,000-metre peak in winter is like a trip to another planet without the support of NASA,' Adam explained. 'We didn't have a whole team of specialists working with us on the expedition. We were regular people who had to do everything ourselves, from choosing gear, logistics, insurance, and finally the climbing itself. So many little jobs to do it's hard to be an expert at anything so improvising is unavoidable. The situation with the GPS was an excellent example.'[15] Janusz suggested building a snow cave for the night, but Artur refused to give up. They finally found the camp at 7.20 p.m.

Over the next two weeks they pushed up the mountain to the Gasherbrum La and over to the base of the Japanese Couloir, where they set up Camp 3. It was there, while setting up the camp, that Ali Sadpara sustained serious frostbite to his toes. The expedition was over for him.

The dynamics on Gerfried's team weren't ideal. Alex and Carlos were functioning as a stand-alone team and friction began to develop between them and their leader. Alex wasn't impressed with Gerfried's leadership *or* the team's progress, and was envious of the Polish team. 'Compared to Artur's expedition ours was a complete catastrophe … His [Artur's] coordination was incredible.'[16]

In mid-February, a storm hit the mountain that surpassed all their previous experience. Except, perhaps, Artur's. Wind speeds reached 120 kilometres per hour – in base camp. For three terrifying days the team struggled to save the expedition. Four tents were lost to the wind forever. Janusz, while sprawled inside his tent, was lifted four metres into the air and hurled down the moraine. The wind was so strong that a seven-and-a-half-tonne helicopter at the nearby military camp was moved twenty metres.

Adam had thought he knew what to expect on Gasherbrum I. After all, he had been on Makalu, the fifth-highest mountain in the world. 'But the things I experienced in the Karakoram were out of this world,' he said. 'In Poland, you can kind of imagine what -40° Celsius would be like, but -60° was kind of an abstract temperature.'[17] Janusz the big-wall climber simply marvelled at Artur's ability to wait it out. He hadn't seen this kind of patience before.

Tamara found the waiting terribly hard. 'I finally understood that winter climbing is some kind of art of suffering and art of waiting,' she later explained. 'You need to be super motivated and mentally strong not to lose your motivation waiting for weeks for better conditions.'

Artur's patience came from experience, as well as planning for the challenges of life at base camp. After his unsuccessful, seventy-five-day Broad Peak winter attempts, which are recounted in the following chapter, he vowed to bring more alcohol to base camp, adding they had been 'too trained, too athletic, too sterile, and in the end, not relaxed enough.' He even considered the possibility of bringing 'a shrink' to base camp to help manage the motivation and fear factors. Ever the joker, Artur concluded that in winter, 'you just have to have much bigger balls!'

On 25 February, the Polish team set off again, hoping for a summit bid during a one-day weather window forecast in two days' time. But when they arrived at Camp 2, they found nothing. The camp had simply disappeared. They retreated to Camp 1 for the night, where Adam suggested skipping Camp 2, going directly to Camp 3 and waiting for a drop in the winds to make a summit bid. Janusz felt they would be too tired for a summit bid if they climbed all the way to Camp 3. Adam disagreed. They argued. Ultimately, Adam and Shaheen went up and Artur and Janusz went down.

Adam and Shaheen faced ferocious winds as they climbed higher: gusts so strong they found themselves being blown *up* the Japanese Couloir. Completely disoriented and off balance, they descended, thankful for the fixed lines that Louis and Gerfried had placed the previous summer, in anticipation of Gerfried's descent. On the way down, they discovered their cache of tents and equipment, which *had* been at Camp 2, had since been dragged 300 metres away. They retrieved the gear and once again attached it to the mountain with ice screws. This time, more securely.

Gerfried's team had headed up as well, sensing an opportunity. The entire group climbed up to Camp 1, where Darek, who had the previous year climbed K2 in just a down suit and without a sleeping bag, found conditions on Gasherbrum I to be 'absolutely borderline'. Cedric, the most accomplished technical climber on the team, managed to surpass the high point of 2010, but the news wasn't good. The steep headwall was awash in light, sugary snow: incredibly difficult to ascend and too insecure for an ice screw. Back in base camp late that night, Gerfried recorded a short video, expressing his frustration. 'I am of course disappointed because I would have been glad if I had finally come home to my girls … we will see the next days, how it goes on. But it is terribly depressing!'[18]

Members of Gerfried's team who later watched this footage felt that would have been the right moment for the expedition to end. The exhaustion and stress were obvious in Gerfried's lined, thinning face. His teammates recalled his 18 February blog entry: 'Who wants to stew here in the cold and give up his loved ones at home? … I miss my two adorable little daughters and my patient, but now also very stressed, woman. Every phone call with my older daughter, Hannah, who constantly asks when I will finally get home, is like a punch in the stomach. It is beautiful to hear her voice, but depressing to fulfil her wishes … Is it possible to reconcile the thirst for adventure and the longing for a "normal" family life?'[19]

Base camp was not a happy place. On the descent with Artur, Janusz had fallen into a crevasse, injuring himself. Shaheen became ill, suffering from a severe peptic-ulcer attack. Adam and Janusz couldn't agree on a strategy.

Janusz, who was accustomed to big-wall teams, where everyone either got up the thing, or everyone retreated, couldn't accept Adam's concept, which was that if even one climber summited Gasherbrum I in winter, the expedition would be deemed a success. It wasn't necessary that everybody get to the top, just *somebody*. Their relationship soured. Reliving his experience of getting airborne in his tent, and still smarting from the injuries he sustained, Janusz actually slept in his harness at base camp, attached to the glacier beneath his tent with a couple of ice screws. The bad weather continued and the winds hammered base camp. Going up in these conditions would have been pointless.

Winter alpinism is all about waiting but weather windows are so infrequent and brief that the waiting is neither restful nor relaxing. It is instead a suspended form of tension, with climbers constantly ready and alert for the merest hint of a change in the weather, a day or two of calm, a bit of sun: anything at all that might offer some hope of going up. The international team waited. The Polish team waited. They read. They ate. They slept. And they checked the weather forecasts with multiple forecasters, hoping for at least one that sounded remotely promising.

Their days would begin around 8 a.m. with breakfast in the double-walled mess tent. The temperature inside ranged from -5° to -10° but would occasionally dip to -15° Celsius. Lunch was served at 2 p.m., followed by the daily battle with the generator. If they could coax it to work, they would enjoy electricity in the evening. If not, they didn't. And then it was time for dinner. They watched movies and read books, sent messages back home to their families and friends. A few brave souls took baths, a process that involved chopping ice, melting and then boiling the water, pouring that into a bucket and finally bathing with it, at which point it had cooled. Winter expeditions are long, but Adam recalled taking only three showers. Because of the cold and the altitude, the 'aroma' of their bodies and their socks seemed manageable.

When three independent meteorologists forecast a weather window for 8 March lasting twenty-four hours, everyone mobilised two days earlier so as to be 'in position' on the magic day. It was less a 'window' than a 'crack in the blind'. The Polish team would climb from the north-west side and Gerfried's team would climb from the south side. If everything proceeded smoothly, they would meet on the summit on 8 March, both teams sharing the first ascent.

Gerfried, Cedric and Nisar set off for Camp 1 on 6 March with Tamara and Darek. Darek later returned to base camp because he was feeling weak. Tamara got a message from Darek that Alex was ready to join her if she wanted to continue. 'As I was feeling good, I agreed,' she said. On 7 March, Gerfried and his two partners crossed the ridge of Gasherbrum South and reached the upper basin of Gasherbrum I, where they bivouacked at around 7,100 metres. Cedric sent an SMS message to his wife that they were cold but calm, that they planned to make the summit bid the next day, that he was fine. Gerfried called on the satellite phone that evening to say it was cold, visibility was poor, but thankfully, there was little wind. 'We will start at about 3 a.m., we hope to have reached the summit in the afternoon,' he said.[20]

The Polish team was also on the move. Adam, Janusz, Artur and Shaheen reached Camp 1 on the afternoon of 6 March. They had planned to skip Camp 2 the next day and go directly to Camp 3, but strong winds blew them back to Camp 2 where they settled in for the night of 7 March. In constant communication with Agnieszka back in base camp, they learnt there was a slight chance that the window might last until 9 March. Their decisions made that evening in the tent at Camp 2 proved critical. Artur announced he would remain at Camp 2 as backup. Adam admired Artur for his decision, since it was the first time Artur wasn't positioning himself for a summit bid. 'When we went for the final stage he said, "Okay guys, I will turn back because I will slow you down." Obviously right, but he didn't need to do this.' Janusz was impressed with Artur as well, but for a different reason. 'Rather, I was afraid for him when he was up there at 6,000 metres … and could simply vomit after breakfast when he wasn't feeling great, but still didn't think to go down … It goes to show his unbelievable bravery and strong mental state.'[21]

The other three – Adam, Janusz and Shaheen – would go to Camp 3 as early as possible the following day, 8 March. Shaheen would help them set up the tent, and then return to Camp 2. Adam and Janusz would try to rest that afternoon before attempting a summit bid on the night of 8 to 9 March: a nocturnal ascent. In winter. It was a highly unusual tactic considering night-time temperatures in the Karakoram, but they were desperate to use this weather window. There might not be another one before the season ended and if they succeeded, they would be back at Camp 3 before the storm arrived.

With unbelievably bad timing, a geomagnetic phenomenon now occurred in the Gasherbrum group. A solar flare sent a storm of highly energised particles that blocked out radio communications. As a result, the outside world knew nothing of what was happening at Gasherbrum I just as loved ones and friends became fully aware that summit bids were in motion and tension on the mountain was building. Gerfried's wife, Heike, was at home in Austria, trying to cope, suffering her own version of hell. She wrote down her feelings, something she had never done before, but which she planned to share with Gerfried when he returned.

Thursday, 8.3.12, 10.36, local time Liezen: I'm sitting here with Helena on the couch and trying to distract myself. Since yesterday … great is the fear that something happens to Gerfried … I try not to think of something bad. But I hardly succeed. I'm writing down my feelings now, since when it's all over, I'll push them back and the memories of the bad hours will quickly fade away. Gerfried is probably fighting his way up the last few metres to the summit. I am sitting down next to my 18-month-old daughter and face fears of death. I prefer to be alone in such hours … I wish everything was over! Time does not pass!! … Now the church bells ring! … It feels like punching your stomach. I feel weak, sick, helpless, unable to act … The clock is ticking; I'm staring at it. A look at the internet makes me nervous again. It is already half past 4 in Pakistan. It's getting tight, they have to come down! When does he finally call again??? The head cinema is getting worse … Is he still alive? … I know, Gerfried thinks of us every step of the way. Oh God, when will the redeeming call finally come?[22]

Adam and Janusz settled into their tent. They boiled water. They drank tea. They ate a bit of food. They burrowed under one sleeping bag, trying to sleep. At 10 p.m. they began packing for their summit bid. At midnight, they crept out of the tent into a cloudless night illuminated by a benevolent full moon, so bright they didn't need headlamps. The wind blew less fiercely than forecast, but the temperature was about -35° Celsius. They had to keep climbing and as fast as possible; stopping for even a couple of minutes was out of the question. Except they did because Adam needed to 'take a dump', as he termed it. Once the mission was accomplished, they moved quickly, confidently, their crampons and axes biting into the wind-packed snow. The higher they climbed, the colder it became, since there was still no warming sun. It was now -40° Celsius and the wind had picked up, gusting up to forty kilometres per hour. 'That means with the wind-chill it would have been about -60°,' Adam explained. 'Today, I know that this is close to my limit.'[23]

Dawn found them nearing the summit ridge on a hundred-metre stretch of glassy ice: the last obstacle on the way to the top. Adam described the chaotic brainstorm in his head. 'At 8,000 metres, I get this visual of status bars, like in a computer game: one bar for hydration, second for hunger, how much oxygen, how much sleep I'm missing ... I keep analysing the weather, what's happening with my partner, keeping track of time, and focusing on simple things like one foot in front of the other. You can't let yourself feel fear or else everything will topple.'[24] He continued, his ears filled with the rasping sounds of his breath, the chafing of his high-altitude suit, the hammering of his pulse.

Adam arrived at the top at 8 a.m. on 9 March. 'I spent around eight minutes on the summit, mostly communicating with our base camp via the radio and taking a few photographs,' Adam reported. 'I was also – unfortunately without success – searching for any traces of Gerfried's international team.'[25] After the initial joy of Adam's summit report, the second part of the news was disturbing. When he told base camp there was no sign of Gerfried, Agnieszka's face collapsed in shock. Then Artur piped up, singing from Camp 2: 'Even if it's raining, even if it's freezing, the Poles don't let us down.' A sliver of a smile returned to Agnieszka.

Ten minutes later, she received a radio message from Gerfried's team. They were camped about 300 metres below the summit on the south side of the mountain; Gerfried, Cedric and Nisar were preparing to start up. Darek grabbed the radio and exclaimed, 'Gerfried, you don't know how happy we are to hear you.' Agnieszka slumped to the ground in relief. The solar storm had ended, so she called Heike to give her the news. Heike was somewhat relieved – but not for long. 'How can a human being do this to another?' she wrote. 'Why? ... I cannot stand this uncertainty!! Gerfried, you have no idea what you are doing to me!!'[26]

Later, Darek would ponder on Gerfried's message, which mentioned that 'their packs were heavy, because they were carrying everything they needed to bivouac on the other side.' His words seemed odd to Darek, because the original plan had been to use the Polish team's tent on their descent. For some reason, the strategy had changed. 'These three kilograms of extra weight mean nothing for a tour in the Alps,' Darek said. 'On an 8,000er, especially in winter, they change a lot! Above all, you have to make a lot more effort … On the other hand … with more luggage on [your] back, you feel safer. You risk more, because you think you have more reserves in bad weather. But this is deceptive: it's almost impossible to stay up high in winter.'[27] And Darek would know.

Almost at the summit, Janusz was still about twenty minutes behind Adam who, because he was now shivering, started back down, moving as quickly as he could on the steep, wind-blasted slopes, crampons scraping, maintaining his balance with the greatest care. He exchanged words with Janusz when they met a few minutes below the top and when Adam reached a comfortable spot below the ice wall, he sat down on his pack, soaked up some of the sun's warming rays, poured himself some tea and waited until Janusz had reached the summit and descended the steepest part of the wall.

Then Adam resumed his descent, picking up speed as he reached easier ground. He arrived at Camp 3 two hours ahead of Janusz, made some tea and waited. They rehydrated together then continued down, leaving the tent with food and fuel for Gerfried's team as they descended from the summit. They hardly noticed how quickly the weather was deteriorating, the front edge of the storm already enveloping them, so immense it seemed to cover the world.

Alex and Tamara, climbing separately from Gerfried's summit team, had reached 7,250 metres before returning to Camp 3 on the previous day. Now, while Adam and Janusz were descending on the other side of the mountain, Alex and Tamara tried moving up again but soon returned to their little tent to wait for the sun, which finally arrived at 11 a.m. Having retreated from their summit attempt, they instead climbed to the summit of nearby Gasherbrum South (7,109 metres). Then, at 2 p.m., the weather changed dramatically. Hurricane-force winds blew in from the north and the temperatures plunged to -50° Celsius. They fought their way down through the blowing snow and sub-zero temperatures, Tamara as far as Camp 1 and Alex all the way to base camp. Darek, also in base camp, suffered terribly as he waited for news of Tamara, who didn't arrive until the following day. She had succeeded in reaching 7,250 metres on the mountain: the highest point for a female alpinist in the Karakoram in winter, a record that stands to this day.

Adam and Janusz continued down in the blizzard, which was intensifying with each passing minute. They could see nothing, and tried not to think about what it was like up high on the mountain. They felt a gnawing dread that something was wrong, something impalpable: inescapable. By 5 p.m. they were back in Camp 2. There would be no more messages from Gerfried.

Next day the entire Polish team descended to base camp. Both Adam and Janusz had suffered some frostbite but they had survived. Their unusual night climb strategy had worked. After forty-nine days of waiting, working on the mountain, enduring long periods of punishing winds and bitterly low temperatures, they had climbed Gasherbrum I in winter. When Artur walked in to camp with the others, he said, 'the guys did a big thing. But Gerfried and Cedric and Nisar aren't here. So that's why we won't sing.'

Back in Austria, Heike was waiting to hear from Agnieszka but when she did, the news wasn't good. 'Saturday, [10.3.] 7.00 CET: Inward despair is spreading ... The phone call with Agna was hell! She could not tell me anything new. Nobody has seen or heard anything since 12 o'clock.'[28]

In desperation, base camp called Pakistan's military mountain rescue service Askari Aviation and requested a helicopter fly over Gerfried's route to look for movement, anything at all. Poor weather prevented helicopters taking off until 15 March. They flew as high as 7,000 metres, but saw nothing. Given the bullet-hard conditions experienced by Adam and Janusz on their descent, and the speed of the oncoming storm, the final assumption was that Gerfried and his team were either blown off the mountain or frozen in place, possibly in a crevasse used to shelter from the storm.

Suffering from frostbite, Adam and Janusz flew out from base camp after the rescue operation was abandoned. After sixty days on the mountain, their sudden return from the sterile, inhuman, freezing, odourless, monochromatic world of Gasherbrum I, its one incessant accompanying sound the wind, to the low-altitude, oxygen-rich, organic world of the living was unsettling. 'All of a sudden there was green grass, smells, sounds of insects and birds,' Adam said. 'It's an intense experience. Little things that I don't normally pay attention to were hugely important.'[29]

When Janusz recalled his experience on Gasherbrum I, it was the wind that remained his strongest memory. 'These winds were as strong as in Patagonia but lasted longer, almost without any quiet periods. They forced us to spend weeks at base camp without any possibility of climbing, which was probably the hardest part. It was difficult to maintain the will to climb and the belief in success. The route itself was perhaps not so technically difficult, but hard ice and little snow cover made it tiring and dangerous.'[30]

Back in Quebec, Louis had followed the progression of the international team, almost beside himself with desire to be there. 'Don't get me wrong,' he said. 'I'm no masochist. It's just that winter climbing in the Himalayas is one pure, unpredictable adventure, and a unique way to climb. I think the Himalayan pioneers of the 1920s probably felt a little bit the same: real isolation, bitter cold, hunger, broken equipment, problems to solve, low chances of success, unpredictable weather ... It's a mix of challenges, mountaineering and surviving.'[31] Despite his love of winter mountaineering, the tragedy of Gerfried and his team shook Louis to the core. It changed his life. He would never look at risk the same way, at his family the same way, at the balance between climbing and the rest of his life in the same way.

Adam Bielecki was pragmatic about the experience of winter climbing. 'Winter climbs – it's hard to speak about pleasure. Normally I am into the experience, but in winter I do it because it's not been done before. That's the main reason.' And yet, even Adam admitted to some aesthetic value. 'The mountains are so spectacular. The Karakoram in winter is so incredible. Deep sense of isolation. The mountains are only for you. I like to be there. It's special.'

Artur was, above all, relieved. Without the success of this climb, it's likely the entire winter programme would have collapsed. He wrote: 'It's nice to hear about this expedition in the international media and that Poles have returned to their winter throne. I had my moments of doubt that it would even happen, but my friends weren't contaminated with early failures. They didn't know that this summit was unattainable, so they just went for it.'[32]

Artur's Himalayan schedule was soon rivalling that of his youth. Two or more expeditions a year, interspersed with months of planning, fundraising, organising. Plus, he was running an outdoor equipment business on the side, and he had a family. His wife, Iza, seemed accepting of the situation: 'Artur's winter expeditions, when I was left by myself in a big house full of things, appliances that could break any time, and of course did break, with an enormous car that you had to brush the snow off, were all extremely taxing for me ... But they weren't life issues that kill a relationship. As soon as he was back, they disappeared – it wasn't a reason for a divorce.'[33] Some people in Poland criticised Artur for using the Himalayan programme for his own personal goals, both to re-enter the alpine arena and to increase profits for his business. Certainly, his pattern of multiple expeditions in quick succession brought to mind the desperate, tragically ill-fated plan of Wanda Rutkiewicz, when she tried to climb eight 8,000ers in an eight-month period, a plan that was heavily criticised by Artur at the time. Yet now he was doing the same.

Other than a meeting with the president of Poland, the Polish Gasherbrum I team returned to normal life: family, friends, training. Adam recalled something he had read, which was attributed to Polish winter legend Maciej Berbeka. Maciej had written about the 'other side of the looking glass', the moment when you have gone right to the edge, not beyond it, but close enough to see what awaits you on the other side. Maciej had been there, as had Jurek and Darek and many, many others. 'If you don't see how fragile life is, if you don't experience situations at your limit, then you will never truly value your life,' Adam said. 'A brush with death means you love life even more. And then, when you eventually get to have a picnic with your girlfriend, drink a beer, you will fully appreciate the moment.'[34] Adam had taken a look. And what Maciej had said was true. 'The true meaning of life isn't in getting these 8,000-metre peaks. It's what I get to come back to,' Adam said. Sadly, for Gerfried, Cedric and Nisar, there was no coming back.

Life after Gasherbrum I was one that Heike, as the wife of a Himalayan climber, had prepared for; even, in her darkest moments, anticipated. At first, she was aided by shock. Numb, she couldn't fully fathom what had happened, what was happening, what would happen. 'I couldn't think in a correct way,' she said. 'I needed a lot of time to handle this.' As grief settled in, she admitted that it sapped her strength, as she ricocheted from anger to sorrow, from worry to acceptance, and back again to despair. She stayed in touch with the Hählen family, sending photos back and forth. As the years passed, so did the acuteness of the pain. 'The days around the 9th of March are still sad, but to see the girls living their lives and their great motivation give me the strength that I need for every day.'

12

BROAD PEAK

Unfinished Business

I was being drawn toward the mountain in a search for adventure, by a desire to explore my own limitations and to also be immersed in a world so deeply beautiful that it would forever be etched into my memory.
Marc-André Leclerc

Karakoram, March 1988. Polish climber Maciej Berbeka is requesting permission from his leader, Andrzej Zawada, to make a dash to the summit of Broad Peak while his climbing partner, Alek Lwow, descends.

'Hi Andrzej, Maciej here. Over.'

'Yes, yes I'm here. I've just heard what Alek has to say. But how are you feeling? Over.'

'I want to go. I want to go.'

'Do you have down gear and … what's it called … anoraks? Over.'

'I have a down jacket and down pants. Over.'

'Does Alek have the same? Over.'

'Alek does have the same. Over.'

'Tell me, is it your opinion that Alek can make it back down alone? Over.'

'Absolutely.'

A third voice now broke into the radio conversation, that of Zyga Heinrich at a higher camp. 'Don't let Maciej go. There's a difficult section on the ridge, the climb up the ridge. Camping there is … it will be extremely difficult for him to survive. And then there is the descent. Stop him if it's possible. Over.'

Andrzej replied, 'Okay. I hear what you have to say. Anything else? Over.'

'At that height you stop thinking well, you're programmed for the summit,' Zyga added. 'You have to direct them. Over.'

'Good point,' Andrzej added. 'Thank you. Over.'[1]

But when Andrzej tried calling Maciej a couple more times, there was only the hiss of empty static. Maciej was no longer talking on the radio. He was climbing.

If there is one mountain and one individual climber forever linked in the history of winter climbing, they are Broad Peak and Maciej Berbeka. Maciej from Zakopane: he was the son of a mountain rescue specialist, and would become one himself. Maciej the Ice Warrior: one of Andrzej Zawada's boys back in the 1980s. Maciej, who made the first winter ascents of Manaslu and Cho Oyu. That Maciej.

His long and tortuous relationship with Broad Peak began simply because of its proximity to K2. The two Karakoram giants sit adjacent to each other and Broad Peak, with its ten kilometres of airy ridge linking its three summits – the 8,051-metre Main Summit, 8,011-metre Central Summit, and 7,490-metre North Summit – is clearly visible from K2 base camp.

Maciej had never intended to climb Broad Peak in the winter of 1987–88. He was on a K2 expedition at the time, together with Andrzej Zawada and fifteen of Poland's best mountaineers. Conditions were atrocious; storm after storm hammered the team and attempts on the mountain were more heroic than reasonable. By the middle of February, their chances had faded to almost zero. Maciej described the level of frustration the team experienced. 'None of them felt sick ... you had fifteen guys hell-bent on climbing the mountain, each of them was a rock star, each with great potential and abilities, and each eager to claim the top.'[2]

And then, something changed. Krzysztof Wielicki, who was also on the team, couldn't quite recall how it happened, but suddenly, there was mumbling about Broad Peak instead of K2. It seemed crazy to him: two guys talking about climbing an 8,000-metre peak they hadn't even climbed in summer. Ludicrous. Suicidal. He made a note in his journal: 'What is this ... It doesn't seem to be the best use of time.'[3] Alek Lwow was one of the two. 'I couldn't get Broad Peak off my mind,' he said. 'You can see the three summits from [K2] base camp and a seemingly easy path to the summit. It was tempting me the entire time. It also seemed that Broad Peak had better weather. It was 600 metres lower, and you could see the summit more often than the summit of K2.'[4] Most on the team were confused and even angry at this apparent abandonment of K2. They still held out hope, even after ninety days on expedition and sixty-four days in base camp, where temperatures hovered between -30° and -35° Celsius with 100-kilometre-per-hour winds on a regular basis.

When Maciej was, once again, blown off one of the high camps on K2, he confided in Alek, wild-haired, heavily moustached Alek, that he felt the mountain was out of the question this season. But what about Broad Peak? It was right across the way ... much lower, seemingly better weather, unclimbed in winter. Alek was all for it, so the two approached Andrzej. At first, he was adamantly opposed to the idea. But Andrzej was not only a dreamer and a visionary; he was also a practical man. He knew their chances on K2 were growing smaller every day. It had been an outrageously expensive expedition, and he was hungry for success. Broad Peak could be the consolation prize. The problem was he didn't have a permit for Broad Peak; the team's permit was for K2 only. So he fired off hopeful messages to Islamabad requesting an additional winter permit for Broad Peak. It's not as if anyone else was around: the mountain was gloriously empty.

Maciej and Alek were convinced the permit would arrive eventually; in the meantime, they needed to get started. The pair left K2 base camp on 3 March and skied over to Broad Peak, a completely self-contained unit, taking all they would need on their backs. Neither Maciej nor Alek had ever been on Broad Peak before. What they were attempting was unprecedented: the first winter ascent not just of Broad Peak but of any 8,000-metre peak in the Karakoram, on sight and in pure alpine style.

Having stowed their skis at the base of the mountain, their first challenge was a maze of séracs and crevasses, where with each step they sank to their knees in soft snow. They stopped at dusk at around 6,000 metres and that evening learnt that thanks to Andrzej Zawada's diplomatic skills, President Zia's office had assured them of the Broad Peak permit. The weather deteriorated the following day, but they continued on up in the face of strong winds and thinning air choked with swirling snow and spindrift avalanches. When they reached a short rock step, they roped up for the first time and at 6,500 metres stopped for their second bivouac.

The morning of 5 March dawned gloriously clear: one of the most beautiful days of the entire expedition. Here they were, the two of them, on this magnificent mountain, together but otherwise completely alone. After a few tricky rock pitches, they topped out on an icefield where they spied some old fixed lines that seemed sufficiently intact to use. After making great progress, they set up their next camp at 7,300 metres, overwhelmed by their good luck and their prospects. They both felt fit and strong, fully acclimatised from their weeks on K2: everything was perfect. From their perch on Broad Peak, they could gaze over at their original objective and wonder what might have been. The mood had now shifted over at K2 base camp; the team was watching through a telescope, amazed at their progress, cheering them on. Go on, boys. You can do it!

That night was cold, the black sky heavy with stars. They emerged from their tent at 8.30 a.m., calculating they were about eight hours from the summit, enough time to return to the tent before dark. The sun rose on cue and warmed them enough to remove their bulky down suits. Moving quickly on the firm snow, they initially made good progress, but as they climbed higher the snow conditions worsened: heavy slabs and deep drifts. Their pace slowed. Alek started to worry around noon. Not Maciej. At 2 p.m. they radioed K2 base camp for details about the route ahead. Some from the K2 team had been there before, and knew what to expect. Krzysztof Wielicki, who had soloed the mountain in an efficient twenty-two-hour sprint, focused the telescope on their position and offered some specific advice.

Shortly after the radio call, Maciej and Alek arrived at a gaping crevasse that split the entire width of the couloir they were climbing. It looked impossible to find a way across and if not impossible, certainly time consuming. Alek was concerned they were losing precious time. It seemed increasingly unlikely they would reach the summit and return to their camp before dark. A high-altitude bivouac looked certain. 'I didn't want to do that,' Alek said. 'As I was debating all these options, Maciej caught up to me. We started walking back and forth along the crevasse. I told Maciej about my concerns and Maciej responded in a way which indicated that we must keep climbing.'[5] Maciej found a way around the crevasse, but they were still 300 metres from the col. Even so, they continued and at 3.45 p.m. the distance to the col was less than 100 metres.

Alek radioed K2 base camp. The conversation that followed – the one that opened this chapter – would determine events on Broad Peak and change Maciej's life. Alek had already made his decision: he would descend. Maciej decided he would carry on a bit higher, so he took the radio from Alek, who started down, slowly and carefully, keeping an eye on the tiny dot way, way down below: the tent. Maciej knew that Alek had made the right decision: for Alek. But not for him. 'The top was so close, and we had put so much effort into the whole expedition, both into the attempts to claim K2, as well as, now with Alek, into the attempt to reach Broad Peak's summit, alpine style, in winter. For me it seemed impossible not to complete the quest.'[6]

Yet the weather was now changing, and fast. The winds were blowing at full force and the air was choked with snow. Visibility was reduced to twenty metres. Alek reached the tent and huddled through the night. All he could do was wait for Maciej's return. Without a radio and completely cut off, he knew nothing of Maciej's communication with K2 base camp that night.

'Maciej, Maciej, how are you? Over.'

'I'm … the radio is breaking up. I feel not bad. Only it's bloody late. Over.'

In the background, Leszek Cichy's voice could be heard: 'He's on the Rocky Summit.'

'Don't worry about that yet,' Andrzej responded to Leszek. Back to Maciej, he asked again, 'How are you? Over.'

'Rather well.'

'Roger, roger. Are you coming back? Will you start descending? Over.'

'Yes, I'm starting the descent. If it's still windy I will dig out a hole. Over.'

'Okay. Take some photos. Take some photos at the top. Over.'

A recording was made of that historic moment at base camp, and in the background you could hear queries, even doubts. Was he on Broad Peak's Main Summit, or the Rocky Summit, a mere seventeen metres lower but still at least an hour from the true top and possibly more in those conditions? Andrzej reassured them Maciej had said he was on the summit, so he *must be* on the summit. Krzysztof knew it was the responsibility of those familiar with the mountain and the route to tell Andrzej that Maciej was *not* on the summit, and he later claimed they did. But Andrzej said nothing to Maciej. It was late in the afternoon, much too late to carry on to the Main Summit. Perhaps Andrzej knew that Maciej would die trying.

Alek waited all evening for Maciej. He waited throughout the night as well. Still no sign. Gusts of wind lifted the tent so forcefully that Alek wondered if he would be blown off the mountain. There were moments when the darkness seemed aggressive, predatory. 'At one point I started feeling a mixed emotion of being scared and also not caring anymore. Indifferently fearful. I didn't think a feeling such as this could exist … It felt like there was no way out.'[7] At noon the following day, Alek began considering the possibility of a solo descent. The chances of Maciej returning were dwindling with each passing hour. 'I was surprised at myself, at how calmly

I was thinking, and how much I didn't care in the face of the tragedy. Subconsciously I could feel the hopelessness of my situation. But I wasn't afraid, probably because people who don't have a choice can't be scared. I wondered whether that makes it easier to die. I decided to wait until morning, but after that, no matter what happened, I would rescue whatever was left to rescue: myself.'[8]

Andrzej had, in the meantime, contacted Poland to share the good news: Maciej Berbeka had reached the summit of Broad Peak. The first winter ascent. Alpine style. Solo. Maciej's wife, Ewa, was elated. She knew the protocol: no calling friends or relatives or the press until everyone is safely back in base camp. A couple of hours later she received another call. Maciej was still descending. He was nowhere near base camp. Crushed, she clung to the hope he had at least made it back to the tent.

He hadn't. As he descended from his 'summit', the wind grew too strong, so he dug a small hole in a snowdrift and took shelter. Andrzej made radio contact again, urging him to hold on, to put on all of his clothing, including his down pants. Maciej responded in a distressingly weak voice: 'I don't have the strength to put my pants on. It's too hard, Andrzej.' The K2 team was horrified because they were being hammered by such a violent storm at base camp that they couldn't imagine what Maciej was enduring high on Broad Peak, all alone and with no tent, not even a bivvy sack.

Hours later, Maciej and base camp communicated again. Maciej now thought he might be near the tent. There had been a brief break in the murky fog and blowing snow, but everything whited out again in an instant. He was unsure which way to move. He was frozen in place, frozen in fear. His voice was even weaker than before, shaky and desperate with fatigue.

Later that evening, Alek was wrapped in his sleeping bag, the hood pulled over his head, feeling small and alone, almost in a stupor. He heard a sound. Was it the wind? A shout? Was he hallucinating? He crawled partway out of his sleeping bag, unzipped the door of the tent, and slashed at the darkness with the beam of his headlamp. Left and right. Nothing. Only the wind. He began to edge back into the tent when he heard another sound: a shout. Then he saw a faint light. At 7 p.m. Maciej stumbled towards the tent. 'He appeared, without a word, in the tent's entrance, covered in ice,' Alek recalled. 'He looked like anyone would after spending over twenty-four hours in a hurricane at over 8,000 metres. In winter. In the Karakoram.'[9] Maciej crouched in the vestibule, waiting for Alek to remove his crampons so he could crawl inside. He was so exhausted he couldn't speak.

'It seems that it flies in the face of what is normally expected in terms of survival,' Krzysztof later commented. 'Surviving in these conditions is an individual thing. The most important part is that it's hard to sit and wait. Psychologically it's almost impossible. I have experienced it and I know what it's like.'[10] Maciej also reflected on his near fatal descent: 'The ordeal I went through during that time … well, I seldom come back to that. I don't like to talk about it as nobody enjoys talking about how you slowly die in the mountains. And I think it's still not the right time for it.'[11]

Alek helped him into the tent, placed a cup of tea in his frozen hands, took off his ice-encrusted boots and wrapped him in a sleeping bag. The radio crackled into life. Alek retrieved it from Maciej's pack and heard Andrzej's voice.

'Alek do you copy, Alek do you copy? Tell Maciej that his wife called. What should I tell her? Over.'

Maciej leant over to the radio, and in a trembling, raspy voice, answered, 'All is well. Over.'[12]

Only then did Alek and Maciej learn that three of their teammates had started up Broad Peak to rescue them. Together, they endured one more night at 6,000 metres and on 9 March descended to the base of the mountain. Maciej could barely walk, lurching and stumbling, destroyed by his epic on Broad Peak. Shortly after, he was evacuated to Skardu.

Krzysztof didn't know why Andrzej had sent a premature message to Poland announcing the first winter ascent of Broad Peak. But he could speculate: 'For Andrzej it wasn't important who and how, but that it was a success. For him it was important that the peak was climbed. This was the kind of military approach to Himalayan climbing, and for this [new] generation, probably difficult to understand.'[13]

Yet the announcement was not only premature; it was also wholly in-accurate. Everyone except Maciej and Alek knew that Maciej had only reached the Rocky Summit, a mere seventeen metres lower than the Main Summit, but an hour away. When Maciej radioed from the 'summit', Leszek Cichy had heard the transmission down in base camp. Leszek knew Broad Peak's detailed topography, and he knew exactly where Maciej was. You can hear him clearly state this in the expedition tape recordings, but he said nothing afterwards to Maciej. Not at that moment, not during the descent and not in base camp. Not before Maciej was helicoptered to Skardu for medical attention and not even when they all met up again in Rawalpindi.

For some inexplicable reason, not one member of the K2 team felt compelled to tell Maciej Berbeka that he had climbed Broad Peak's Rocky Summit, but not the Main Summit. That he had endured the worst high-altitude storm of his life, permanently damaged his feet with frostbite, risked everything, but had not reached the summit. Instead, Maciej returned to Poland a hero. He was given a medal for sporting achievement and another one from Pakistan for the first of their 8,000ers climbed in winter. He shuffled around his house in slippers, suffering from the frostbite earnt high on Broad Peak. Then he lost a toe. Infection set in. Time passed. Nobody said a word.

And then, Alek did. He published a piece in the Polish climbing magazine *Taternik*, stating that Maciej had reached the Rocky Summit of Broad Peak but not the Main Summit. The reaction was swift and fierce. Maciej was horrified, ashamed, humiliated and confused. How could they not have told him? How cruel that they did not deal with this in private, in Pakistan, before coming home. These men were not merely his climbing companions: they were his closest friends. He had been fiercely loyal to them, and he expected loyalty in return. 'It went inward, deep into him,' his friend Ryszard Gajewski observed. When asked why he hadn't first talked to

Maciej Berbeka's triumphant arrival in Poland after it was reported that he had made the first winter ascent of Broad Peak. *Photo: Maciej Berbeka Archive.*

Maciej before publishing the article, Alek answered, 'We weren't close friends.'[14] Maciej's immediate response was bitter: 'If I had stayed there, I would have been a hero.'[15] His words were not only bitter: they were also prophetic.

Most from the K2 team agreed with Alek's article, but they were privately relieved it hadn't been them who wrote it. Andrzej Zawada was angry. His success story was shattered. He attacked Alek's credibility, which, to be fair, wasn't squeaky clean. Somewhat of a rebel, Alek had made a few 'illegal' ascents in the Himalaya and wasn't always on the 'A' list of mountaineers chosen for national expeditions. But Andrzej couldn't dispute the facts. Maciej Berbeka had made the first winter ascent of the Rocky Summit of Broad Peak, in pure alpine style with no prior knowledge of the mountain. He had been the first to break the 8,000-metre barrier in the Karakoram. It was undoubtedly a remarkable achievement. But he hadn't climbed Broad Peak.

Maciej felt duped by his friends, betrayed by Alek, humiliated by his team, and used by Andrzej. He vowed to abandon high-altitude climbing and refused to climb with Andrzej Zawada again. He concentrated on healing his feet, building a new home for his growing family, guiding, climbing in the Tatras and abroad. He climbed the Seven Summits. He climbed in the Himalaya, but avoided state-sponsored Polish national expeditions. His reputation as an empathetic and careful guide brought him plenty of work. The debacle on Broad Peak had changed the course of his life, not that he abandoned the mountains, but in how he functioned as a family man, a community man, a man committed to his church.

The years passed. There were five more attempts on Broad Peak in winter, expeditions from Spain, Italy and Poland. Then came an announcement that another Polish expedition to Broad Peak was planned for the winter of 2012–13. When asked if it tempted him in any way, Maciej answered directly: 'No, not at all. I'm finished with Broad Peak.'

A few months later, at a press conference in Warsaw to announce the final team for the Polish national expedition to Broad Peak in winter, Artur Hajzer dropped a bombshell. 'I have led six expeditions with this [new Polish winter] programme but this time I'm not going because I have tried to summit Broad Peak in the winter twice already and my faith in climbing this peak is a little faded. What's needed is fresh, unwavering bravery.'[16] Then he read out the list of climbers who would be going: the leader would be veteran Ice Warrior Krzysztof Wielicki and his team included Adam Bielecki, Artur Małek and Tomasz Kowalski. And the fourth member of the team would be none other than fifty-nine-year-old Maciej Berbeka from Zakopane. It was a stunning turn of events.

Now sixty years of age, Krzysztof readily accepted leadership of the Broad Peak attempt, provided Artur take full responsibility for its organisation. As far as Artur was concerned, it was simply another expedition in his winter programme. Krzysztof remained on the periphery during the planning stage, trusting Artur's choice of equipment, food and team members: except when it came to Maciej. It was Krzysztof himself who approached his old teammate and friend, asking if he had some 'unfinished business' on Broad Peak. After an initial refusal, Maciej reconsidered and called Krzysztof back. 'Is there still room on the team?' he asked. 'Absolutely,' Krzysztof said. When Ewa learnt of his decision, she 'collapsed'. But she didn't try to dissuade him. She knew that the splinter deep inside Maciej could only be excised on the summit of Broad Peak.

Adam Bielecki was an obvious choice for the team, given his success on Gasherbrum I the previous winter, and a summer ascent of K2 that same year. When he learnt that Krzysztof would lead the team, he was awestruck. 'He was another one of my heroes,' Adam said. 'I grew up with his auto-graphed poster hanging above my bed. If somebody had told me then that I would go on an expedition with him, I wouldn't have believed them.'[17]

Artur Małek, a young physiotherapist from Katowice, was the most technically proficient of the group, particularly on ice. Tomasz (Tomek) Kowalski, the youngest at twenty-eight, had proven himself to be strong and fast on a number of high alpine traverses. When he arrived in Skardu, he recorded his feelings on his blog: 'I can't believe it … I feel as if I was some young guitarist in a start-up band and all of a sudden am playing with Mick Jagger and the Stones in a full stadium in Wembley.'[18] Joining them in a support role was Karim Hayat, a highly experienced Pakistani mountaineer.

Krzysztof had no delusions of grandeur for himself on Broad Peak. His role would be as leader and adviser. He knew the best chance of success lay with the younger, faster alpinists. And hopefully, with Maciej. Not because he was young and quick, but because his motivation was unmatched and his experience was priceless. The team seemed ideal: two legendary Himalayan climbers with a vast amount of experience, three young, strong, motivated guys with everything to prove, and local knowledge from Karim. Artur's strategy was for the expedition to arrive late in January rather than December, reasoning that the best weather windows usually appeared in early March. Why let the team fester in base camp for six weeks?

Everything went according to plan at the start. Camp 1 was in place on 27 January and by 16 February Camp 4 was ready. The first weather window arrived early, on 17 and 18 February, which was when the team began launching a series of summit bids. But who would climb with whom? Adam and Tomek had been partners up to this point, but at Krzysztof's suggestion, the pairing now switched to Adam and Artur. Tomek wasn't happy, since it seemed he had been demoted to the backup team. Adam was clearly the fastest in the group and Maciej the slowest. But Maciej was also the most experienced and Tomek the least. There were obvious advantages to these new pairings and everyone finally agreed. First to go up were Adam and Artur; a day later, Maciej and Tomek. Both teams were stopped by the giant crevasse below the col, but they gained valuable knowledge about the terrain above Camp 4. Early on, issues emerged regarding radio protocol. Krzysztof expected more contact than the team appeared willing to provide, a disagreement that would dog them the entire expedition.

When the weather deteriorated, they were forced into the usual waiting pattern. Possibly the only downside of accurate weather forecasts is the involuntary idleness in base camp. Sitting around, losing fitness, becoming impatient: all contributed to rising levels of frustration. The storm would last for the next thirteen days.

Krzysztof's plan, for when the weather finally improved, was that two teams of two would attempt the summit on two successive days. This would ensure a backup team was available if anything went wrong, a strategy Krzysztof had learnt from Andrzej Zawada. The tactic had worked well in those days when expeditions had ten or twelve highly experienced mountaineers available, all of whom understood that only one or two members would likely summit. The situation was different now. As Krzysztof explained, 'On Broad Peak there were four contenders, four hungry for success. And no one during the expedition fell out of the running.'[19] When the long-awaited good-weather forecast did arrive, it was predicted to last for only one day: 5 March.

The four climbers came up with their *own* plan, regardless of what Krzysztof had in mind. They would all leave base camp on 3 March, reach

Camp 4 next day, and climb to the summit on the one good day, 5 March. And they would go as a team of four, not two teams of two. 'On this expedition, I didn't take any authoritative decisions,' Krzysztof explained. 'When we discussed the plan of attack, I concluded that, in this situation, this configuration was the safest and most sensible way to go. If any one of them felt weak, then another could go down with them and the remaining two would continue. That's why I supported their proposal of a simultaneous attack.'[20] As backup, he sent Karim to Camp 2 with oxygen. Just in case.

By the afternoon of 4 March, the four men had made it to Camp 4. Two tents faced each other: Adam and Artur in one, Maciej and Tomek in the other. While brewing tea and prepping for the summit bid, they discussed tactics. Adam wanted to replicate his Gasherbrum I strategy, leaving the tent at night. He suggested a 2 a.m. departure. Maciej protested he would have to turn around within two hours if they did that, simply because of the sensitivity in his feet from his previous frostbite. He suggested leaving at 7 a.m. Adam disagreed, and they finally settled on 5 a.m. They radioed base camp to inform Krzysztof, who immediately objected to the 5 a.m. departure. He was convinced they wouldn't get out the door at five, but Maciej reassured him they would. It seemed to everyone that Maciej was now in charge of the most important decisions on this climb. Adam calculated they had fourteen hours until sunset if they left at 5 a.m. Ten hours up and four down: it should be enough.

They awoke at 3 a.m. and started melting snow, drinking as much as they could and eating a little. Everyone was quiet, concentrated: nervous. Adam packed a few energy gels, a flag and a sponsor's banner, along with half a litre of hot liquid. They started climbing at 5.15 a.m. All those years of guiding kicked in as Maciej set a steady pace. Adam recalled watching him moving up the slope. 'He was walking the same as Artur [Hajzer] – never stopping. His base camp speed was the same as at 8,000 metres. Super solid. Slow but nonstop.'

The terrain was easy so they didn't rope up. 'After ten steps I threw up my breakfast,' Adam said. 'It was my first high-altitude vomit.' He comforted himself by recalling Artur Hajzer, who would vomit on a regular basis at altitude, and then promptly resume climbing. 'It was his ritual, like brushing his teeth,' Adam said. But it wasn't normal for Adam. Nevertheless, he ignored it, since the day looked promising and they were on their way up.

He glanced up at Maciej, still out front, marvelling at his vigour. 'The thought crossed my mind that I would like to have his fitness at that age.'[21]

Maciej radioed Krzysztof to say everything was going well.

'How about your feet?' Krzysztof asked.

'They're fine. We are getting a bit of sun now.'

'Yes, from now on you will have sun. I told you guys you should have left earlier.'

'No, this is fine. If we had left earlier, I would have had to turn around.'

When they reached a large crevasse, Adam and Maciej fixed a line across a wobbly snow bridge, securing it with a snow picket on the other side. Adam took a few sips from his hot drink, and promptly threw that up as well. Worried about dehydration now, he was puzzled why his body was rejecting everything he swallowed.

They reached the col on the summit ridge of Broad Peak at noon. Two hours too late, in Adam's opinion. Before leaving, they had agreed they would need to reach the col before sunset on their descent. It might still be possible, but the hours were passing quickly. They radioed in to Krzysztof, who encouraged them. 'Fuck, I hope you make it. We are all pacing back and forth down here. Remember, Maciej, to stay roped up there on the ridge. Remember to look back on the younger guys and make sure they don't make any mistakes.'[22]

Krzysztof was concerned. They were moving too slowly. He couldn't understand why their pace was so much slower than previous days. He kept comparing the times to his own ascent of the mountain, which, to be fair, had been a solo speed ascent and in summer. He speculated that the terrain was more difficult in winter, with more exposed ice and rock. Certainly, the weather wasn't an issue. It was a rare, bluebird day with almost no wind.

High on the ridge, Adam and Artur arrived at a ten-metre rock outcrop. Adam climbed it first, securing the rope in a couple of places for the others. Then the ground eased and the two continued up together. Twenty steps. Stop and lean over your ice axe. Ten steps. Stop and rest, catch your breath. Adam's radio was turned on throughout this time. 'Krzysztof took advantage of this more than I would have wanted,' he later said.[23]

'Adam, Adam, come in. I have a question. Is everyone feeling okay?'

'We are doing the same thing we were doing five hours ago – going up. We're still going up.'

When Adam neared the Rocky Summit, Krzysztof called again. Adam stopped to respond and to rest. When the others caught up, they all stopped, the first real break of the day. Adam asked Krzysztof the time. It was 3 p.m. 'I started counting,' Adam said. 'No matter how I counted, we would inevitably be coming back in the dark.'[24] Krzysztof wanted to talk to Maciej so Adam told the others to turn on their radios: he was sick of all the radio chatter.

Krzysztof had been counting, too, and at this point he suggested they turn back. 'Maciej replied that they hadn't come here simply to turn around, but to get to the summit,' Krzysztof recounted. 'It seemed that these words turned out to be decisive for all of them because Maciej was for them an undisputed authority and no one took up the discussion after that. From my perspective … it was hard to dictate to them from base camp.'[25]

Adam felt a ball of fear forming in his gut. He knew the summit was near, but they were moving too slowly. They weren't going to make it down in daylight. He threw it out there again: should they go down? Maciej raised his head slightly, looked at Adam, and started moving up. 'I felt stupid about that,' Adam later said. 'This guy could easily be my father, and he is doing fine. And I am the one backing out? We unroped. And stepped into the other side of the looking glass. We began our race with the sun. We were racing for our lives.'[26]

Freed from the rope, Adam now sped ahead, fuelled by fear and his residual conditioning, but also what he later called sheer stubbornness. He reached the Rocky Summit at 4 p.m. The way ahead looked confusing, so he called Krzysztof. Krzysztof calmed him down, instructed him to stay close to the ridgeline and reassured him the Main Summit was no more than twenty minutes away. Adam doubted his timing but headed up the ridge. When he reached the summit, his first feeling was overwhelming relief that he needn't punish his body for one more upward step. The second emotion was fear. It was 5.20 p.m.

The air seemed to quiver as he watched the others inching up towards him. He took some pictures and a short video and then called Krzysztof on the radio. Krzysztof didn't answer. He tried again, fiddling with his handset. The frequency had changed. But how? He took off his mitts to change it back. It still didn't work. He turned the radio off, turned it back on. Nothing. His fingers were becoming numb so he gave up, stuffing his hand back into his down mitt hoping he hadn't frozen it.

Krzysztof was fretting in base camp. 'Five p.m. passed and there was

Self-portrait on the summit of Broad Peak, 5 March 2013. Adam Bielecki was followed by Artur Małek, Maciej Berbeka and Tomasz Kowalski, all four making the first winter ascent of Broad Peak. *Photo: Adam Bielecki.*

complete silence,' he said. 'I was at a loss for what to do because I thought something had happened.'[27]

Adam started down. He met Artur first, then Maciej and finally Tomek, all in relatively close proximity. He spoke to each of them briefly. 'I'm so happy you made it,' he said to Maciej. 'Nobody deserves it more than you.'[28] Maciej nodded. Adam recalled that everyone looked 'okay', but it was difficult to tell, smothered as they were under all those layers of down, their faces masked by ice. Adam asked Maciej to radio Krzysztof on the top to explain that his radio wasn't working and that he was heading down.

Krzysztof later regretted they hadn't radioed in at that moment, rather than waiting until they had all summited. It was only a difference of twenty minutes or so but every minute counted. The summit had been climbed. Was it necessary for all four of them to reach it? Then again, Krzysztof understood that when you are twenty minutes from a summit and you are about to make history, it's almost impossible to turn around. Even if he had suggested it – ordered it – it's doubtful they would have agreed. Artur reached the summit next: 'Seeing that sunset, I understood one of the most important moments of our lives was beginning. The moment where we begin to fight our way back to living.'[29]

When Maciej radioed in from the summit, Krzysztof responded:

'I'm listening, Maciej. Where are you, goddamn it? Over.'

'At the top. At the top.'

'Be careful during the descent, Maciej. Congratulations. Great. But slowly. Belay each other.'

'Yes, Krzysiek, yes. So long.'[30]

When Krzysztof asked about Adam, Maciej explained he had already summited half an hour earlier and was on his way down. Krzysztof answered: 'Well that's good, but that goof could have at least said something. He could have radioed in. Aside from that, he should have waited for you.'[31] The comment reveals a subtle shift in attitude, from advising Maciej to look after the young ones to wanting Adam to wait for the rest of the team on the summit. The shift was not so much about leadership but about capacity. Artur recalled meeting Maciej below the summit after he had already begun his descent. Maciej suggested he wait for Tomasz and him to summit so they could all rope up on the way down. Artur said no because he was simply too cold to wait. Like Adam, he needed to move.

Fifteen minutes after speaking with Maciej, Krzysztof was announcing on Polish national television that the summit had been climbed, adding this was not a complete success because they still had to get down. He later admitted to being terribly afraid at that moment.

Adam was still above the col when darkness fell. He turned on his headlamp, continued down to the col and stopped to rest. The most difficult part of the descent was over. He peered up the ridge into the darkness and could see a light descending from the Rocky Summit. He assumed it was Artur. He took a few sips of tea and vomited. Looking up once more, he could still see only one light moving down; and after ten minutes, he began shivering uncontrollably so started moving again. As he looked down the couloir, peering into the inky moonless night, he suddenly realised that several hundred metres of séracs and crevasses were between him and the tent and he had no idea how to find it.

Dry-heaving as he stumbled down, grabbing odd bits of old fixed lines, staring into the darkness, he suddenly spied a yellow light. What on earth? Confused now, he assumed Karim was coming up from Camp 2. It must be Karim. But it was an odd colour for a headlamp. Too yellow. Then it disappeared. Devastated, he slumped to the snow. He switched his headlamp to the highest beam and scanned the slopes, both up and down. That's when he saw a single light, high on the ridge: much, much too high. Adam realised the descent was not going as planned. The other three should be at the col by now, or at least near it. This light was closer to the Rocky Summit than the col. He began to shiver again. He had to move. Suddenly there was a flash of light, the tiniest flicker. It was, he realised, the reflection of his headlamp on the guy-line of a tent. But that didn't make sense: it was in the opposite direction of the yellow light. Was he hallucinating? No, he was not. The yellow light was not Karim's headlamp: it was a bonfire at base camp, Krzysztof's idea to motivate them, to warm them psychologically on their long descent through the darkness. If Adam had continued following the light, he would have fallen several kilometres down the face of Broad Peak.

He collapsed into the tent at Camp 4 at 11 p.m. and grabbed his radio. Punching buttons, turning dials, changing batteries, he finally got the thing to work. The first thing he heard was Krzysztof talking to Tomek. 'To this day, it's hard for me to talk about this,' Adam said. 'Krzysztof was telling him to try and descend. But Tomek didn't have the energy.'[32] Adam joined in, trying to motivate him to descend. But they both knew the situation was hopeless. It was too late. He was too high. 'I was talking with a friend who was fated to die,' Adam said. 'Nobody knew what was happening with Maciej. Tomek said he was alone.'[33]

Adam could see Artur's light nearing the tent, bobbing, weaving: even disappearing at times. There was no radio communication with Artur; his radio had also malfunctioned, probably frozen. He needed to remove his gloves to fiddle with it and feared frostbite. When he eventually arrived, he also collapsed in exhaustion. The radio conversation with Tomek continued through the night. He had lost his crampon, he said. He was slipping down the slope. His hand was cold. He couldn't find his mitt. His speech began to slow. He seemed unaware of how serious his position was. When he told Krzysztof he was still near the Rocky Summit, Krzysztof's stomach dropped. By 6 a.m. Tomasz had stopped responding.

Krzysztof recalled the agony of that night. 'I was talking to this guy who was fighting for his life and it was obvious his chances of saving it were small and I couldn't do anything about it.'[34]

There had been no communication with Maciej throughout the night. Krzysztof kept calling, 'Maciej, Maciej, Maciej, are you there?' It was confusing at first, because Tomek said that Maciej was with him but didn't want to talk on the radio. Later, it seemed more likely the two of them weren't together, and that Maciej no longer had a radio. Adam, however, was sure that Maciej *did* have a radio but was equally sure it wasn't turned on.

'Maciej never turned his radio on – I could clearly see that the radio wasn't his thing,' Adam later said. 'He just wanted to climb.'

Krzysztof wasn't overly worried about Maciej. He had so much experience and so much strength and stamina, he would survive. After all, he had done so in 1988. He would again. Adam and Artur were also expecting him to show up at the tent right through the night, convinced, like Krzysztof, that it was only a matter of time till he came knocking. What they had all forgotten was the passage of time: exactly twenty-five years – to the day – had passed since Maciej's epic descent and survival on Broad Peak.

The cook at base camp thought he glimpsed movement immediately below the col early next morning, offering a glimmer of hope. Karim started up from Camp 2 with an oxygen bottle and Krzysztof told Adam and Artur to start back up the mountain to look for Maciej. They quickly turned around, citing exhaustion. When Karim arrived, having broken his all-time altitude record, they somehow convinced him to go higher, using the oxygen. He did, against his better judgement. 'I left Camp 4 and when I got to the catchment below the last sérac it felt very lonely. In my mind, questions started to arise. What would happen if I fell into a crevasse or slipped off the mountain? At this altitude, nobody will help me. But I continued climbing as far as I could. I got to 7,700 metres or maybe a little lower but I didn't see anyone.'[35] Everyone now considered the possibility that Maciej wasn't coming back.

Ewa Berbeka was awaiting news when she underwent a terrifying experience. 'I was there on Broad Peak, I died along with Maciej. I felt it physically. I was suddenly extremely tired and my lips and tongue started tasting salty … huge amounts of salt. That's when I understood that I was present with Maciej during his last moments. I suffered with him. I struggled with every step along with him.'[36] Soon after, she received a call from their friend Ryszard Gajewski, telling her to turn off the television. It was three months before she dared turn it back on.

Returning to Poland was a nightmare. Even before the team arrived, the speculation had begun. Zbyszek Piotrowicz, editor of Poland's climbing magazine *Taternik*, published an article foretelling their reception.

I am loath to think of the coming days when the media will pass judgement on Artur Hajzer, the leader behind the Himalayan winter programme, and Krzysztof Wielicki, the leader. Experts will appear; comments and moral judgements will be passed. It will be a race to be the most principled, the quickest to pass judgement. Those who will be the most vocal will likely be the least capable of understanding what actually happened … I call on people to respect the climbers' decisions to do what they were doing. Pointing fingers is useless, especially not at the leaders.[37]

Adam later commented that the editorial was ninety per cent correct. The ten per cent error was where people pointed: it wasn't Artur or Krzysztof who was blamed; it was Adam.

There was a commission, led by the PZA, as there usually was for a nationally sponsored expedition that had suffered fatalities. The report had five authors, two of whom had been to 8,000 metres but only in summer. Strange inconsistencies in the various narratives began to emerge: differing versions of radio protocol, opposing accounts of which conversations were taped and how some tapes had disappeared, the unwillingness of Adam and Artur to mount a rescue for Maciej, Tomek's inexperience, the switch in leadership from Krzysztof to Maciej. There was no shortage of criticism.

Only after the report was released to a newspaper, was Adam given a copy. 'First I cried,' he recalled. 'My second reaction was aggression. I almost destroyed a cabinet in anger. And then everything ricocheted from anger to fear. The most overwhelming feeling was one of unfairness. The feeling that I had been made a scapegoat.'[38]

Ryszard Gajewski agreed with much of the report but added, 'If anything, it's too soft.'[39] He averred that Adam should be barred from any nationally supported expeditions for five years, and that Artur and Krzysztof used bad judgement when they put together the team. In Ryszard's opinion, neither Artur Małek nor Tomek Kowalski was qualified for a winter ascent of Broad Peak.

Alek Lwow, who had been with Maciej on the 1988 Broad Peak attempt, was equally blunt about the report, but arrived at a completely different conclusion. 'I think the report is entirely useless. The report is based on basic principles that above 7,500 metres in winter, simply don't work.' Alek refrained from laying the blame on Adam, but pointed out a number of key moments where he felt mistakes were made, laying the burden of guilt on all of them. 'The fundamental mistake was that they moved as a team of four. The second pair should have gone as a backup. The second big mistake was that they didn't turn around because of the late hour. The third was when Bielecki got to the summit and the others didn't turn around.' According to Alek, Adam's acts of self-preservation reflected the reality of the situation. 'The cause of Berbeka's and Kowalski's death is that they misjudged their abilities,' he continued. 'The report talks a lot about the team and teamwork. That's dumb. If anyone broke up the team it was those who didn't turn around.'[40]

Krzysztof was convinced it wouldn't have mattered what he had said or how forcefully he had said it: all four would have gone to the summit. Furthermore, he understood why. He would have done the same. 'You must remember ... our community is made up in large part of powerful personalities,' he said. 'At the Rocky Summit, there were four individuals who could have advised each other but ultimately everyone made their own decision.'[41]

Adam remembered that decisive moment at the Rocky Summit as well. When he realised how late it was, he had become scared. When he tentatively suggested they might consider going down, nobody answered him. 'I felt that Maciej, who made the first step towards the summit, was making decisions for the whole group,' he said. 'I think something weird happened. Normally, when someone proposes turning around, there is a discussion. Somebody reacts. But my question wasn't answered, as if it wasn't important. I had faith in Maciej's strength and experience, and that was my mistake. On the Rocky Summit each of us had to look deep inside and answer for themselves, can I make it? Tomek and Maciej overestimated their capabilities but no one should judge them for it. It was their decision. They had every right to it.'

The memory of those moments when Adam met the others on descent remained painfully fresh. 'I was assigned blame for breaking apart the group at the Rocky Summit. But the guys passing me on the way to the top could easily have turned around and come down with me. The expedition was already successful, but they had decided otherwise, even though they knew I wouldn't be able to wait for them. They chose to make individual ascents. Mountains denude us. They take away our masks. In the moment when you are hungry and fighting for your life, it becomes clear what you have inside of you. You can't hide. Broad Peak showed me what the price of ambition could be. All of us wanted to get to the summit and each one of us paid for it.'[42]

The tragedy on Broad Peak split the Polish climbing community in two: or more accurately, four. There were those who blamed Adam and Artur. Others pointed the finger at Krzysztof. And then, there was the mastermind of the entire enterprise, Artur Hajzer. There was plenty of blame to go around, and plenty of grief. Each of them handled the grief and pressure differently. Artur Hajzer became quiet, the edge gone from his voice, obsessed with reading everything posted about the expedition. He played the role of the emotionally controlled person, even using humour to mask his reeling emotions; but those who knew him well understood he was suffering. Krzysztof became evasive. Artur Małek appeared in shock and avoided public appearances. Adam retreated, knowing he was persona non grata, particularly in Zakopane, Maciej's hometown. The Kowalski family could hardly fathom that their son had died in the prime of his life. And after years of worry, Ewa Berbeka was finally a widow: 'My life without Maciej is now very empty … I try to be strong for my sons.'[43]

The practical effects continued for two more years. The Polish winter programme's main sponsor pulled out. Maciej's brother organised an expedition to Broad Peak to find the bodies; only Tomasz's body was found, and was moved slightly off the main ascent route. Ewa travelled to the mountain to say her final goodbyes, even though she was already terminally ill. She died shortly after. Artur Hajzer returned to the Karakoram the following summer and was killed in a fall in the Japanese Couloir on Gasherbrum I. Many said he had never recovered from the shock and the guilt of losing two climbers on Broad Peak. Artur Małek said: 'I think the most important lesson to learn from Artur Hajzer is [from] Gasherbrum I, when he died. It was his last message from the high mountains. People die in the mountains, even the best ones.'[44] So much death.

Krzysztof later said he wished it had been a full-blown hurricane on the Broad Peak summit day. That would have forced them all to turn around and everyone would still be alive. He recalled a saying of his mentor, Andrzej Zawada: 'A successful expedition is one when you reach the summit and a happy expedition is one on which everyone comes back.'[45] The Broad Peak winter expedition of 2013 was certainly successful, but it couldn't have been less happy.

Simone Moro, who had twice attempted Broad Peak in winter, wrote a letter to the Berbeka family. 'Broad Peak is a metaphor for dreams, and life itself … That Broad Peak can actually be climbed in the winter was the great lesson that Berbeka taught us. Nobody wants to die for their dreams. The only thing we truly want is to have a dream so strong it lets us feel young and alive. Maciej taught me this as well. That it's never too late for dreams, and no dream is so big and so beckoning or so icy it's impossible. Thank you, Maciej.'[46]

Stanisław, Maciej's son, remembered the last time he saw his dad. He had been packing for Broad Peak. The ritual was the same for every trip. Maciej would lay out all his precious items: the clothing, the gear, the goggles, his favourite helmet, his special foods. Nobody but Maciej was allowed to touch them. While watching his dad sorting and re-sorting, he wondered why they had never talked about the first Broad Peak trip: a father-to-son talk. 'I was curious about what he had experienced there and how he had coped during the descent,' Stanisław said. 'What he was thinking about. And generally, what does one think about in a situation like this, when you can die at any moment? Do you think about your home, your family, about the kids, about your wife? Do you want to get back to them?'[47] Stanisław and Maciej would likely have had that conversation, eventually. Maciej could have told him about his epic survival story and his high-altitude bivouac. About what drew him back – back to the tent, to Poland, to his family. And about what ultimately compelled him to return to Broad Peak.

Maciej was so well liked and respected throughout Poland that many people developed theories about what had happened to him, and why it had happened. Almost all of the theories were based on his character, rather than the facts: his caring nature; his patience; his maturity as a mountaineer. Most theories assumed it was because he was looking after Tomasz that he died on Broad Peak.

Alek Lwow thinks differently and, though his words seem harsh, they reflect the fact that Maciej and Tomasz were far apart when they died. 'I'm not saying Maciej did anything wrong by not giving up on his summit bid. I'm saying that in the final report there is no room for monuments ... with certainty his headlamp was seen around the col when Kowalski's body was found on the ridge.'[48] Still, it's equally possible that Maciej waited too long for Tomasz before he began descending alone, fighting for his life.

Stanisław is haunted by the enduring mystery of what happened to his father. Did he fall? Did he die of exposure in a crevasse? Exhaustion? What were his last moments? What were his last thoughts? Where is his final resting place? There are simply no answers.

13

NANGA PARBAT

The Magnificent Obsession

Nanga Parbat. The mountain all alpinists respect, even fear. Its name translates as the 'naked mountain' but it's known also as the 'killer mountain', even the 'king of the mountains'. And its reputation is justified.

Of all the 8,000-metre peaks, Nanga Parbat has seen the greatest number of serious winter attempts: thirty-three to date. Thirty-four, if you count the 1950 British expedition, which ended in tragedy when two of the three climbers disappeared on the mountain during a storm. Since they started in early November and perished at the start of December, it should more correctly be called an autumn attempt, although their intention was to 'see what winter temperatures, snow and avalanche conditions would be like,' as the sole survivor Captain Richard Marsh explained.[1] It was a bold effort, considering Nanga Parbat hadn't been climbed in *any* season at that time.

The Nanga Parbat massif forms the western corner of the Himalaya and is, at 8,125 metres, the second-highest mountain in Pakistan. With three magnificent faces, there is plenty of choice for climbers: the easier-angled Rakhiot face, the steep and rocky Diamir face, or, on the southern side of the mountain, the mighty Rupal face. Each one is impressive, both in scale and height, but the Rupal is especially so, spanning 4,500 metres from base to summit.

It was this face that tempted a group of Poles from Zakopane to make the first serious winter attempt in the 1988–89 season. The team's leader was Maciej Berbeka, a year after he had reached the Rocky Summit of Broad

Peak, becoming the first person to have been over 8,000 metres in Pakistan in winter. The Poles climbed 2,200 metres on the glistening ice of the Rupal face before abandoning the attempt. Maciej returned two years later with a team of four Brits and seven Poles, their goal a winter ascent of the central spur, the route Reinhold Messner had climbed in 1970, ascending the full height of the magnificent Rupal face. Unsuccessful on the 1970 route, and with the winter season drawing to a close, Maciej tossed out a radical suggestion: change tactics and change routes. They switched to the easier Schell route and, climbing alpine style, reached 6,600 metres before admitting defeat. They got away with their bold attempt, but lightweight pushes on a mountain like Nanga Parbat in winter would prove extremely dangerous – even lethal – for the similarly ambitious teams that followed.

A small French team tried the Schell route in 1993 and Andrzej Zawada brought a strong Polish expedition to the mountain in 1996–97, strong enough to reach 7,875 metres on the Diamir face, at which point the two summit climbers suffered crippling frostbite and had to retreat. Andrzej returned the following winter but was defeated, this time by heavy snowfall. Krzysztof Wielicki gave it a try in the winter of 2006–07, but was plagued throughout the attempt by winds so strong Krzysztof described their plan as 'pure science fiction'. Deeply disappointed, he speculated it would be a long time before anyone reached the summit of Nanga Parbat in winter, and he hoped they would 'not lose their humility in the face of this mountain'.[2]

More teams followed: from Poland, Italy and Russia. In the winter of 2011–12, two arrived, both on the Diamir side. Marek Klonowski, a Polish climber living in Ireland, had joined forces with another expat, Tomasz Mackiewicz (known as Tomek), also living in Ireland. Tomek was a man who needed strong emotions to feel alive and, before he discovered climbing, drugs had offered him that. His wife, Anna, recalled how, 'My first impression was his energy. And his eyes – like a glacier on fire. Tomek shook me with his energy … you feel you want to be close to him because of his energy.' She had met Tomek while he was still in therapy for heroin addiction. Both married at the time, they extricated themselves from their unhappy partnerships and eventually moved to Ireland, where there were more opportunities for work.

Tomek hadn't been trained like most Polish climbers: no PZA courses, no moving up through the ranks, the Tatras, the Alps, the Himalaya. He and Marek had made a complete traverse of Canada's highest mountain, Mount

Tomek Mackiewicz and Anna Solska-Mackiewicz. *Photo: Anna Solska-Mackiewicz Archive.*

Logan, but his climbing trajectory was unconventional: as far as the Himalaya was concerned, he went straight in at the deep end on Nanga Parbat in winter. It became his obsession. As Anna explained, 'He learnt about climbing during the years on Nanga – on the job training.' His lack of formal training and his free-spirited, rebellious nature eliminated the possibility of support from the PZA, even after the winter Himalaya programme was in full swing. Following his first trip to Nanga Parbat, Tomek had written to Artur Hajzer for advice and information. Artur had responded in his typical, somewhat sarcastic fashion. 'Most definitely I would advise the following:

1. Complete a winter mountaineering course in the Tatras (previous to that, a summer course and a season of climbing on your own in the Tatras).
2. Climb for two winter seasons independently in the Tatras – 5 routes each season, minimum of Grade V and minimum of 400 metres of climbing.
3. Go to an 8,000-metre peak in a non-winter season and, before that, it would be best to go to the Pamirs above 7,000 metres.
4. Only then, consider winter in the Himalaya.'[3]

The next time Tomek wrote to Artur, there was no response at all. He then tried Krzysztof Wielicki, but received in return only a brief message that was almost as dismissive as Artur's. Tomek was simply not considered a serious alpinist. He was a confirmed rebel: a misfit within the Polish climbing community. Tomek and Marek were clearly on their own.

They were now in Pakistan with Łukasz Biernacki for their second attempt of the mountain's Diamir face. Theirs was an ambitious project on a shoe-string budget. Both free spirits, their style contrasted sharply with that of the season's other contender, Simone Moro. Simone came with his usual, meticulously planned approach: big budget, good food, comfortable base camp, high expectations and his favourite partner – Denis Urubko. They had been climbing together for more than a decade and had already made first winter ascents of two 8,000-metre peaks. They were, as *PlanetMountain* reported, 'revving their engines and getting an idea of their Nanga Parbat, in its winter vest via the Diamir face.'[4]

Many in Poland queried Tomek about attempting Nanga Parbat at the same time as such a famous and well-established alpinist like Simone, but he simply laughed at their scepticism. After hosting a jam-packed press conference in Milan, Simone and Denis headed for Pakistan but, like so many before them, were thwarted by the massif's punishing winter storms. They reached 6,800 metres before being turned back, only 200 metres higher than the renegade Poles.

The following winter of 2012–13 saw a marked increase in traffic on the mountain, more like summer in terms of numbers, with four teams vying for the first winter ascent. The penny had dropped among the world's high-altitude climbers that the chances of a first winter ascent of an 8,000-metre peak were dwindling fast. While Simone and Tomek had been on Nanga Parbat, Gasherbrum I had been climbed, leaving just three mountains left. Tomek and Marek formed one of the teams, returning for their third attempt on Nanga Parbat, this time via the Schell route on the Rupal face. They called themselves the 'Justice for All' expedition. Anna explained that 'they wanted, maybe naively, to convey a message to people, to try to change the world to a better place.'

Undaunted, they started up the mountain, fixing ropes they had purchased at a local farm-supply store in Poland. Higher on the mountain, Tomek posted on his blog that he thought they might be on a partially new route. This caught Artur's attention and he went online to express his scorn. 'They simply don't know where they are. The photos on their blog are photos taken on the Schell route. There is no doubt. Even the piton of which they write is characteristic of the 1950s and is precisely on the Schell route.'[5]

Despite the disdain the established Polish climbing community showed the pair, they were certainly keeping a close eye on their climb.

Tomek ended up spending four nights alone in a snow cave, hallucinating and communing with the mystical powers of Nanga Parbat. In total, he spent twenty-one days above base camp, an astonishing amount of time to survive at altitude in the harshest season. Back in Poland, Voytek Kurtyka for one identified strongly with Tomek's appetite for suffering. 'The ability to prove that I am stronger than my suffering is a source of huge joy and emotional strength ... If I can be stronger than myself, then I raise the art of suffering to new heights.'[6]

Others were also raising the art of suffering. While Tomek and Marek were on the Rupal face, the Italian alpinist Daniele Nardi teamed up with French climber Élisabeth Revol for an ambitious objective: an alpine-style ascent of the Diamir face via the difficult and extremely dangerous Mummery Rib. Daniele, who had plenty of experience at altitude with five 8,000ers in his CV, had announced it was only the unclimbed Mummery Rib that interested him: a direct line to the summit. Luckily for him, Élisabeth was one of the few alpinists who could match his speed and ability.

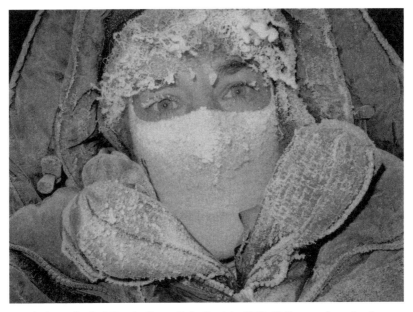

French alpinist Élisabeth Revol at Nanga Parbat in winter 2012–13. She was attempting the unclimbed Mummery Rib with Italian climber Daniele Nardi. *Photo: Élisabeth Revol Archive.*

Élisabeth, known as Eli, was a gymnast as a child but had turned to alpinism while still a teenager. The petite athlete showed great promise, and was soon in Bolivia with a French expedition. She returned with nine summits, five first ascents and an insatiable appetite for high mountains. On her first expedition to the Karakoram in 2008, she climbed the Rocky Summit of Broad Peak, Gasherbrum I and Gasherbrum II within the span of sixteen days, all without supplemental oxygen. The following year, her partner Martin Minařík died of altitude sickness and exhaustion as they descended from a fore-summit of Annapurna. Devastated by the tragedy, Eli avoided the high mountains for almost four years. Now she was back, on Nanga Parbat in winter, on a yet-to-be-climbed route with Daniele.

Nanga Parbat was oblivious to their experience and fitness. On their final attempt, winds of 100 kilometres per hour and temperatures as low as −48° Celsius turned them back at around 6,400 metres. Daniele expressed his disappointment in his dispatches from the mountain. 'Unfortunately, our story of the Nanga Parbat in winter on the Mummery Ridge ends here. The mountain decided. It closed its doors once again. I accept it. It was the most extraordinary human and alpinist experience I've ever made in my life … It's because it spared my life, it let me taste its violence and its honey, the Queen of the Mountains … the killer mountain … How much did I learn? A lot more than I can digest at the moment!'[7]

It wasn't enough to dissuade him from pursuing his dream of the Mummery Rib, although 'obsession' might be more accurate. The winter of 2014–15 saw him make his third attempt on this dangerous, avalanche-prone route. Daniele wasn't the only one obsessed with Nanga Parbat. That same season, Eli was paired with Tomek, now on his fifth attempt of the mountain. Newcomers from Russia and Iran brought the number of teams to an astonishing five, all vying for the first winter ascent of Nanga Parbat, by then one of just two 8,000ers left.

Tomek and Eli called themselves 'Nanga Light' as they inched up the mountain, one camp at a time. Their spirits were high, they were eating well and their acclimatisation was good. Tomek seemed to thrive in this environment, never rushing, savouring the isolation, the cold, the companionship. His wife Anna recalled how, 'Tomek liked to be *on* the mountain – not simply *climb* the mountain. He was not in a hurry.' But at 7,800 metres, he and Eli ran out of time. So close to the summit they felt they could almost touch it, the pair turned back.

Krzysztof Wielicki had been monitoring the situation on Nanga Parbat: 'Five teams on the same 8,000-metre peak – it's without precedent up until now in winter Himalayan climbing. You could imagine that if there is a fairly well-defined weather window then more or less everyone would go up at the same time … I could be wrong, but I have a feeling this year Nanga will finally fall.'[8] He was wrong. Tomek and Eli's attempt would prove to be the high point that season.

Five teams returned for the following winter of 2015–16 but the combinations had changed. Eli was still with Tomek, but Marek had a new team, and Daniele was with Basque climber Alex Txikon and the accomplished Pakistani mountaineer Ali Sadpara, who had already climbed Nanga Parbat twice in summer. Simone came with his new partner, Tamara Lunger, and Adam Bielecki was there with Jacek Czech, hoping to do a lightning fast, alpine-style ascent of the Kinshofer route, the regular route on the Diamir face. Each team was accompanied by a couple of Kalashnikov-armed soldiers, courtesy of the Pakistani government, in response to the shocking slaughter of ten foreign climbers and a local cook in 2013.

Kalashnikov-bearing soldiers accompanied the 2015-16 climbers at Nanga Parbat base camp. *L to R*: Simone Moro, Tamara Lunger, four soldiers (names unknown), Alex Txikon and Ali Sadpara. *Photo: Tamara Lunger Archive.*

If it sounds confusing, it was. And it became more so as the season progressed.

Daniele, Alex and Ali were installing a line of fixed ropes on the Kinshofer route, while Adam and Jacek were nearby on the same route, but climbing alpine style. Simone and Tamara, while on the same side as Daniele and the others, were on Messner's 1978 route up the Diamir face, the same as Tomek and Eli. Marek was on the other side of the mountain in the Rupal Valley.

When Adam and Jacek arrived at base camp on 29 December, having acclimatised in the Chilean Andes, the others were already established on the mountain. Adam and Jacek wasted little time. On 2 January they reached 4,900 metres and set up their tent. The following day they simul-climbed up the Kinshofer Couloir and left a stash of equipment at 5,700 metres. On the way down they fixed 300 metres of rope and were back in base camp by 9 p.m. Their acclimatisation in Chile was paying good dividends. But when the weather deteriorated, they began to lose it. Base camp was low, and every day that passed contributed to a loss of acclimatisation and fitness.

The atmosphere in base camp was complicated. Simone's roomy, comfortable tent was a favourite gathering place, in part because of Tamara's fine Italian coffee machine. Many hours were spent around the coffee maker, sharing stories, planning, scheming and joking. A common target of their jokes was 'the Italian media, which claimed Simone was probably sleeping with Tamara and that statistically, someone would inevitably die on the mountain. Simone joked the season's sub-title should be "Race, Fuck, and Die."'[9]

Yet the mood wasn't altogether lighthearted. Alex seemed more serious than usual. He and his partner Daniele weren't getting along, in part because of their constant posting on social media. Each would arrive at Simone's tent and complain about the other's behaviour, not a good sign for what lay ahead. Tomek and Eli were not always welcome in Simone's tent either. Tamara explained that although she admired Tomek's 'light' style, it was often *too* light. 'They didn't have enough things to climb the mountain,' she said. 'We gave them a lot of supplies – a generator, gas, food. Every day they came and asked for something different.'

When it became clear that Adam and Jacek were stalled, they joined forces with Alex's team. After all, they were on the same route. But they couldn't agree on the terms of their cooperation. Alex wanted Adam to chip in on the cost of his equipment and porter fees, as well as the 300 metres of rope he had already fixed. They negotiated and argued and finally came up

MAKALU

Above left: Katia and Jean-Christophe Lafaille. *Photo: Katia Lafaille Archive.*

Above right: Simone Moro and Denis Urubko staying in touch with the world during their winter 2008-09 Makalu expedition. *Photo: Simone Moro.*

Below: Simone Moro on the summit of Makalu, 9 February 2009, when he and Denis Urubko made the first winter ascent of the mountain. *Photo: Denis Urubko.*

GASHERBRUM II

Top left: Denis Urubko during the 2010-11 winter expedition to Gasherbrum II. *Photo: Cory Richards.*

Top right: Sub-zero tent scene during the Gasherbrum II winter expedition in 2010-11. *Photo: Cory Richards.*

Bottom left: Cory Richards filming during the first winter ascent of Gasherbrum II. *Photo: Cory Richards.*

Bottom right: Cory Richards self-portrait, after surviving a massive avalanche while descending Gasherbrum II. *Photo: Cory Richards.*

GASHERBRUM I

Top: Alex Txikon and Gerfried Göschl moving supplies across gaping crevasses on their winter attempt of Gasherbrum I. *Photo: Louis Rousseau.*

Above: Storms hit Gasherbrum I base camp on a regular basis during winter 2011-12. Two teams were there: an international team led by Gerfried Göschl and a Polish team led by Artur Hajzer. *Photo: Darek Załuski.*

Left: Extreme fatigue after the failed attempt to climb a partial new route on Gasherbrum I in winter 2011. *Photo: Gerfried Göschl.*

GASHERBRUM I (CONTINUED)

Top: Adam Bielecki, Janusz Gołąb and Artur Hajzer strategising about their summit attempt on Gasherbrum I. *Photo: Darek Załuski.*

Above: Tamara Styś after her unsuccessful attempt at summiting Gasherbrum I in winter 2012. She did, however, reach 7,250 metres, a female record for the Karakoram in winter. *Photo: Darek Załuski.*

BROAD PEAK

Top: Maciej Berbeka being helped into camp after having survived an open-air bivouac near the Rocky Summit of Broad Peak in winter 1988. He had just made the first winter ascent of the Rocky Summit, and the first winter ascent over 8,000 metres in the Karakoram. *Photo: Alek Lwow.*

Above: Maciej Berbeka at 6,300 metres, below Camp 2 on the 2013 Polish Broad Peak winter expedition. *Photo: Adam Bielecki.*

BROAD PEAK (CONTINUED)

Top: View of the summit, as Adam Bielecki approaches it after 5 p.m. on 5 March 2013. *Photo: Adam Bielecki.*

Above: Ewa Berbeka visits Broad Peak base camp after her husband disappeared on the mountain while descending from the summit. *Photo: Maciej Berbeka Archive.*

NANGA PARBAT

Top: Multiple teams at Nanga Parbat in 2015-16, all hoping for the first winter ascent of the mountain.
Top: Tamara Lunger, Élisabeth Revol and Daniele Nardi. *Middle:* Simone Moro, Jacek Czech, Adam Bielecki and Ali Sadpara. *Bottom:* Alex Txikon and Tomasz Mackiewicz. *Photo: Tamara Lunger Archive.*

Above: Élisabeth Revol and Tomasz Mackiewicz on Nanga Parbat in winter 2017-18. *Photo: Élisabeth Revol.*

NANGA PARBAT (CONTINUED)

Denis Urubko, Élisabeth Revol and Adam Bielecki, during the dramatic rescue on Nanga Parbat.
Photo: Adam Bielecki.

K2

The Polish 2017–18 K2 winter expedition team. *Photo: Darek Załuski.*

with a compromise that suited neither. Adam and Daniele headed up, planning to fix more lines. Before leaving base camp, Adam glanced at the rope supplied by Alex. 'What is this shit? Is this supposed to be a climbing rope?' he scoffed.[10] Daniele agreed it wasn't ideal. The rope was still in its packaging, which clearly indicated a maximum weight capacity of 118 kilograms: hardly adequate for a fixed climbing rope.

Still, up they went. At 5,700 metres they set up a belay and Adam started up, fixing the Spanish rope as he climbed. After sixty metres, he placed two ice screws and carried on up the fifty-five-degree slope until the coil of rope ran out. Adam described what happened next. 'I shouted down to Daniele, "Why don't you come up? We can simul-climb." Daniele untied from the stance and climbed up to the first ice screw. It was fifteen metres below me. The idea was to always have two points of security between us, so I stopped and pounded in a good piton and tied the fixed line through it. I wanted to rest so I tied a knot into the fixed line on my side of the piton and clipped it to my harness. I rested on it. The line broke.'[11]

Adam flew through the air. His head hit the ice and he momentarily lost consciousness. When he came to, he was still falling, head first. After seventy metres he stopped. Hanging upside down in his harness, he saw that his hand was damaged, probably from grasping the rope in the hopes of slowing his fall. Still confused about what had happened, he looked down at the karabiner attached to the belay loop on his harness and saw the broken piece of fixed line. His first reaction was rage. Rage at himself for having used a line he knew was inadequate. Rage at Alex for having brought inferior equipment. Rage that for him the trip was over. His hands were so burned he could barely grip his ice axe.

Alex and Ali continued working on the Kinshofer route, fixing lines and moving their camps ever higher. Tomek and Eli, meanwhile, had reached 7,400 metres on the Messner route and were poised for the summit. The temperature dropped to -50° Celsius in their tent that night: the only time Tomek had ever seen Eli afraid. As they discussed whether to attempt the summit the following day, Eli admitted, 'The likelihood that we wouldn't come back was too high.'[12] They were further discouraged by a weather forecast Simone had provided that warned of ferocious winds in the very near future. Daniele, who was also on the mountain at the time, was confused, because his independent weather forecast predicted a relatively calm period for several more days. But he said nothing.

In light of the forecast and the intense cold, Tomek and Eli decided to descend. Their climb was over. But the aftermath of their retreat deteriorated into a nasty tangle of resentment and distrust. Tomek accused Simone of exaggerating how poor the weather would be in the forecast he'd shared, and in doing so influenced their decision to descend. Eli was now out of time so she returned to France, but Tomek decided to try again. He travelled to Gilgit where he extended his permit and raised some money for his unpaid expedition expenses. When he returned to base camp, intending to head back up the mountain alone, he and Simone traded insults. Each account refutes the other's so it's impossible to know where the truth lies, but everyone who was at base camp agrees that Tomek was no longer in any shape to climb. Thin, ill, dehydrated and having lost his acclimatisation, his determination to climb Nanga Parbat was fuelled by something other than reason. 'I realised I was taking part in some giant shit-show on this mountain,' he finally concluded.[13] Defeated and demoralised, he left base camp for home.

Simone and Tamara, who had been climbing the lower part of the Messner route, now abandoned their climb because of sérac danger. Marek's team reached just over 7,000 metres on the Rupal side, before they also retreated. It appeared that only the team of Alex, Daniele and Ali would continue with their winter attempt on the Diamir face. Then things got interesting. According to Tamara, Alex invited her and Simone to join forces with them. 'At the beginning we didn't want to,' Tamara explained. 'They had already fixed a lot of ropes and it wasn't so elegant from our side to join them now. They had worked a lot.' Daniele had not been consulted and was livid. Secretly recording conversations at base camp, he offered a different scenario, in which Simone was the one to suggest the alliance: an alliance he was willing to pay for. Disgusted, Daniele left the mountain.

A new team of four now formed. And as unbalanced as it might seem, each member brought value to the relationship: Alex's team had done much of the hard work. Simone, in particular, brought an immense amount of winter tactical experience. They waited until the forecast offered a slim strand of hope, and headed up as a team of four.

They clicked immediately. 'I felt at home with this team,' Tamara recalled. 'I felt like one of them, not the woman who is behind, or the *woman* climber – I was *a climber*.' Their night at Camp 3 was like a dream: cold, but with a full moon bathing their tent with an ethereal light and illuminating the summit. By 25 February they were at Camp 4 at 7,100 metres. It was obvious to all of

Camping high above the clouds on Nanga Parbat, winter 2015-16. *Photo: Tamara Lunger Archive.*

them that history was about to be made: the first winter ascent of Nanga Parbat, and the first winter ascent of an 8,000er in Pakistan by a woman. Alex and Ali left first. Tamara was half an hour behind, and Simone fifteen minutes after her. 'When I left the tent, I felt that my muscles weren't in such great shape,' Tamara recalled. 'I don't know if I was actually sick – I had my period – but when Simone passed me, I realised, oh my God, I'm not in good shape this day.' Simone was taking twenty-five steps before resting but Tamara could only manage twenty.

Alex's partner, Igone Mariezkurrena, who was watching them through a telescope at base camp, sent up encouraging messages: 200 metres from the summit, 150 metres from the summit, 100 metres from the summit.

One hundred metres from the summit, Tamara stopped to rest. She had been vomiting much of the day and was now exhausted. She peered up at her teammates spread out on the slope above her. Ali appeared to be on the summit, waving his arms. The other two had stopped, slumped over their ice axes. Then they started up again. Tamara, who is deeply religious, was conversing with Jesus. 'Every time I go up the mountain, I speak with this guy,' she explained. 'He's the only one who is nearby me in these extremely exposed moments. He knows what I need to do. When I went up from Camp 4, I spoke with him constantly: "Please switch off this wind. I can't live with this wind just now." When I came to the point where Simone climbed into the couloir and I could no longer see him, I lost all of my motivation. I said to Jesus, "I give you five more minutes to switch off the wind. If you can't do it, there must be a reason and I have to turn around."' Jesus did not switch the wind off.

Tamara sensed danger. She sensed death. 'This was such a strong feeling that if I wanted to survive, I needed to go down.' She looked up; she looked down. She wept in frustration. She was quite sure she could make it to the summit, but was equally convinced she would need help getting down. She couldn't place that burden on her teammates. Shortly after starting down, she fell flat on her stomach from exhaustion. She lay there, gazing at the stupendous view, waiting to die: *willing* herself to die in this magnificent place. Yet the will to live was stronger. It forced her to shift her weary body, lean on her ice axe and stand. Then Tamara continued to Camp 4 on her own while the others joined Ali on the summit. It was 3.17 p.m. on 26 February. The summit climbers were back in Camp 4 by 8 p.m. the same day, and the entire team made it all the way to base camp on 27 February.

The prize had been claimed. Nanga Parbat had finally been climbed in winter and the media became crazed with the dramatic story: Alex, Simone and Ali were heroes, and Tamara was universally praised for her sound judgement. Despite her initial disappointment, she later reflected it had been the right decision. 'Only now that the expedition has ended, do I realise that all the difficulties we tackled have changed me deeply,' she wrote. 'I have become a new Tamara, more mature and more courageous. A Tamara who knows she made the right choice by giving up on the summit and thanking God for listening to her voice. A Tamara who looked death in the eye and is still alive, who felt the cold but now knows she can deal with it ... Now I know with certainty, that my real home is ... there, amidst the highest mountains, in solitude and simplicity.'[14]

The mountaineering world celebrated with them, bestowing them the respect they deserved. Simone was elated, stating, 'In some respects, it was my career's highest point ... not so much for the feat itself, but mainly because it represents all the ingredients which allowed me to get where I am now: insight, patience, pioneering, perseverance, commitment, friendship, and the ability to suffer.'[15] Tamara was equally satisfied. 'Nanga Parbat was the most important expedition in my life, even though I nearly lost my life,' she later said.

But the saga of Nanga Parbat in winter was far from finished.

Not everyone was happy about the victorious winter ascent of Nanga Parbat by Alex Txikon, Simone Moro and Ali Sadpara. Daniele Nardi felt abandoned by Alex and turned inward with his disappointment. Pragmatic Eli simply planned to return; she wanted to climb Nanga Parbat in winter in alpine style. That prize still remained, as did the first female winter ascent.

Tomek was destroyed. His Nanga Parbat dream had morphed into a nightmare. He had been sure that his sixth try would be the lucky one, that he would be the first. It's what he had been living for all these years. He had found the perfect partner in Eli, but now the dream was over. Tomek began publicly criticising Simone's claim, seeding doubts about his honesty and demanding proof: a video from the summit. Simone responded in kind, saying that the only way Tomek could justify his ongoing obsession with the first winter ascent was to refute the success of others. They traded insults and accusations on the internet, for the whole world to see. Eli came to Tomek's defence, saying, 'In 2016, Simone destroyed Tomek. He made him feel like dirt.' When Tomek returned to Poland, he resumed a self-destructive pattern that had nearly killed him years earlier: alcohol, drugs, bitterness.

His wife, Anna, tried to provide some context for his behaviour, admitting freely that he was not an easy person. But she also knew, as did Tomek's therapist, that alpinism was therapeutic for his drug addiction. 'My life story with him is the story of Nanga,' she said. 'I was almost married to Nanga. It was my choice. I knew it. I didn't have quite a full understanding of his love affair with Nanga, but I accepted it.' Yet his extended trips to Nanga Parbat, year after year, did cause her to wonder: 'I had a feeling somewhere deep inside that he was escaping: from me, from this life of ours. And it hurt. But I also understood he couldn't live without this. And I couldn't ask him not to do it because this was his life. He needed it badly.' He stayed in close touch with her during his climbs: phone calls, sharing impressions and emotions, asking questions, even about the route. 'Maybe he needed to go away to see how much he needed me and how much he loved me.' When Eli told Tomek that she was going to try Nanga Parbat again, he agreed to join her. 'I had a feeling he shouldn't go this year,' Anna admitted. But she said nothing to dissuade him.

And so it transpired that in the winter of 2017–18, Eli and Tomek were back on Nanga Parbat. It was Eli's fourth attempt and Tomek's seventh. They were such a curious team: Eli, the highly trained athlete, petite, self-disciplined, quick, focused, and rather quiet; Tomek, the free spirit, who loved to talk. They typically climbed some distance apart when they weren't roped together since Eli was so much faster than Tomek. As Anna explained, 'He never wanted to be fast. She hardly walks – she flies. She is so tiny and fast.'

Because of security issues, they were forced to set up base camp in a summer settlement 400 metres lower than the usual base camp. At least with no other climbers in the area, it was blissfully silent. The allure of Nanga Parbat in winter had magically vanished following the first ascent. The enforced lower base camp was but one of their problems. As Eli explained: 'Nothing seemed to work that year. We didn't have a true base camp. We didn't have a cook. We didn't have a generator. We didn't have electricity. We had to be frugal with our energy for all of our devices. The satellite phone quickly became useless.'[16]

They began acclimatising by carrying gear and food to the base of the mountain: four and a half hours up from base camp. Eli, as usual, was more concerned than Tomek about a systematic acclimatisation programme. 'It took a lot of time to explain to him that our bodies work differently,' she said. 'I weigh several dozen kilograms less than him which means my reactions to elevations are more extreme. Tomek seems to not lose a lot of energy on the mountain while everything above base camp was a big energy expenditure for me.'[17]

When they started up the Messner route, Eli noted a couple of changes in Tomek. It was the first time she had seen him refrain from smoking on an expedition. And he was far fitter than usual. He confessed that he had actually trained for this climb, something he rarely did, since he despised training. But it was his change in attitude that most caught her attention. 'It was a different Tomek this year; he only talked about Simone,' she recalled. 'He said he hadn't reached the top, that he had no proof. He was obsessed with Simone and it coloured his time on the mountain. This was a tragedy.'

They set up Camp 2 at 6,000 metres, near the technical sérac portion of the route. After a difficult day of climbing and complex route finding, they positioned their camp in a crevasse where they could find shelter from the wind. Here, they began discussing two options for their final route to the summit. Eli wanted to climb to around 7,500 metres and then traverse a massive snowfield to the top of the Kinshofer route at the base of the summit pyramid. Tomek preferred a longer and more ambitious route, first climbing Nanga Parbat's north peak at 7,800 metres and then continuing up the original 1953 Hermann Buhl route to the main summit. The idea worried Eli. 'For Tomek, the most important thing was to show people he was able to climb up a legendary route in winter. He was sure no one else would repeat an effort like that.'[18] She finally suggested they climb together to 7,400 metres, set up their last camp, and then carry on with their individual climbs. He agreed, but Eli was afraid. If anything were to happen to either of them, they would be unable to help each other.

When bad weather moved in, they dismantled their tent, secured it to the inside of the crevasse with a shovel, and descended to base camp. The forecast predicted high winds for the next twenty days: twenty days of enforced rest but at an altitude that was much too low to retain their acclimatisation. Tomek called Anna, who recalled that he seemed surprisingly calm and in good spirits, though impatient about waiting. He regaled the locals in base camp with tales about his previous attempts, his determination to succeed this year, and how he doubted Simone's claim to have reached the summit.

On 18 January, Tomek and Eli decided the time had come to go back on the mountain. As a treat before leaving, the cooks prepared them some fresh bread, but after eating it Tomek suddenly began vomiting. 'They have poisoned me,' he exclaimed to Eli. 'I am going to take a piece of this bread back to Poland and have it chemically analysed. They are trying to kill me!'

'Calm down, Tomek,' Eli replied. 'The bread is fine. Look at me. I'm not sick.'

Anna wasn't surprised by the incident. 'When his psychological state got worse, he would have anxieties, he would really suffer, and couldn't handle the visions he would experience,' she said. 'He would become distrustful.'[19]

When the forecast changed to a much smaller window of good weather, Tomek agreed to join Eli on her preferred route. It was shorter and faster, offering a better chance at the summit and a safe return to their highest camp. Their final trip up the mountain started badly for him, though, since he was constantly vomiting. Yet despite his heaving stomach, they continued up to Camp 3, where they found their little tent wedged in the crevasse but no sign of the shovel. 'Must be Feri,' Tomek commented. Feri was a legendary figure to the local shepherds, a chameleon-like phantom, who could appear in different forms: a person, a demon, a mountain spirit. She could be a force for either good or evil and Nanga Parbat was her home. Tomek had first become acquainted with her on his fifth expedition to the mountain, and had developed quite a close relationship, according to Eli. He would often communicate with her, but only when he was alone. Eli sometimes wondered if this was why he preferred to climb at a slower pace.

High winds pinned them down at 6,600 metres so they remained in their tent on 22 January: a full day of rest that helped settle Tomek's stomach. They talked and laughed, as in the old days. Simone was forgotten, at least for the moment. The following day they reached 6,900 metres but could hear a violent wind screaming over the Mazeno Pass directly above them at 7,000 metres. Eli remembered the following day of climbing as dreamlike; every moment was perfect. They found a sheltering crevasse at 7,300 metres and, late in the afternoon, began preparing for their summit bid.

On the morning of 25 January they crept out of their tent at 6 a.m. The cold sucked at their body heat, but miraculously there was no wind. Nevertheless, within minutes, Tomek had lost feeling in his extremities and they had to return to the tent to warm them over the stove: it wasn't until 7.30 a.m. that they resumed climbing. At least the snow was firm: ideal conditions. They crossed a large plateau, traversed to the base of the summit pyramid, and began the final climb to the top. The distance between Eli and Tomek grew. She stopped to wait. Was he speaking with Feri? She took out her camera and filmed the vast panorama below her, sweeping left and right, finally settling the lens on Tomek, edging up towards her.

Now finally in the sun, Eli put on her sunglasses and when Tomek arrived, she said: 'Tomek, you should put something over your eyes. The sun is strong. You should take care.'

'Thanks, I feel good,' he answered.

'Whatever you want,' she replied.[20]

A short while later, Eli applied sunscreen to her face. Again, Tomek said he didn't need it. At 8,035 metres, she stopped and waited for Tomek, who was a quarter of an hour behind. She photographed him as he climbed slowly towards her, then checked the time on her satellite tracking and messaging device. It was 5.15 p.m. They were less than 100 metres from the summit.

When Tomek reached Eli, she pointed to the clouds surging up over the Mazeno Ridge. Tomek nodded. 'How are you feeling?' she asked.

'Good. I'm good today. I want to keep going.'

When Eli recalled this short exchange six months later it seemed completely routine. 'We made the decision together, as usual. He wasn't complaining about anything. I also couldn't see any signs of trouble with breathing or with his stomach. He wasn't fast, but he was no slower than usual.'[21]

They climbed up the couloir another fifty metres to the summit ridge, where the wind slammed them with a terrific force. No longer protected by the summit pyramid, they quickly became chilled. Eli stopped to put on her face mask. Tomek did not. He was moving even more slowly than before, so she stopped several more times to wait. At 6.15 p.m., Eli reached the summit in failing light. Tomek arrived shortly after in almost complete darkness.

When she asked Tomek how he was feeling, he answered, 'I can't quite see you … It's hard for me to see your headlight. Eli, I don't see you.'

Eli reassured him: 'Don't worry. Grab my shoulder. We're going down.'[22] At first, she thought he had snow-blindness, but it was soon clear he was also suffering from altitude sickness and frostbite. 'Everything around started to feel threatening,' Eli recalled. 'I had to concentrate a lot, be careful where I placed my feet, because after my footstep would be Tomek's. We walked like a pair of robots. We were as careful as cats, close to the rocks and using our ice axes to prop us up.'[23]

When she turned around to monitor his progress, she was surprised to see Tomek had removed the face mask she had finally convinced him to wear to protect his face from the cold. She pressed him to put it back on but he resisted, saying he couldn't breathe with it over his mouth and nose. This comment triggered more alarm bells for Eli so she decided to inject him with the steroid dexamethasone to help relieve the symptoms of altitude sickness. The needle broke when she tried to penetrate his multiple layers of clothing and, since there was no spare, she resorted to tablets, which she doubted would be as effective. She kept talking to Tomek, trying to distract him from his condition, telling him stories about Anna, about his children, about Ireland, anything to keep him moving. But she had no idea if he could hear her.

Tomek soon lost the ability to move on his own. Eli helped him descend, his arm draped over her shoulder, his body leaning heavily on her tiny frame. 'I was pushing, pushing all the time,' she recalled. 'I hated to do that – it was kind of cruel – but I had to do it to keep him moving.' Finally, Tomek stated, 'I will take some other pills – the small ones that are in the little bag.'[24] Unsure at first which pills he wanted, she then remembered Tomek telling her that if she ever felt she was about to die, she should take these pills, because they would allow her to continue moving. She gave him two 20-milligram doses of what she later learnt was ephedrine, a central nervous system stimulant. It was a desperate measure. When he next spoke, it was to tell her he had lost all feeling in his hands and feet.

When they reached a crevasse at around 7,280 metres, Tomek announced he could go no farther. 'So, I took a piece of rope and made a belay for him in the crevasse,' she explained. Tomek's breathing was laboured, blood was seeping from his mouth and his nose was white with frostbite. At 11.10 p.m., Eli used her satellite device to send text messages: to her husband, Jean-Christophe; to Tomek's wife, Anna; and to a close climbing friend, Ludovic Giambiasi. The message was simple: Tomek was in trouble. He could no longer move. He needed to be evacuated.

Eli's messages spiralled outward through the interconnected cyberworld of the international mountaineering community. But it was inevitable they would eventually settle less than 200 kilometres away at K2 base camp, where an elite Polish team was attempting the peak, the last 8,000er yet to be climbed in winter.

The team's leader was Krzysztof Wielicki, one of the original Ice Warriors. When he heard the news, he knew there were but a handful of people in the entire world sufficiently acclimatised and close enough to try to rescue Tomek and Eli. All of them were at K2.

Krzysztof turned to his team and asked if anyone would be willing to interrupt his climb to go to Nanga Parbat and help with a rescue. 'Every single one said yes,' he recalled. He chose Adam Bielecki, Denis Urubko, Piotr Tomala and Jarosław Botor. It was not a decision taken lightly. All four were key players on the K2 team; Adam and Denis were considered their best hopes for the summit. Choosing Adam and Denis to go to Nanga Parbat could be a crippling blow to the K2 effort.

Adam Bielecki was an obvious choice for the first summit team for a number of reasons. He had already climbed K2 in summer and had made first winter ascents of both Gasherbrum I and Broad Peak, all within one calendar year. He was young, fast, and seemingly impervious to the suffering integral to high-altitude winter climbing. When Adam first learnt of the situation on Nanga Parbat, he was terrified. He had survived enough dicey winter situations to understand how serious it was. So when the opportunity arose to help with the rescue, Adam didn't hesitate, despite the potential impact on his chances for K2. 'At that moment I did not care about K2,' he said. He may have been thinking, as well, about the finger-pointing that followed his winter ascent of Broad Peak, when two of the four summit climbers, including Maciej Berbeka, died on descent. Adam had taken the brunt of that blame and was not keen to repeat the experience.

Denis Urubko, the military-trained Russian alpinist with nineteen 8,000-metre summits to his name, including two in winter, was the arrow in the quiver for the K2 team. Everybody knew that. Denis was close friends with many on the Polish team, had climbed with them, socialised with them and was as deeply committed to the K2 winter ascent as any of them. His reputation was impeccable. He either summited peaks, or rescued people trying to summit peaks. His dramatic rescue of Anna Czerwińska on Lhotse, the rescue attempt of Iñaki Ochoa on Annapurna and several more success-ful rescues on Gasherbrum II were the stuff of legend. Denis felt no qualms about turning his back on K2, at least temporarily, in order to help his fellow climbers.

High on Nanga Parbat, Eli was battling to keep Tomek alive and moving down. 'I lost track of time,' she said of their struggle to survive. 'We fought all night long. It was extremely cold. I had never experienced anything similar in my life … In body he was with me, but in his thoughts, he was elsewhere. Maybe he was trying to communicate with Feri. I don't know.'[25] She helped him take shelter in a cramped ice cave near the crevasse where she placed his legs in his pack. At first, she tried to cuddle him, to warm him. But the cave was too small so she sat outside for several hours, sending messages and thinking. 'I couldn't sleep. I sat on my pack and looked at the stars. I wondered what we should do. What was even possibly left to do.' When she received a message from Anna, saying, 'Don't worry. Tomek is strong. He will live through this. We are organising help. It will be okay,' Eli was momentarily encouraged.[26]

At 6 a.m., she began searching for the crevasse where they had stashed their sleeping bags during the ascent. After two hours, she returned empty-handed. Tomek begged her to help him out of the ice cave and into the sun. His hands and feet were completely frozen, so all he could do was shuffle along on his knees, with Eli's help. She finally managed to drag him into the sunlight where she attached him to a section of fixed line.

Eli now had to face the most difficult decision of her life. Later that afternoon, after she had wrapped Tomek in warm clothing, he insisted that she start descending. 'I don't know if Tomek pushed me to go down to save my life,' she later reflected. 'I knew only I had to go down to save his. And I knew if I descended the Kinshofer route, I could get safely to Camp 3 – no crevasses in that stretch, and quite easy. But after Camp 3, I also knew I could go no farther. It was a prison at Camp 3. From there I would need a rescue. So, it was a risky decision.'

She reached Camp 3, but was devastated to learn there would be no helicopter rescue that day. Ludovic radioed her to tell her to stay at Camp 3, that help would arrive in the morning. 'In that case, I will go back to Tomek,' she answered. 'No, Eli, the helicopter might come early in the morning. You have to stay where you are.' Frustrated and angry now, she later recalled: 'Everything I was doing at this point was against my will. It was awful. When you go to the mountains you are alone, you take risks and you agree to those terms. But when there's a rescue mission, you have to rely on others … I had no control. And not just over my own life.'[27]

As the sun slipped below the horizon, Eli felt the intense cold seeping into her body. After some time, she felt strangely warm, safe: peaceful. Her considerable experience in the mountains saved her from the seduction, that painless surrender to death by hypothermia. She fought the illusion of warmth but was soon hallucinating. A woman offered her a hot cup of tea, for a price. Eli would need to offer a boot. Slipping in and out of consciousness, she woke to see her boot lying beside her. She had no idea how many hours her foot had been exposed to the cold. All the next day, Eli waited for the sound of a helicopter, for a message announcing they were on their way. For anything at all.

She was now close to panic. Her phone batteries began to die and night was closing in. She sent a message to Ludovic at 5.28: 'My battery is failing. I will die if help doesn't arrive.' At 6.07 p.m. she sent one last message.

'Descending.'[28]

Eli had endured two high-altitude bivouacs – one without her boot on – and was now about to attempt a dangerous, solo descent of seventy-degree ice in the dark. Her warm mitts were with Tomek; she had only her thin inner gloves.

In places where the old fixed lines were buried in the ice and snow, she had to unclip and down-climb slowly and carefully, relying completely on her crampons and axes for balance on the glassy, fragile ice. It had been sixty hours since she sipped a drop of water. Then, her headlamp died.

Extremely tired, she stopped at times and leant on her axes, licking bits of snow and ice in an attempt to quench her raging thirst: but not for long, because the wind picked up and she chilled off quickly. The wan light of the moon peering through the clouds guided her. Down she went, continuously down. Slowly. Carefully.

'I told myself I didn't want to stay here. I didn't want to be left here. I focused on every step to descend this section without a belay. My brain didn't want to give up. I mastered it with thoughts of survival,' she recalled. 'I tried to find the last bits of energy deep inside me.'[29]

While Eli struggled on her lonely descent and Tomek remained high on the mountain, two helicopters and four rescuers lifted off from K2 base camp. On 27 January at 5.10 p.m., the pilots deposited the rescuers on a small rocky platform 100 metres below Camp 1 on Nanga Parbat. 'The helicopter pilot took a very strong risk for this mission with his life,' Denis said. 'It saved me and Adam, and other members of the rescue team, around five to six hours.'[30] They quickly came up with a strategy: Piotr and Jarosław would remain at the landing site as backup while Adam and Denis started climbing the Kinshofer route.

Twenty minutes after landing, Adam and Denis began racing up the mountain. At 6.22 p.m., they were at 5,219 metres. At 9 p.m. it was 5,670 metres. At 9.44 p.m., 5,814 metres. Up and up they went, to 6,100 metres. Benefiting from the light of the same moon that was illuminating Eli's descent, they climbed 1,200 metres in eight hours. Denis explained their extraordinary pace: 'Adam and me, we were very well trained before the expedition on K2, and of course we were already acclimatised … it helped us to expend, in short time, a lot of efforts.' They both knew the route from previous expeditions, but ascending it at night was another game altogether. They climbed as light as possible: no sleeping bags, only a bit of food, some liquids, a bivvy sack, a stove, gas and spare mitts.

Along the way, they broke one of the cardinal rules of mountaineering: no grabbing on to old fixed lines. 'I also have this rule that I don't climb on old fixed ropes,' Adam said. 'And here I am, climbing at night, in the same place I almost lost my life and the only help is old fixed ropes … It's not such a common thing to climb at night … we know how to do it. But we usually don't do it in winter at altitudes above 5,000 metres because it's too cold. But this time we literally had no choice.'

Denis reached Eli shortly before 2 a.m.

'One moment I heard him screaming, "Adam, I can hear her!"' Adam said. 'A moment later he shouted, "Adam, I got her! I got her!"'

Denis brought Eli over to Adam, who checked her condition. 'She was seriously frostbitten and was unable to manipulate her hands. She couldn't clip and unclip the karabiner.' Eli was travelling even lighter than Adam and Denis: no headlamp, no pack, no sleeping pad and only thin gloves on her frostbitten hands.

They moved her to a ledge where they could sit together, replaced her gloves with warm mitts, and then heated some water and gave her drugs to stimulate her circulation. Eli told them of her lonely descent, of her hallucinations, of having removed her boot for a phantom woman who demanded it in exchange for a warm cup of tea. She told them of Tomek, his frightening state.

They spread out the bivouac sack and tried to shield it from the wind, nestling Eli between them. 'She put her legs on me and she lay down on Adam's side,' Denis explained. They watched as she slept and talked quietly about what to do. Should they take her to a safe spot, secure her to the mountain, and continue up to Tomek? Eli had explained that Tomek was unable to move: he would need to be carried. 'We understood that if we left Eli and continued up for Tomek, she would die,' Adam explained. They also knew that the two of them couldn't carry Tomek down. And he was too high for a helicopter. Tomek, they slowly realised, was beyond help. 'That's a thought that doesn't sink in right away,' Adam said. 'You have to sit with it awhile.'[31]

'We chose to rescue Élisabeth,' Denis said.

With her damaged hands, she was unable to rappel down the steep terrain below them. Luckily, her legs still worked reasonably well, so she could move independently while on moderate ground. They took turns lowering her, doing tandem rappels and descending next to her on the snow slopes. At 11.30 a.m., they reached their teammates and the helicopters at Camp 1. First they flew her down to base camp for some basic first aid, then to the hospital at Skardu and on to Islamabad the following day. On 30 January, she flew back to France to begin treatment for her frostbite. During all this time, Eli assumed the rescue had continued for Tomek. 'I didn't realise that he [had] died until I was back in France,' she later said. 'I was convinced he could survive. He always survived. I was so sure he was alive.'

Eli spent two months in a rehabilitation centre in Grenoble and many more months of slow, painful recovery. Eli is an athlete, so her physical rehabilitation was manageable. She had the self-discipline to put in the hours required and the intelligence to manage her expectations and set reasonable goals. Emotional recovery is something else entirely, and on this front, she struggled. In a message on her Facebook page, two weeks after being rescued, she tried to express her feelings.

Tomek and I knew the summit would not be easy ... I have infinite gratitude for Tomek, for his mystical fascination with this mountain ... that for those uninitiated it may be difficult to comprehend and to accept that a winter ascent of this mountain is what has always excited him ... My thoughts go to Anna, Tomek's wife, and his three children. Perhaps, they will consider this quest of a summit frivolous in relation to a loss of their dad ... I do not know how to resolve this dilemma and it is not my place to provide a view ... I know that the passion of their father was so noble that one would struggle to come up with the 'right' answer.

Everyone seemed to have an opinion about Tomek. For many established Polish climbers, he was an object of mockery: untrained, undisciplined, uneducated, ill-equipped and with visions of grandeur. But Voytek Kurtyka saw something else in this wild-spirited man. 'I see an artistry in his behavior,' he said. 'His loss is [a] very sad thing.'[32] Adam was generous as well in his assessment. 'He was a pro. He climbed Nanga Parbat in winter! That is an incredible achievement. Tomasz had a right to play this game according to his own rules. His strategy was completely different than mine, but I respect it.'[33] Many others weren't as kind.

Anna spoke later about Eli and Tomek. 'The great thing about this story is that it was a man and a woman,' she said. 'She was so delicate and he was fascinated about that. I love it that she was a woman, they were a great team, they had different strengths, but they had a common passion.' In the midst of her grief, Anna searched for some meaning to justify the loss. 'I have the feeling it had to happen. It was our fate in a way. I don't know why, maybe it's a way to understand his death. Some kind of destiny. A man who loved freedom and had a right to choose his way of life, even to the end. Freedom until death. The right to die for this idea. He chose his way, right up to the end.' She sighed, adding, 'I somehow need to understand the finer sense of this loss.'

For Eli, the grief and the survivor guilt were almost too much to bear. 'From the first moment we met, we clicked,' she said. 'He said there was nobody in the world he could talk to as freely as me. He talked and talked to me about everything – his life – his emotions – his love for Nanga. On the mountain we talked all the time in the tent ... We never stopped talking and laughing. He told me everything about Anna. She is a beautiful person and she was his anchor – his balance. He cared so much for her that he wanted to protect her from himself.' Eli, who met Anna for the first time only after the tragedy, described the meeting. 'When I first met Anna, I knew everything about her from Tomek,' she said, smiling. 'And she was exactly as he said: beautiful, peaceful, kind, strong, wanting to take care of everyone. A wonderful person.'

When Eli tried to recall the last hours with Tomek, she crumbled with emotion. 'I don't know when he crossed the moment of no return. I didn't see it,' she said. 'We always climbed alone. We had a different pace. I was much faster and besides, he needed to be alone to speak with his Feri. He was always making "calls" to his Feri, and you can only do that when you are alone. I also liked to be alone.' It was like that on their summit day of Nanga Parbat in 2018.

Still suffering terribly from PTSD, Eli finally wrote a farewell letter to Tomek.

> Today I write you a farewell letter, but I prefer not to finish it by saying goodbye, because it is something that is still impossible. I have experienced unique moments with you, I have felt extraordinary things and we have done together beautiful and authentic things ...
>
> You were a great man, a monument, a myth, a genius of winter ...
>
> I don't know the moment you crossed the extreme line: If only I could have seen that sign. I don't know when I started losing you, when you crossed the point of no return, if yourself, did you feel it?
>
> Meeting a person like you remains rare, exceptional. You were the gentleman of the Nanga ... You had the energy and strength to live your dream and go to the end of your dream.
>
> The Nanga was your writing, your inspiration and the book of your life ...
>
> Thank you Tomek for being what you've been.

In the months that followed the rescue, the public response to Denis and Adam, Piotr and Jarosław, at Polish mountain festivals in Zakopane, Lądek and Kraków, was staggering. Two thousand people rose to their feet to honour them, to thank them. Tiny Eli entered the stage, still suffering terribly from post-traumatic stress, fragile and emotional, engulfed by Denis and Adam's embrace. And finally, Anna, Tomek's widow, approached Eli, her husband's last climbing partner, and the rescuers who ultimately had to leave him on the mountain of his dreams. A poignant reunion, it was filled with affection, gratitude and grief, and in those sad moments, some healing seemed to take place.

When the American Alpine Club presented the rescuers with the rarely given David Sowles Award for 'coming to the aid of another,' Adam spoke on behalf of the team. 'Even though we are not going to the mountains for the risk itself, the risk is always there. We have to embrace it, we have to accept it; we have to be fully aware of it. In our pursuit of achieving our climbing goals we face our fears and we test our limits. But that also sometimes puts us in a situation where we are on the wrong side of our limits. These are the moments when we need help of fellow climbers.'

A few months later, the French government bestowed its highest civilian honour – the Legion of Honour – on the rescue team.

One year later, the drama repeated itself. Daniele Nardi returned to Nanga Parbat for the fifth time, again for the Mummery Rib, this time with young British alpinist Tom Ballard. The son of Alison Hargreaves, who died on K2 in 1995, Tom was born to climb. He joked that he was a climber even *before* birth, since his mother had climbed the North Face of the Eiger in 1988 while six months pregnant with him. But Tom hadn't been Daniele's first choice. He had first invited Louis Rousseau from Quebec, trying to convince him with his passion for this unclimbed route on Nanga Parbat. 'I love the line of the Mummery Spur and I tried and tried to climb it and now I have the experience to know what is needed to climb it and open a new route in winter. So, if you join this great adventure, to go there again, follow the step of Mummery and write an important page of high-altitude climbing, it can be wonderful.'

Louis said no. His answer was both thoughtful and prophetic. 'Nanga is a mountain that hypnotises climbers. I too was hypnotised. I know now that every person who tries Nanga must eventually pay the price. Anyone I know who has been hypnotised has either lost his life or lost a part of himself eventually … I believe in the curse of the killer mountain. It is a mountain that is not like the others … ' Louis tried to dissuade Daniele from his plan. 'If I were in your shoes, my friend, I would not insist on a winter ascent of Nanga. I know it's attractive, but you've already gone several times. The real challenge, even more difficult, is … to give it up and choose another dream … The Mummery Rib will always be your idea, your vision, your inspiration, but you must accept to become something else by turning this page for good. Inside our biggest dreams are sometimes hidden our worst nightmares, Daniele. This I learnt on Nanga. Nanga Parbat winter will not be my next dream. Sorry.'

Daniele accepted his decision, but not his advice, answering, 'I want to climb Mummery, I want to close this chapter … I hope to change the world, not only some thoughts.'

The last radio contact with Daniele and Tom was on 24 February 2019. They were at 6,200 metres on the Mummery Rib. An aerial search was delayed after Pakistani airspace closed during an increase in tension between India and Pakistan. But when the Pakistani Army eventually sent helicopters to K2 base camp on 4 March to whisk Alex Txikon and his teammates to Nanga Parbat to scan the peak, they found nothing. Even after twelve passes along the Mummery Rib and the adjacent Kinshofer route, they saw no sign of the pair. Days of searching followed, on foot, by helicopter and with drones. Finally, on 9 March, the bodies of Tom and Daniele were spotted through a telescope above Camp 3 on the Mummery Rib at around 5,900 metres. There was talk of recovering the bodies, but the Ballard family requested that no one should place themselves in any more danger. The search was terminated.

Then Simone Moro weighed in, saying initially that the Mummery line was a 'suicide route', and 'trying the Mummery Spur in winter is like playing Russian roulette.' He later softened his statements, saying 'there are difficult routes and there are dangerous routes. The Mummery route was a dangerous route, proven by the fact that in 125 years, it had yet to be climbed.' He continued, in an interview with Darío Rodríguez. 'Why, Nardi, in his five attempts, has gone with five different partners? Because nobody wanted to return.'

The Italian mountaineering author Vinicio Stefanello reflected on Daniele's passion for the Mummery Rib. 'Finding the strength and constancy to try again every year … knowing exactly what lay in store, is not normal … Nanga Parbat in winter, but also the legendary Mummery Rib, was something that Nardi could not, evidently, do without.'[34]

Daniele had craved a truly historical climb, one that would go down in the annals of Himalayan history; one that in his words would 'change the world.' Sadly, all it did was change the worlds of his family, Tom's family, their friends, and the mountaineering community that cared about them.

Daniele Nardi's family later asked that his words, penned before leaving for Nanga Parbat, be made public. He had written: 'I would like to be remembered as a young man who tried to do something amazing, impossible … If I didn't return, the message I would leave my son would be this: don't stop, don't give up, do your thing, because the world needs better people to make peace a reality and not just an idea … it's worth it.'

Not all would agree.

14

K2

A Mountain for Thoroughbreds

But there is another kind of elevation that I am seeking here, a humility that recognises the fundamentally earthbound aspect of climbing ... I seek an altitude of the spirit – a relentless bearing down on the limits of the flesh. In the smallest margins, on a microscopic and bewildering level, I search for a phantom summit that I might have glimpsed decades earlier, one that I have never quite lost sight of.

Peter Beal, 'Escape Route: Chaos Canyon, Colorado'[1]

K2 is a mountaineer's mountain. Overwhelming in size, majesty, complexity and steepness, it stands alone above its neighbours in the most dramatic mountain range on Earth – the Karakoram. So massive it creates its own weather, the summit is often wreathed in an icy horizontal cloud formation created by an unforgiving jet stream. Terrifying ice avalanches, weighing many tons, crash down its slopes and explode into millions of pieces, creating a thick fog of pulverised ice and snow. The south face is a mythical vision of perfection, its buttresses and ridges marching ever higher until that final summit pyramid. The south-west face thrusts upward like a fang, slicing the indigo sky. Its east face is draped in a sagging blanket of ice while the west face is stripped bare, revealing the mountain's bony, jagged structure. American alpinist Steve Swenson, who climbed it in 1990, described it as 'Absolute symmetry between chaos and order ... Sharp ridges and sheer faces alternate like the facets of a giant crystal, forming contour lines that seem like the perfect embodiment of an alpine dream.'[2]

K2 is known as the 'Savage Mountain', the highest mountain in Pakistan and second-highest in the world. Steep on all sides, it retains an aura of mystery from its initial, almost anonymous designation as one of the 'K peaks'. But mystery is alluring, and as British author Robert Macfarlane noted, 'The unknown is so inflammatory to the imagination because it is an imaginatively malleable space: a projection-screen on to which a culture or an individual can throw their fears and their aspirations. Like Echo's cave, the unknown will answer back with whatever you shout at it.'[3]

But perhaps the most evocative reflection on this crystal mountain of geometric perfection is from Italian author, photographer, academic and mountaineer Fosco Maraini. 'K2 may owe its origin to chance, but it is a name itself, and one of striking originality,' he wrote. 'Sibylline, magical, with a slight touch of fantasy. A short name but one that is pure and peremptory, so charged with evocation that it threatens to break through its bleak syllabic bonds. And at the same time a name instinct with mystery and suggestion: a name that scraps race, religion, history and past. No country claims it, no latitudes and longitudes and geography, no dictionary words. No, just the bare bones of a name, all rock and ice and storm and abyss. It makes no attempt to sound human. It is atoms and stars. It has the nakedness of the world before the first man – or of the cindered planet after the last.' [4]

The grandfather of winter Himalayan climbing, Andrzej Zawada, had always intended to climb K2 in winter. He knew it would be difficult, would require meticulous planning, as well as considerable luck with the weather. And money, of course. He just didn't know *how* hard it would be to combine all of these elements.

Polish climbers have a strong historical connection to K2. The first woman to climb it was Polish alpinist Wanda Rutkiewicz in 1986. The same season, Jurek Kukuczka and Tadek Piotrowski climbed a daring, new and unrepeated line on its south face, while Janusz Majer led a team that climbed the futuristic 'Magic Line' on the mountain. It seemed fitting that Polish alpinists would make the first winter ascent of the second-highest mountain on Earth. They had dispatched the highest one – Everest – in short order on their first try back in 1980. But located at the far western edge of the Karakoram, K2 is farther north than Everest and in the direct line of attack from the ferocious Siberian winter storms. Its upper slopes are often stripped bare by the jet stream roaring in from the north-west. It's impossible to erect a tent in these conditions and, even if one were in place, winds such as these would swat it aside like an unwanted fly.

Its more northerly location presents another problem, one not so obvious at first glance. The Earth's atmospheric pressure decreases with increased distance from the equator. K2 is at the latitude of 36° north, making it the most northerly 8,000er and consequently the farthest from the equator. Michał Pyka, who has studied the Karakoram meteorological anomaly closely, explains: 'The thickness of the troposphere on the equator is about fourteen kilometres, while in winter, at the north pole, it is only six kilometres thick.' Because of K2's geographical location and its elevation, the air pressure above 7,500 metres is exceedingly low, particularly in winter: much less than at a similar elevation on Everest, or any of the 8,000ers farther south. Simply put, there is less atmosphere in which to find oxygen. Furthermore, Pyka insists that the low pressure creates a situation of great instability, making sudden drops in pressure a high likelihood. 'In my opinion, those who want to climb high on K2 will have to check the pressure and the temperature very precisely and frequently, just like astronauts.' Karl Gabl discounts this theory almost completely. Although he agrees that declines in pressure at 8,000 metres are possible, they're not sufficient to impact significantly on a climber's performance.

Despite all of these challenges, Andrzej Zawada still dreamed of climbing it in winter.

In 1981, Andrzej travelled to Montreal for a lecture tour. While he was in Canada, Poland collapsed into chaos, with martial law being imposed on its citizens. Andrzej stayed on, bunking in with Polish mountaineer Jacques Olek, who had fled Soviet-controlled Poland on foot, immigrated to Canada, and made a new life for himself and his family. It's no surprise they became friends, for Jacques was mentoring a generation of young Quebec climbers while Andrzej was doing the same in Poland. As their friendship deepened, Andrzej invited Jacques to be part of his K2 dream. The first step was a reconnaissance of the mountain; in the winter of 1983, Jacques and Andrzej journeyed to the Baltoro to take a look.

The Pakistan government was initially uneasy about granting a winter permit for K2, but when Andrzej impressed the authorities – and President Zia – with his previous winter ascents of 8,000-metre peaks, they agreed. Affectionately known as the 'K2-million-dollar-helicopter expedition', the 1987–88 trip was a lavish affair. Andrzej obtained financial support in Canada, as well as from the outdoor equipment company Karrimor, which provided their high-altitude clothing. No more flannel, button-up shirts. The expedition included twenty-four Poles, seven Canadians and four Brits. Andrzej had arranged for their equipment to be carried to base camp by 250 porters in October, but when heavy snowfall brought the caravan to a stand-still partway up the Baltoro Glacier, the porters abandoned their loads. When the team arrived in late December, equipment was strewn across the glacier halfway to the mountain. Andrzej hired twenty more porters to help move the loads to base camp, but it was clear this effort wouldn't be enough. The only answer was helicopters. Thanks to Andrzej's diplomatic skills and the efforts of the Polish, British and Canadian ambassadors, President Zia authorised the helicopter ferries. Expedition costs mounted dramatically and as a consequence pressure grew for Andrzej to return with a victory.

The weather refused to cooperate. The infrequent fair-weather windows lasted no more than a day or two, not enough to climb high on the mountain. 'At night there were beautiful stars and everyone would get ready to go but that fantasy would always end,' Krzysztof Wielicki recalled. 'We would barely make a step on the mountain and the weather would break again … Despite this, we believed in success for a long time.'[5]

Battling adverse conditions, the team managed to establish Camp 1 on the Abruzzi Spur at 6,100 metres on 5 January. A few days later, Krzysztof and his Everest winter companion Leszek Cichy set up Camp 2 at 6,700 metres. Then the storms rolled through, week after week, pinning them in base camp until 2 March, when Krzysztof and Leszek could finally set up Camp 3 at 7,300 metres. 'It was unbelievable, because in the summer you can get to this elevation in four days,' Krzysztof exclaimed. 'It took us two months.'[6] They were joined by Roger Mear and Jean-François Gagnon on 6 March, but that night, hurricane-force winds struck their camp and both Roger and Jean-François had to be helped down the following day, suffering from frostbite.

Alek Lwow remembered the expedition primarily as one of waiting, and waiting some more. Which was why, after ninety days of effort, he and Maciej Berbeka absconded to Broad Peak, the start of another adventure, and one that began an obsession for Maciej that would end many years later with his death. Andrzej's endorsement of their scheme threw the team into turmoil. Krzysztof – and others – were determined to climb K2: 'although I don't know if there was reason to be motivated,' he wryly added. 'We thought the climbing on K2 was getting to kind of a threshold stage and we wanted all hands on deck. And then we found out Zawada was sending these guys to Broad Peak, as if he wasn't believing in our success. Up high we were really serious. Our friends in base camp were also pretty mad.'[7]

Leszek Cichy climbing in House's Chimney on the Polish 1988 winter attempt of K2. *Photo: Krzysztof Wielicki Archive.*

The change of plan brought an end to the K2 expedition, which had experienced only ten days of 'good' weather in over three months. 'The weather cheated us,' Andrzej later said. 'But we didn't blame ourselves because we did everything we could and that was humanly possible … It was bitter, but at the same time it caused me to reflect, unlike the euphoria of success. So, what did this nerve-racking, utterly tiring days of base camp teach us? What did the days above base camp teach us? For me, how to not take my partners for granted because it was them who wanted to climb, even in the worst conditions. They never lost their sense of humour, their smiles. At the time it meant so much to me.'[8]

Andrzej didn't abandon his dream of K2 in winter, but instead shifted his attention to the Chinese side: a terribly expensive alternative. It would be over a decade before another attempt was made on K2 in winter, and it would not be led by Andrzej.

To climb K2 from the north, Andrzej needed to know if an expedition could reach base camp in winter using camels. He planned a reconnaissance in 1999 with Jacques Olek to find out, but became ill and couldn't travel. Darek Załuski went in his place. The Chinese initially refused to allow the use of camels, but when Darek and Jacques placed $4,000 on the table, the official whisked the cash into a drawer and the camels appeared. As they soon discovered, the camels had no problem reaching base camp.

In February 2000, Andrzej's health deteriorated further; in six months he was dead. The Polish community reeled with shock. Andrzej, their indestructible leader: gone. He had often said he would rather die in the mountains than of some long, drawn-out disease. He was granted half his wish. His cancer progressed so quickly his wasn't a slow decline. Darek said in admiration that, 'I would go anywhere with Zawada.' Jacques agreed: 'He was the ultimate confirmation of someone pushing ideas with deep respect for the human soul and a capacity for sharing that goes beyond the ordinary.' Krzysztof, who had spent New Year's Eve with Andrzej, struggled to accept his loss. 'Andrzej was very much the life of the party ... He was the last to leave the dance floor,' Krzysztof remembered. 'He always had something interesting to say. And on top of it all, he was incredibly cultured. He inspired those younger than him to put their best foot forward in any situation ... He had exceptional charisma and was able to motivate a team.'[9]

Still grieving his mentor, Krzysztof Wielicki assumed Andrzej's mantle to lead a fourteen-member team to K2 in 2002–03. An Eastern Bloc effort, it included mountaineers from Poland, Georgia, Kazakhstan and Uzbekistan. Netia, Poland's largest TV company, was there too, sending daily reports to be aired on prime-time news. With additional support climbers, the team swelled to more than thirty.[10]

After flying to Bishkek, the capital of Kyrgyzstan, the Poles met up with the others before continuing to Kashgar where they took jeeps to the Chinese border police station at Yilik. From there, a colourful, seventy-camel caravan carried their six tons of equipment and food across the 4,805-metre Aghil Pass, descended to the Shaksgam river and continued up the Qogir Valley. By 30 December they were at base camp at 5,100 metres.

They started work immediately on the Japanese north ridge route, well known by Krzysztof since he had climbed it in summer. Those alpinists from the former Soviet Union, including Denis Urubko, proved to be a driving force, fixing hundreds of metres of line to Camp 1, located inside a large snow cave at 6,000 metres. The winter winds had stripped the mountain of snow, a good thing from the perspective of avalanche danger, but this left ice that was hard as concrete and black as slate. There would be no easy snow plodding on this route. Storms cycled through for two weeks after which

Krzysztof, together with Jacek Berbeka (brother of Maciej), fixed 200 more metres of rope through the Rock Barrier. In late January, Maciej Pawlikowski and Darek Załuski were sleeping at Camp 2 when violent winds destroyed their tent, forcing them to descend at sunrise. The weather deteriorated so badly everyone fled to base camp.

But something was amiss between the Poles and the rest of the team. When three of the four climbers from the former Soviet Union, Gia Tortladze, Ilyas Tukhvatullin and Vassiliy Pivtsov, left the expedition, they struck a devastating blow. 'It was a surprise,' Krzysztof said. 'It was a result of a completely different philosophy of participation in the expedition … although the official reason for them leaving was a lack of meat … curious because it was unwarranted – simply made up.'[11] Denis, however, chose to stay. Krzysztof was relieved, since Denis's strength and determination were essential for the team. 'He could give advice and help with logistics … he could truly be creative,' Krzysztof explained. 'I saw he had a great future career because he showed true leadership and was a workhorse in the group.'[12]

Denis continued climbing with the Poles on the north ridge of the mountain, helping to establish Camp 3 at 7,200 metres and Camp 4 at 7,650 metres. Success looked possible: not probable, but a remote chance. Then, the weather hammered them again and they huddled in base camp. By this time, most of the climbers were either suffering from frostbite or some kind of respiratory illness, or were simply not well enough acclimatised to go high on the mountain. Piotr Morawski, a young alpinist at the time, who wrote the final report of the climb and later died on Dhaulagiri, explained that there were only four climbers still strong enough to go above Camp 3, himself included. But when the expedition doctor told Piotr his frostbite was so serious he would need to give up or risk losing his toes, Piotr stayed below, adding wryly, 'So, I stopped and fortunately in the end lost only one toe.'[13]

When the winds finally abated, Krzysztof announced a summit bid on 21 February. The strategy was for Jerzy Natkański and Jacek Jawien to start climbing first, stocking the upper camps with food. Marcin Kaczkan and Denis would follow the next day. Three days later, when Marcin and Denis reached Camp 4, they found it annihilated by the high-altitude winds. Instead of the relative comfort of the tent that had been placed there, Denis and Marcin were forced to spend the night in a small bivouac tent, crammed into one sleeping bag spread over a mat of ropes.

During the night, Marcin started suffering from cerebral oedema; by morning he was unable to move or communicate. Denis radioed base camp and a rescue team headed up. It took Denis several hours to dress Marcin and start descending, but with every metre of elevation lost, his condition improved. Krzysztof met them above Camp 3 and by that afternoon they were at Camp 2, where there was a bottle of oxygen for Marcin. Down and down they went, to Camp 1, where they spent the night with Marcin on oxygen. The next day he was able to reach base camp; the expedition was over.

They hadn't succeeded in climbing the mountain, but they had climbed extremely high and were convinced it was possible. Upon his return to Poland on 18 March 2003, Krzysztof announced to the press: 'The mission of ascending the peak has not ended, but rather been suspended. I will not give any dates, but I assure you I will return to K2.'[14] Krzysztof later reflected, 'The truth is, to be ready for a summit bid with any chance of success, we would have needed a second Denis.'[15]

Monika Rogozińska, a reporter assigned to the expedition, wrote of her visit to Andrzej Zawada's grave at the Warsaw Powązki Cemetery. 'Somebody had put a white piece of paper torn out from a notebook behind the plate,' she recalled. 'It said, "Rest in peace there. We're going to K2. Your team."'[16] His team went, they tried, and they returned. Now it was the Russians' turn.

———————

At the end of December 2011, Viktor Kozlov flew to K2 base camp with a powerful Russian team of nine climbers, a coach and a doctor. They reached 7,200 metres before hurricane-level winds forced everyone down to base camp. For climber Vitaly Gorelik, it was too late. He had suffered frostbite while working high on the mountain and when he arrived at base camp, was diagnosed with pneumonia. He was still at base camp when he died on 6 February. The expedition was called off. Vitaly's death was the first tragedy, after three major attempts to stand on K2's summit in winter.

In 2014, Denis Urubko, now quite familiar with the mountain, decided to try it with a small team. He enlisted the help of Polish winter specialist Adam Bielecki, Basque climber Alex Txikon and Russians Artiom Braun and Dmitry Siniew. Denis preferred the Chinese side of the mountain in winter, primarily because he felt it would be more protected from the high-altitude winds. But a few days before departure, Denis learnt that the

Chinese authorities were refusing to issue a permit. Undeterred, he tried another agent. The answer was still no, allegedly because there was a terrorist threat in an area through which they would be travelling. The expedition ended before it began.

Now the ball was back in the Poles' court. After returning from K2 in the winter of 2002–03, Krzysztof had analysed every aspect of their climb: what had worked, what had not, what had been within their control, what was completely up to the weather. He concluded that a two-pronged approach would be more effective: two teams working together. The first team would arrive early in the winter season and equip it as high as 7,000 metres. The second team – the summit team – would acclimatise somewhere else entirely: South America, for example. They would fly to K2 base camp on the Pakistan side, totally acclimatised, at a time determined by the precise weather forecasts. 'The classic military method that we used on K2 – the Russians also used it – doesn't set you up for success because after a certain time people get tired of it,' Krzysztof said. 'After forty days of waiting for a weather window, everybody is exhausted. However, if the mountain were ready, and an acclimatised team shows up … the chances would be much higher. The added bonus is that the summit team doesn't have to be large.'[17]

And yet, the 2017–18 K2 expedition, led again by Krzysztof Wielicki, looked alarmingly similar to that classic military style. The team received a million złotys (approximately $250,000) from the Polish Ministry of Sport and Tourism, and the pre-trip build-up was massive, with press conferences, interviews, television appearances and festival events. With this level of hype and government support, there were certain expectations. One of those expectations was that the mountain would be climbed by Polish climbers.

Ludwik Wilczyński, a Polish Himalayan mountaineer active in the 1980s, reflected on the dangers of this Polish obsession with K2 in winter. 'Collecting Himalayan peaks has become a central narrative in Poland,' he wrote. 'Our first set of Ice Warriors, or collectors, i.e. Jurek, Wanda and Krzysztof, were also excellent climbers. Nowadays, excellent climbers are only occasionally in these same circles. More often you find only average climbers, even weak climbers.'[18]

Sixty-seven-year-old Krzysztof knew the choices were now more limited than in the 1980s, but he still felt he could assemble a strong team. Janusz Gołąb, who had done the first winter ascent of Gasherbrum I with Adam

Bielecki, and was well known throughout Poland as a big-wall climber, would be the climbing leader and help with tactics on the mountain. Adam Bielecki was an obvious choice, having done two first winter ascents of Karakoram 8,000ers as well as K2 in summer. Another proven winter climber was Artur Małek, who had done the first winter ascent of Broad Peak with Adam. Darek Załuski, the filmmaker who had climbed five 8,000-metre peaks, including K2, and been on nine winter expeditions to 8,000ers, was invited, along with seven other Polish Himalayan climbers and one newly minted Pole. Denis Urubko had recently been granted Polish citizenship and Poles joked that the president had been happy to do so to allow him on the Polish national climbing team heading to K2. Denis and Adam were considered the two most likely to make the summit of K2. They were both fast, incredibly fit, experienced in winter, ambitious and willing to suffer for the prize.

The seriousness of the undertaking was obvious since, up until this time, there had only been three serious attempts on K2 in winter compared to over thirty on Nanga Parbat. Adam tried to put K2 in perspective: 'It's as if you climb to the top of Gasherbrum I or Gasherbrum II; then you have to make a camp; and only then do you make a summit push for K2. And on both Gasherbrum I and Broad Peak, I couldn't do anything more when I got to the summit.' Krzysztof was careful to avoid any predictions of success. They would need to be extremely lucky to have enough good weather days at precisely the right time, when two or four climbers were sufficiently acclimatised, healthy and ready for a summit bid.

The greatest problem was the wind, although not the only problem. They first chose the Česen route, which turned out to be a mistake. After two serious injuries from rockfall, they changed tactics and moved over to the Abruzzi route. So much time and effort had been expended in those early weeks that it was as if they were starting over but a month late. The Abruzzi route was laced with old fixed ropes remaining from summer expeditions, but Janusz insisted they install new fixed lines.

'We don't need new lines,' Denis objected. 'I can tell if a line is safe or not. This is a waste of effort.'

'No, it's too dangerous,' Janusz replied. 'We have to manage the risks. Old fixed lines aren't good.' Darek recalled the discussion: 'I was more on the side of Denis because if you are a good alpinist you know what is risky and what is not risky and you decide. On the other hand, Janusz who is very principled felt all fixed ropes must be new.' He added, pragmatically, 'Okay, I understand this, but if you have a choice of reaching the summit or fixing all new ropes, I would choose the summit.' But as climbing leader with responsibility for the team, Janusz didn't have the luxury of choosing that option.

This disagreement and others gradually eroded Janusz's authority with the group. Part of the problem was communication. Everyone but Denis spoke Polish so, naturally, discussions about tactics were in Polish. Yet, Denis was one of the most experienced high-altitude winter climbers in the group, had already climbed to 7,650 metres on K2 in the winter of 2002–03 and was the top contender for a summit bid. Frustrated at being excluded from these discussions, he had to rely on abridged versions of decisions that would inevitably implicate him on the mountain. Denis was such an important authority figure in the group that, eventually, the differences of opinion resulted in a situation where, as Darek put it, 'there was no climbing leader.' Darek added that the fault was theirs, since they should have tried harder to include Denis in the discussions.

The precise weather forecasts further divided rather than united them. Krzysztof was old school and wanted them to climb in marginal weather as well as good weather. Young alpinists like Adam disagreed with this strategy. For Adam, speed and health were important; losing your fitness and strength in bad weather was ridiculous. While the storms continued, the team festered in base camp, where another problem emerged.

Base camp had unlimited access to the internet, as well as a direct phone line to Poland: not only a direct line, but a Warsaw number for the convenience of the Polish organisers and media. Too convenient, as it turned out. The climbers were happy to stay connected with families and friends, but the incessant checking of social media sites to see how their expedition was being viewed by the world became a toxic distraction. Instead of building team spirit, they were more concerned about their external image. Like so many modern restaurant scenes, the individuals in base camp were not interacting, but rather sitting glued to their phones. When news arrived of the crisis on Nanga Parbat, everyone offered to go. Certainly, out of consideration for Élisabeth and Tomek, but it's hard not to speculate that some of the motivation was to escape the noxious atmosphere at K2 base camp.

After the rescue, the situation worsened. There was now a 'celebrity' team and a 'support' team. From the moment the four rescuers returned to K2 base camp, they were inundated with calls, emails and media requests for every detail about the rescue. Swamped with interview requests, their attention was diluted from the task at hand: a winter ascent of K2. 'Almost every day I was in shock about what was happening to the dynamics of our team,' Darek recalled. 'Everybody was talking about what they are thinking about us in Poland … we were on the main pages of all the media – sometimes ahead of the football. We were the headlines. It was crazy.'

The phone continued to ring and as the days sped by, tension grew between Denis and Krzysztof. Denis's definition of winter insisted that the last possible summit day was 28 February. Krzysztof, and the rest of the team, subscribed to the calendar definition of winter, which ended on 21 March. Denis tried to convince Adam to make a lightning-fast summit attempt in the last days of February, but Adam said no: it was premature, and the weather was bad. Denis finally lost his patience and left base camp, without permission and without a radio, heading up for a solo attempt. Krzysztof was justifiably livid. 'What Denis has done is selfish. Denis thinks it's all about him, but it's not. He has put all of us in danger. If something goes wrong, of course we must try to rescue him.'[19] Denis reached 7,600 metres before being turned back by the usual high winds and a fall in a crevasse. His arrival in base camp was met by a sullen silence, and soon after he left for home. The expedition fizzled.

There was plenty of post-expedition reflection. Adam doubted the Nanga Parbat rescue was the cause of their failure on K2. He believed that, in future, a different tactic should be considered: a small team rather than a team that included 'summit' climbers and 'support' climbers. 'On the one hand, I respect that somebody is there to support; but on the other hand, this support mode is better if that person also wants to climb to the summit. The same attitude.' He concluded: 'With a small team, there is more work, but the motivation is also better … everybody needs to go up and fix the ropes because nobody will do it for you. And on K2, there were others who could do it for us. So, we relaxed too much.'

Denis was of the same mind, announcing that, while he was thinking of winding down his high-altitude career, K2 in winter was still on his shortlist. And initially, Adam was on his shortlist for the team. Adam remained equally keen to try K2 with Denis. 'Mentally, he is good for me,' Adam says. 'Except that the level of risk he will accept is higher. Which is why he set off by himself. I wouldn't do that. The point is to be old. I want to have grandchildren.'

While the Poles were dealing with the fallout from their failure and scheming about the future, two teams attempted the mountain in the winter of 2018–19. The first was a joint Russian–Kazakh–Kyrgyz team led by Vassiliy Pivtsov that reached 7,634 metres before admitting defeat. The second was a small team led by Basque climber Alex Txikon, which didn't quite reach 7,000 metres. Alex's team became involved in another rescue on Nanga Parbat, that of Daniele Nardi and Tom Ballard, so was further distracted from the job at hand. Denis watched the expeditions' progress from a distance. 'They have no chance of winning K2 this year,' he announced. 'But there will be more trips, the mountain will wait.'

Janusz Majer, who, together with Piotr Tomala, took charge of the Polish winter programme, announced the next Polish expedition to K2 for the winter of 2020–21. Leszek Cichy then indicated his interest in leading the team. His Everest partner Krzysztof indicated that he too would consider leading the next Polish attempt if asked to do so, but not if he felt the team wasn't strong enough. Not exactly a ringing endorsement. Janusz, however, felt it was time for the leadership to shift to someone younger.

Once again, there was the question of style: would it be a small team of elite alpinists climbing semi-alpine style? Could there be two teams: the first to prepare the route up to Camp 4 and the second to fly in after acclimatising in South America? Which route should it be? The Abruzzi route on the Pakistan side or the north ridge over on the Chinese side? Would it be a national or an international team? Janusz pointed out that if the money came from the Polish government, it would have to be a Polish team. If the sponsor was private, it could be an international team.

Karl Gabl, their trusty weather forecaster, wasn't optimistic. He predicted it would be at least ten years before K2 was climbed in winter, his rationale being that wind and cold have stopped all the previous teams. Windchill temperatures routinely approach -73° Celsius; summit wind speeds are often above 128 kilometres per hour. Darek disagreed. 'I don't believe it. I think now it's much easier to climb than ten years ago,' he said. 'The weather is much better. In K2 base camp we had maximum of fifty-kilometre-per-hour winds and on Gasherbrum I we had 130 kilometres per hour.' The greatest problem on K2 in winter is the length of the weather windows: it's rare to have more than three days. Three days to climb the upper part of the mountain and descend low enough to survive an incoming storm means climbing rapidly.

Darek supported the two-pronged approach, with one team preparing the route and the second team acclimatising in South America and parachuting in for a fast summit attempt. 'Sitting in camp for months on end doesn't work,' he said. Another possibility would be to acclimatise on the less technical Broad Peak before attempting a summit bid on K2. This wouldn't solve the problem of festering in base camp, but would at least provide some variety.

At the conclusion of his 2018–19 attempt Alex Txikon indicated his fascination with the mountain remained. 'K2 has given us unique and unrepeatable moments … we will never forget what we have lived here,' he said. 'I have more than thirty expeditions behind me, but the atmosphere that surrounds the mountain will never cease to amaze me.'

Alex wasn't the only one infatuated with the peak. Simone Moro once promised his wife he would not go to K2 in winter but he, too, began expressing interest. And who would he want on his four-person team? Initially he named Denis Urubko, Adam Bielecki and Janusz Gołąb. But as the rift between Simone and Denis grew, Simone eliminated him as a possibility, suggesting instead that should the Polish team invite Simone, he would go.

More players showed interest in 2019, among them Nepali climber Nirmal Purja, known as Nims. His statements were vague, even coy, but it seemed clear that he would like to add this jewel to his already burnished crown of having climbed all 8,000ers in a seven-month period. Mingma Gyalje Sherpa was much clearer in his intentions, stating that he would lead a team in the winter of 2019–20, consisting of John Snorri from Iceland and Chinese climber Gao Li. All three climbers had extensive experience on 8,000-metre peaks, including two ascents of K2 by Mingma in the summer months. The seriousness of K2 in winter took them by surprise, however, and they admitted that they were not fully prepared, physically or mentally, to cope with it.

And then Denis threw out an even bolder plan: to climb Broad Peak in the winter of 2019–20 and, if sufficiently acclimatised and strong, pop over to K2 to finish the job, alpine style and with just one partner, Canadian climber Don Bowie. Of course, everything would need to be wrapped up by the end of February 2020 to satisfy his requirements. Denis further announced that K2 in winter would be his high-altitude swansong. It was a grand idea, but Denis climbed neither Broad Peak nor K2 that winter season.

Whoever is on the team that finally summits K2 in winter, the challenge to lead them will be titanic. As Himalayan blogger Alan Arnette observed: 'Any climber worthy of attempting K2 in winter will have tremendous skills with an ego to match. It will take strong leadership to manage these thoroughbreds.'[20]

As of this writing, K2 in winter is still waiting for the thoroughbreds.

Porters carrying loads to K2 base camp for the Polish 2017-18 winter expedition.
Photo: Darek Załuski.

Porter caravan approaches Gasherbrum I in winter 2010-11. The international team attempting the first winter ascent included Austrian Gerfried Göschl, Basque Alex Txikon and Canadian Louis Rousseau. *Photo: Louis Rousseau.*

EPILOGUE

Ice Warriors

I'll sing so we will not forget you. I will sing you home.
Maureen, Karen and Teresa Ennis, 'Sing You Home'

The question remains, why? Why do these men and women choose to climb the highest mountains on Earth in the cruellest season? How can they justify the risks inherent in this level of extreme? How do they endure the boredom of waiting, sometimes for weeks, in dark, frigid, lonely base camps? What could possibly motivate them to throw themselves at the mercy of the jet stream? And how can they justify the collateral damage resulting from their winter passion? The answers are as varied as the Ice Warriors themselves.

Many winter specialists were motivated by nationalistic pride, particularly in the early days of high-altitude winter climbing. Andrzej Zawada saw it as a way for Polish climbers to enter the Himalayan arena. It was something new, something they could excel at: take their rightful place in the history of Himalayan climbing. When Andrzej died, Krzysztof assumed his mantle, clearly stating in his Winter Manifesto that it was not only an opportunity, but a responsibility for young Polish climbers to 'finish the job' on the 8,000-metre peaks in winter. Artur Hajzer was even more direct when he secured Polish government support for the winter programme by stirring up nationalistic fervour; he only needed to mention the Russians. He knew it would trigger a response, one with cash attached. Although other countries like Japan and South Korea and Italy flew their nations' flags on those wintry summits as well, none reached the collective fervour of Poland's winter identity.

Some climbers spoke of records: setting them, breaking them. Adam Bielecki, when asked what motivated him most about winter in the Himalaya, admitted that claiming the first winter ascent of an 8,000er was the greatest incentive. He pointed out the obvious, that there is little pleasure to be found at high altitude in winter. Andrzej Zawada was also aware of records, from that first, record-making ascent of Noshaq in 1972 to the heart-breaking failure on Lhotse in 1974. Daniele Nardi was so committed to the Mummery Rib on Nanga Parbat that he felt a winter ascent of the unclimbed route would 'write an important page of high-altitude climbing'. Tomek Mackiewicz needed the first winter ascent of Nanga Parbat, and when that was no longer possible, he tried to set a record by ascending the mountain in winter by a combination of routes that would likely never be repeated. Simply making the second winter ascent in alpine style wasn't of sufficient interest to Tomek. Jurek Kukuczka was fully aware of the record he was setting by climbing two 8,000ers in the same winter.

Setting new standards in the mountains has always inspired serious alpinists, including the Ice Warriors. Andrzej Zawada's vision for the first winter ascent of Cho Oyu included not only a winter ascent by a new route, but one without the use of supplemental oxygen by anyone on the team. Gerfried Göschl's dream for Gasherbrum I was even more ambitious: probably too ambitious, as it turned out. He not only wanted the first winter ascent of the mountain, he wanted it via a difficult new route capped with a complete traverse. That, too, would have set a new standard. Krzysztof Wielicki and Jean-Christophe Lafaille, with their solo climbs of 8,000-metre peaks in winter, set lonely new standards which few have been willing to consider, Denis Urubko an obvious exception. Simone Moro has been obsessed with pushing the standards, defending his strict adherence to the calendar winter season as well as a lightweight approach.

Competition has spurred every Ice Warrior who has placed a cramponed foot on an 8,000er in winter. Some were more vocal (and honest) than others. Jurek was clear that his motivation for climbing both Dhaulagiri and Cho Oyu in one winter was to improve his standing in the race with Reinhold Messner. Artur Hajzer was equally transparent in his competition with the Russians. Tamara Lunger spoke of the competitive atmosphere at Nanga Parbat base camp in the winter of 2015–16, when five teams were vying for the first winter ascent, and Tamara for the first female winter ascent. And ultimately, Tomek's life was destroyed by his rivalry with Simone.

The degree of suffering that these winter athletes seem willing to embrace is hard to comprehend. Tamara Lunger 'feels good' at 8,000 metres in winter. Krzysztof maintains that the additional suffering inherent in winter enhances the experience. 'It is more appealing, more exciting,' he insists. Adam, while admitting that winter Himalayan climbing isn't for everyone, takes a pragmatic, sporting view of it. 'It's how I want to spend my life. I am happy there. It's just another human activity – I'm not saving the world. I don't think it's a better sport than others, but it's the right one for me.'

Denis Urubko adopts a more complex approach. 'I take on the mountain as an athlete first; with beauty as my second priority,' he says. 'My desire is to achieve personal goals as an athlete and to explore my desires as an artist. To gain fulfilment through my own physical and mental achievements.'[1] As it turns out, Denis shares some values with UNESCO, which recently stated that alpinism is not only a physical activity requiring athletic qualities and technical expertise, but also an art. That the personal engagement inherent in alpinism, the sense of self-responsibility, the knowledge and respect for the mountains, and the strength of the social relationships, make alpinism an 'Intangible Cultural Heritage' of outstanding universal human and social value. Indeed.

Although probably not as aesthetically inclined as Denis, even the most pragmatic Ice Warrior knows that winter in the desolate Himalayan valleys and on the soaring, wind-scoured Karakoram spires is something rare and beautiful and wild. As Darek Załuski says, 'Winter is at the end of the world … You can feel this'. Alex Txikon described Everest in winter as having 'stolen his heart'. Following her gruelling solo attempt on Manaslu in winter, Élisabeth Revol said, 'After touching some of the most exposed sections of this planet in some of the most brutal climates, I lived the great Himalayan solitude, it is surely the richest experience of my life.'[2] It seems that Ice Warriors need solitude to perform at their highest level. The crowds of the gentler seasons no longer appeal.

There are countless dramatic moments in the annals of those winter climbs. While many have been tinged with the acrid taste of fear and suffering and tragedy, some had the ingredients of genuine happiness. The first winter attempt on Gasherbrum I in 2010–11, though unsuccessful, was simply an adventure for three friends, who ultimately 'found some peace and happiness in the accomplishment of the task, rather than the goal,' as Louis Rousseau later said.[3] One of the greatest moments of pure joy occurred on the first winter ascent of an 8,000er, back in 1980. When Krzysztof Wielicki reflected on his emotions upon returning to base camp from the summit of Everest, he said he never again felt such camaraderie, joy and contentment on an expedition. When Marianne Chapuisat clung to the summit of Cho Oyu in 1993, becoming the first woman to climb an 8,000er in winter, it was love which brought her there – love for her partner. Her memories of that moment became a kind of mantra for the rest of her life. 'May the rarefied air of high altitude and the joy of the journey bring a breeze of kindness and peace, of tolerance and gentleness in a world that is too often chaotic,' she said. 'Would that the raw beauty of the mountains succeed in soothing, even for a short time, the sometimes small-minded human spirit.'[4] For Marianne, they did.

Close calls and near-death experiences are plentiful throughout the history of 8,000ers in winter. And there is no shortage of tragic endings: Manaslu, Makalu, Annapurna and more. One of the most disturbing was surely on Broad Peak, with Krzysztof's futile attempts to coax Tomasz down off the summit ridge and Maciej's heartbreaking silence.

These icy winter adventures are bursting with intensity and excitement. But what about the collateral damage? The injuries, the deaths, the families left behind. How many toes and fingers have been lost to frostbite? How many lives were cut short, snuffed out in a storm, lost in a fall or buried in an avalanche? How many fatherless children, widows, mothers and fathers and grieving siblings are left to compose well-meaning statements about how they supported their partners who were doing what they loved, about how they will bravely carry on with their lives, because that's what their deceased friend or lover would have wanted? How many lives have been fundamentally scarred, even destroyed, by this obsession with winter in the high mountains?

As Maria Coffey wrote in her book, *Where the Mountain Casts Its Shadow: The Dark Side of Extreme Adventure*, 'The world needs risk takers. They inspire, challenge and encourage. They set off sparks, igniting fires that burn long after their passing. They dare the impossible. But not without cost.'[5] It's hard to imagine the grief borne by the Ballard family after Tom died on Nanga Parbat in 2019. They first lost their wife and mother on K2, and then, a son and brother. Katia Lafaille, even though she fully supported her husband's solo winter climbs, was shocked at the emptiness his death brought. 'We had so much ahead of us,' she said. Heike Göschl suffered terribly from Gerfried's death, ricocheting from anger to grief to loneliness to numbness. His death affected his former climbing partner Louis Rousseau so profoundly that Louis was unable to perceive the relationship between mountaineering and his family the same way again. In the midst of her grief at losing Tomek, Anna Mackiewicz struggled to find some meaning, some higher purpose to this tragedy.

And it's not as if writhing in grief was the sole activity of those left behind: they still had to go to work, comfort their children, earn money, answer questions from the media, wake up every morning knowing their lives would never be the same. As Anna said, 'I feel exhausted, so tired. Sometimes I feel I cannot accept it. He was a part of me. Physically and mentally – it's like someone cut my hand or my heart away. I feel empty.' For those who have been left behind because of tragedy, the acute pain of their loss eventually eases, but the void left by their loved ones remains. There is no language to contain the grief they have experienced.

Winter climbing in the highest mountains is acknowledged as fundamentally dangerous, even by those who are most passionate about it. Like religion, it has saints and martyrs, sacred and forbidden places. Thirteen of those sacred 8,000ers have now been climbed. Will the lure of this special genre of high-altitude climbing fade when K2 is finally climbed in winter? Will the saints retire to their sofas and the martyrs fade into the history books? Or will the quest for better lines, faster times, smaller teams drive alpinists to keep returning in winter? For those who are smitten with the 8,000ers but abhor the growing crowds, will they increasingly choose the quiet season?

An anonymous quote from a Polish climber in the 1980s speaking about winter climbing said: 'I finally recovered from this addiction. What I needed was: martial law, children and weaker health.' Krzysztof Wielicki experienced all three, but his reaction was different. He explained how, for a time, this nomadic, mountaineering lifestyle had been perfect for him. 'Time had no value back then. We did what we wanted: we met at the mountaineers' club, we dreamt, we made plans, and then set out to the mountains! As grown-ups, we were at a permanent party, having quit our professions, not knowing that, in a few years' time, capitalism would also come to us.' Now almost seventy, Krzysztof has still not recovered from his addiction, for he continues to dream about K2 in winter. But not without cost. Three spouses, four children; so much waiting for a husband and father who was rarely present.

Élisabeth Revol did not experience martial law, children or weaker health, but she knows plenty about trauma, both emotional and physical. Even after the death of Tomek on Nanga Parbat, her second loss of a partner, she vowed to return to the Himalaya. 'I know I will go back to the mountains some-time, but I think that, for the Himalaya, it will be alone,' she said. 'I don't want to take the responsibility again with a partner. It's too hard.' In the spring of 2019, she did precisely that, soloing Everest and Lhotse within a two-day period, followed by Manaslu that autumn.

The new generation of Ice Warriors is busy, training and preparing them-selves, lifting weights, pushing weights, squats, lunges, running, yoga, balance work, and even more running. They move like champions, strong and firm, forging their bodies into instruments of steel, so resilient they can withstand all that winter might throw at them at 8,000 metres.

And what of the bold survivors of that pioneering generation of Ice Warriors? Their bodies are bent from years of carrying heavy loads, their knees creaky and sore from countless steps kicked into wind-hardened drifts, their faces as lined as topographical maps. Yet their hearts swell with memories of winters up high and their eyes still sparkle with the passion that drove them to embrace the suffering in those lofty places. Their lives, shaped by uncounted days in the mountains, are richer for having discovered the loneliness of winter at 8,000 metres.

Their stories are neither perfect nor complete. There are unanswered questions, bad decisions, unnecessary risks and broken bonds. There are tales of loyalty and bravery, ambition, commitment and vision. There are friendships wrought under such harsh conditions they can never be destroyed. These imperfect tales are all that we have and, in sharing them, we can try to understand the souls of the Ice Warriors, those men and women who find the greatest fulfilment in the highest mountains in the coldest, shortest, darkest days: the cruel days of winter.

APPENDIX A

Selected List of Climbers

[Phonetic spelling]

Berbeka, Maciej [Bair**beck**uh, **Ma**chek] (1954–2013). Polish climber from Zakopane who made first winter ascents of three 8,000-metre peaks: Manaslu, Cho Oyu and Broad Peak. He died on descent from Broad Peak.

Bielecki, Adam [Bee**let**skee, **A**dam] (b.1983). Polish climber who made two first winter ascents of 8,000-metre peaks: Gasherbrum I and Broad Peak. He was on the unsuccessful 2018 K2 winter expedition when he and three teammates flew to Nanga Parbat for the dramatic rescue of Élisabeth Revol and Tomek Mackiewicz.

Bilczewski, Adam [Bil**chev**skee, **A**dam] (1934–1987). Polish climber from Gliwice; led the first winter ascent of Dhaulagiri.

Boukreev, Anatoli [**Boo**kree-ev, Ana**toh**lee] (1958–1997). Elite Kazakh alpinist who climbed nine of the fourteen 8,000-metre peaks, including Manaslu in (meteorological) winter. He died on a winter attempt on Annapurna on Christmas Day 1997.

Chapuisat, Marianne [**Shap**wesat, Maree**ann**] (b.1969). Swiss mountaineer who was the first woman to climb an 8,000er in winter, Cho Oyu in 1993.

Cichy, Leszek [**Chee**hay, **Lesh**ek] (b.1951). Polish climber who made the first ever winter ascent of an 8,000-metre peak when he climbed Everest in winter with Krzysztof Wielicki.

Czok, Andrzej [**Chok, Ahn**jay] (1948–1986). Polish climber. He made the first winter ascent of Dhaulagiri with Jerzy Kukuczka and died while making an attempt on the first winter ascent of Kangchenjunga.

Gabl, Karl [**Gah**bel, **Karl**] (b.1946). Austrian meteorologist and mountaineer who provides accurate weather forecasts for many Himalayan winter expeditions.

Gajewski, Ryszard [Gai-**ev**skee, **Ree**shahrd] (b.1954). Polish climber from Zakopane; made the first winter ascent of Manaslu with Maciej Berbeka.

Gołąb, Janusz [**Go**wahb, **Yan**oosh] (b.1967). Polish big-wall specialist from Gliwice; made the first winter ascent of Gasherbrum I with Adam Bielecki, and was climbing leader on the 2018 Polish winter attempt on K2.

Göschl, Gerfried [**Goeh**shel, **Gair**freed] (1972–2012). From the Styrian region of Austria; ascents of seven 8,000ers. He disappeared on his second winter attempt on Gasherbrum I.

Hajzer, Artur [**Hai**-jer, **Ahr**ter] (1962–2013). Polish climber. Climbed seven 8,000ers, several by new routes. He spearheaded the Polish winter programme and led the team that made the first winter ascent of Gasherbrum I. He died in a fall on Gasherbrum I.

Hayat, Karim [**Hai**yat, Kahr**eem**] (b.1972). Pakistani mountaineer and guide who attempted to find Maciej Berbeka after the Pole went missing descending from Broad Peak.

Heinrich, Zygmunt (Zyga) [**Hain**rick, **Zeeg**moont (**Zee**gah)] (1937–1989). Polish Himalayan climber; the first, with Andrzej Zawada, to climb above 8,000 metres in winter on Lhotse during the unsuccessful attempt in 1974. He climbed high on Everest in winter during the first winter ascent in 1980 and was on the second summit rope team with Jurek Kukuczka for the first winter ascent of Cho Oyu. He died in an avalanche on Everest.

Korniszewski, Lech [Corni**chev**skee, **Leck**] (b.1936). Polish doctor and climber; led the successful first winter ascent of Manaslu.

Kowalski, Tomasz [Ku**vahl**skee, **To**mahj] (1985–2013). One of the new generation of Polish winter climbers; made the first winter ascent of Broad Peak but died on descent.

Kukuczka, Jerzy (Jurek) [Ku**koosh**kah, **Yai**rjee (**Yoo**rek)] (1948–1989). Legendary Polish high-altitude climber and second in the world to climb all fourteen 8,000-metre peaks. He made first winter ascents of Dhaulagiri, Kangchenjunga and Annapurna, and was on the second rope that made the first winter ascent of Cho Oyu. He died in a fall attempting the south face of Lhotse in 1989.

Kurtyka, Voytek [Koor**tee**kah, **Voy**tek] (b.1947). Polish high-altitude climber; pioneered alpine-style climbing in the Himalaya, making several new routes on difficult lines. He was a frequent early partner of Jurek Kukuczka.

Lafaille, Jean-Christophe (JC) (1965–2006). French Himalayan climber and mountain guide who specialised in difficult routes and solo ascents. He made an early (meteorological) winter solo ascent of Shishapangma and disappeared while making a winter solo attempt of Makalu.

Lunger, Tamara (b.1986). Italian ski-mountaineer and Himalayan climber. She was within 100 metres of the summit of Nanga Parbat before turning back in order to save her own life. Her teammates succeeded in making the first winter ascent.

Lwow, Alek [Lu**voaf**, **Al**ek] (b.1953). Polish Himalayan climber; climbed four 8,000ers and was Maciej Berbeka's partner when Maciej made the first winter ascent of Broad Peak's Rocky Summit.

Mackiewicz, Tomasz (Tomek) [Match**kay**vich, **To**mahj] (1975–2018). Polish mountaineer who made repeated attempts to climb Nanga Parbat in winter. He reached the summit on his seventh attempt, but died on descent.

Małek, Artur [**Maow**-ek, **Ar**tur] (b.1979). Polish alpinist and ice-climbing specialist; made the first winter ascent of Broad Peak.

Messner, Reinhold (b.1944). Italian Himalayan climber. He was the first to climb all fourteen 8,000ers. Together with Peter Habeler, he was also first to climb Everest without supplemental oxygen.

Morawski, Piotr [Morahvskee, Peeotrah] (1976–2009). Polish climber with six 8,000-metre peaks, including the first winter ascent of Shishapangma with Simone Moro. He died in a crevasse on Dhaulagiri.

Moro, Simone [**Mo**ro, See**mon**ay] (b.1967). Italian alpinist who has climbed eight 8,000ers. He was the first non-Pole to climb an 8,000er in winter and is the only climber to have made first winter ascents of four 8,000ers: Shishapangma, Makalu, Gasherbrum II and Nanga Parbat.

Nardi, Daniele [**Nahr**dee, Danee-**ell**] (1976–2019). Italian alpinist who made several attempts on Nanga Parbat's unclimbed Mummery Rib in winter. He died on the route, together with British climber Tom Ballard, in 2019.

Okopińska, Anna [Oko**pin**skah, **Ann**a] (b.1948). One of a group of pioneering female Polish Himalayan climbers active in the 1970s, she was on the unsuccessful 1974–75 Polish winter expedition to Lhotse.

Pawlikowski, Maciej [Pahvli**kov**skee, **Ma**chek] (b.1951). Polish mountaineer from Zakopane; made the first winter ascent of Cho Oyu with Maciej Berbeka.

Piasecki, Przemysław (Przemek) [Pee-ah**setch**kee, **Shem**iswav (**Shem**ik)] (b.1952). Polish alpinist and Andrzej Czok's partner on the tragic Kangchenjunga winter expedition. He climbed the Magic Line on K2 in 1986.

Piotrowski, Tadeusz (Tadek) [Pee-ah**trov**skee, Tah**day**ush, **Tah**dek] (1939–1986). Made the first winter ascent of Noshaq with Andrzej Zawada and was on the 1974–75 Lhotse winter attempt. He died on descent after summiting the as yet unrepeated Polish route on the south face of K2 with Jerzy Kukuczka.

Pivtsov, Vassiliy [**Peev**tsoh, Vah**see**lee] (b.1975). Kazakh high-altitude climber who has climbed all fourteen of the 8,000-metre peaks. He was on the 2002–03 Polish–International winter expedition to K2 and led a winter expedition to K2 in 2019. Neither expedition reached the summit.

Revol, Élisabeth [Re**vohl**, **Eliz**abeth] (b.1979). French high-altitude climber who has summitted seven 8,000-metre peaks, including Nanga Parbat in winter. She was rescued on descent in 2018 by members of the Polish team on K2.

Richards, Cory (b.1981). American climber and photographer; made the first winter ascent of Gasherbrum II with an international team.

Rutkiewicz, Wanda [Root**kay**vich, **Vahn**dah] (1943–1992). Polish Himalayan climber who climbed eight of the fourteen 8,000ers, including the first female ascent of K2. She was on the Polish winter expedition to Annapurna but didn't summit. She disappeared on Kangchenjunga in 1992.

Sadpara, Muhammad Ali [Sahd**pah**rah, Mu**hahm**ahd Ah**lee**] (b.1976). Pakistani high-altitude climber who has climbed seven 8,000ers, including the first winter ascent of Nanga Parbat in 2016 with an international team.

Sadpara, Nisar Hussain [Sahd**pah**rah, **Nees**ahr Hoo**sain**] (1975–2012). Pakistani high-altitude climber who climbed all five of the 8,000ers in Pakistan. He died on the international winter expedition to Gasherbrum I in 2012.

Sherpa, Pasang Norbu [**Sher**pah, **Pah**sang **Nor**boo] (b.1949). Sherpa climber who was with Zyga Heinrich high on Everest during the first winter ascent.

Styś, Tamara [**Steesh**, Tah**mah**rah] (b.1978). Polish alpinist; she climbed Gasherbrum II and was on the international expedition to Gasherbrum I in 2012. She did not summit but holds the female winter altitude record in the Karakoram.

Tanabe, Osamu [Tah**nah**bee, Oh**sahm**oo] (1961–2010). Japanese Himalayan climber. He climbed six 8,000ers, including a winter ascent of Everest and a winter ascent of the south face of Lhotse, although only to the summit ridge. He died in an avalanche on Dhaulagiri.

Tomala, Piotr [To**mahl**ah, Pee**o**trah] (b.1972). Polish alpinist on the Polish K2 winter expedition in 2018; he flew to Nanga Parbat to participate in the rescue of Élisabeth Revol.

Txikon, Alex [Tsee**kohn**, **Ahl**ex] (b.1981). Basque high-altitude climber and youngest of thirteen children. He has done ten 8,000ers including the first winter ascent of Nanga Parbat in 2016 with an international team.

Urubko, Denis [Oo**roo**bko, **Den**is] (b.1973). Ethnically Russian, he has held Kazakh and Polish passports. Denis has summited 8,000-metre peaks twenty-two times. He made the first winter ascents of Makalu and Gasherbrum II and was on several K2 winter expeditions. In the winter of 2018, he was part of the successful rescue of Élisabeth Revol on Nanga Parbat.

Wielicki, Krzysztof [Veel**its**kee, **Kreesh**tof] (b.1950). Polish Himalayan climber. He has climbed all of the 8,000ers including first winter ascents of Everest, Kangchenjunga and Lhotse.

Yamada, Noboru [Yah**mah**dah, Noh**boh**roo] (1950–1989). Japanese high-altitude mountaineer. He climbed nine 8,000ers, including Everest three times, once in winter. He died on a winter expedition to Denali in Alaska.

Załuski, Darek [Zah**woos**kee, **Dah**rek] (b.1959). Polish Himalayan climber and filmmaker. He has climbed five 8,000ers, including K2 and two ascents of Everest. He has been on nine winter expeditions to 8,000-metre peaks.

Zawada, Andrzej [Zah**vah**dah, **Ahn**jay] (1928–2000). Polish Himalayan climber who first envisioned climbing 8,000-metre peaks in winter. He led several successful winter expeditions to 8,000ers, including the first winter ascent of an 8,000-metre peak, Everest.

APPENDIX B

Summary of First Winter Ascents of 8,000ers

Everest (8,848 metres): 17 February 1980. Polish expedition led by Andrzej Zawada. Summit climbers: Krzysztof Wielicki, Leszek Cichy.

Manaslu (8,163 metres): 12 January 1984. Polish expedition led by Lech Korniszewski. Summit climbers: Maciej Berbeka, Ryszard Gajewski.

Dhaulagiri (8,167 metres): 21 January 1985. Polish expedition led by Adam Bilczewski. Summit climbers: Andrzej Czok, Jerzy Kukuczka.

Cho Oyu (8,188 metres): 12 February 1985. Polish expedition led by Andrzej Zawada. Summit climbers: Maciej Berbeka, Maciej Pawlikowski. Second summit team: Jerzy Kukuczka, Zygmunt Heinrich.

Kangchenjunga (8,586 metres): 11 January 1986. Polish expedition led by Andrzej Machnik. Summit climbers: Jerzy Kukuczka, Krzysztof Wielicki.

Annapurna (8,091 metres): 3 February 1987. Polish expedition led by Jerzy Kukuczka. Summit climbers: Jerzy Kukuczka, Artur Hajzer.

Lhotse (8,516 metres): 31 December 1988. Belgian–Polish expedition led by Herman Detienne. Summit climber: Krzysztof Wielicki.

Shishapangma (8,027 metres): 14 January 2005. Polish–Italian expedition. Summit climbers: Piotr Morawski, Simone Moro.

Makalu (8,485 metres): 9 February 2009. International expedition led by Simone Moro. Summit climbers: Simone Moro, Denis Urubko.

Gasherbrum II (8,034 metres): 2 February 2011. International expedition led by Simone Moro. Summit climbers: Simone Moro, Denis Urubko, Cory Richards.

Gasherbrum I (8,080 metres): 9 March 2012. Polish expedition led by Artur Hajzer. Summit climbers: Janusz Gołąb, Adam Bielecki.

Broad Peak (8,051 metres): 5 March 2013. Polish expedition led by Krzysztof Wielicki. Summit climbers: Maciej Berbeka, Adam Bielecki, Artur Małek, Tomasz Kowalski.

Nanga Parbat (8,125 metres): 26 February 2016. Two amalgamated teams led by Simone Moro and Alex Txikon. Summit climbers: Alex Txikon, Ali Sadpara, Simone Moro.

K2 (8,611 metres): To be continued.

ACKNOWLEDGEMENTS

The seeds of this book were planted twenty-six years ago in Katowice, Poland, when I first met Andrzej Zawada at a gathering of the original Ice Warriors. Over the next few decades, I grew to know a number of these climbers well. Their fascination with winter and the art of suffering intrigued me. The stories they told of their adventures at the highest elevations in the coldest temperatures were fascinating, sometimes hard to believe. The tragic endings to many of their expeditions saddened me. With the encouragement of a few close writing friends, I decided to chronicle the history of winter climbing in the Himalaya and Karakoram that focused on the characters who propelled this history. I can't adequately thank the Ice Warriors and surviving family members and friends who so kindly supported me throughout this long and interesting process. It is because of their written accounts, their letters and photos, their libraries, and the untold hours they spent with me in person at their kitchen tables, on the phone and on email, that this book exists.

But just to be clear, this is not the *definitive* history of winter climbing at 8,000 metres. Thanks to exhaustive research done by Bob A. Schelfhout Aubertijn, with assistance from several others, including Eberhard Jurgalski, Rodolphe Popier, Louis Rousseau, Richard Salisbury and Jochen Hemmleb, I was buried by an avalanche of almost 200 winter expeditions to the highest peaks. Obviously, not a book. More like a library. I chose to concentrate on certain personalities and specific climbs rather than cramming the details of this vast, complex and impressive history into one volume. Many significant ascents and fascinating individuals are not included. I apologise to any who might feel slighted or ignored.

I want to thank those who agreed to talk with me, sometimes for days.

Some of these interviews took place years ago, in preparation for another book, *Freedom Climbers*, and through my previous role as director of the Banff Mountain Film Festival. Sadly, many of these characters are no longer with us. Sincere thanks to all of you: Adam Bielecki, Alek Lwow, Alessandra Carati, Alex Txikon, Ali Sadpara, Anatoli Boukreev, Andrzej Zawada, Anna Czerwińska, Anna Kamińska, Anna Milewska, Anna Okopińska, Anna Solska-Mackiewicz, Artur Hajzer, Artur Małek, Bartek Dobroch, Bogdan Jankowski, Brian Hall, Celina Kukuczka, Cory Richards, Danuta Piotrowska, Darek Załuski, Denis Urubko, Dominik Szczepański, Dr Peter Hackett, Élisabeth Revol, Erhard Loretan, Ewa Berbeka, Ewa Matuszewska, Federico Bernardi, Gerlinde Kaltenbrunner, Heike Göschl-Grünwald, Jacques Olek, Janusz Gołąb, Janusz Kurczab, Janusz Majer, Jerzy Kukuczka, Jerzy Porębski, Jochen Hemmleb, John Porter, Karl Gabl, Katia Lafaille, Krzysztof Wielicki, Lech Korniszewski, Leszek Cichy, Linda Wylie, Lindsay Griffin, Louis Rousseau, Ludwik Wilczyński, Maciej Berbeka, Maciek Pawlikowski, Maria Coffey, Marianne Chapuisat, Monika Rogozińska, Pemba Gyalje Sherpa, Piotr Drożdż, Piotr Tomala, Przemysław Piasecki, Reinhold Messner, Roman Gołędowski, Ryszard Gajewski, Ryszard Pawlowski, Simone Moro, Stanisław Berbeka, Steve Swenson, Tamara Lunger, Tamara Styś, Tom Hornbein, Tomek Mackiewicz, Victor Saunders, Voytek Kurtyka, Wanda Rutkiewicz and Wojtek Dzik.

If only we had an unlimited budget, we could have included more of the hundreds of photographs that were offered. Thanks to all who were so generous: Cory Richards, Élisabeth Revol, Jacques Olek, Lech Korniszewski, Ryszard Gajewski, Jerzy Porębski, Przemysław Piasecki, Bogdan Jankowski, Alek Lwow, Piotr Drożdż, Leszek Cichy, Marek Pronobis, Adam Bilczewski, J. Barcz, Mirek Wiśniewski, Darek Załuski, Piotr Morawski, Simone Moro, Denis Urubko, Louis Rousseau, Mirek Wiśniewski, Gerfried Göschl, Artur Małek, Sergey Boiko, Linda Wylie, Andrzej Zawada Archive, Janusz Kurczab Archive, Marianne Chapuisat Archive, Artur Hajzer Archive, Katia Lafaille Archive, Göschl Family Archive, Tamara Lunger Archive, Anna Solska-Mackiewicz Archive.

A huge thanks to Bob A. Schelfhout Aubertijn, whose Himalayan-database of a mind scoured the manuscript for climbing history errors. I take full responsibility for those that remain. And thanks to Alessandra Raggio and Jochen Hemmleb for helping me find those mysterious reference page numbers.

I'm grateful to those who provided early critical reads: Bonnie Hamilton, Alan McDonald and Geoff Powter. And I owe a huge debt of gratitude to Amanda Lewis for her editorial leap of faith in taking this project on, and to Jon Barton and his team at Vertebrate Publishing for believing in and supporting the book: John Coefield, Ed Douglas, Lorna Hargreaves, Sophie Fletcher, Cameron Bonser, Jane Beagley, Nathan Ryder and Emma Lockley. On this side of the pond, it was a thrill to once again work with the team at Mountaineers Books.

And once again, for our third book project together, Julia Pulwicki deserves my heartfelt thanks. My research included a couple of dozen hefty tomes in various languages. Several were in Polish. Despite her hectic schedule, she carved out many hours to work with me over a series of months, translating countless pages of fascinating stuff. Anne Ryall also helped with French translations, and I even have to give Google Translate a high five for the odd, emergency translation.

I'm sometimes taken by surprise when ideas suddenly appear at various stages of a project. In the case of the cover design and title, it was my roomies on a climbing trip to El Potrero Chico who helped me decide. Thanks for your sage advice, Marni, Barb and Sharon.

And finally, thanks to my husband, Alan, whose patience with me when I disappeared into the frigid world of Himalayan climbing in winter warmed my heart.

NOTES

INTRODUCTION

1   Bolesław Bierut was a Polish Communist leader, NKVD (secret police) agent and hard-line Stalinist who became president of Poland after the defeat of the Nazi forces in the Second World War.

2   Adam Bielecki and Dominik Szczepański, *Adam Bielecki* (Warszawa: Agora, 2017), 129.

1: EVEREST

1   Andrzej Zawada, 'Winter at 8250 metres: Polish expedition to Lhotse 1974', *Alpine Journal* 1977: 28.

2   Andrzej Zawada, '25 Years of Winter in the Himalaya', *Alpine Journal* 2000: 35.

3   Andrzej Zawada, 'Mount Everest – the First Winter Ascent', *Alpine Journal* 1984: 50–51.

4   Piotr Drożdż, *Krzysztof Wielicki: Mój Wybór. Wywiad-Rzeka Tom 1* (Kraków: Góry Books, 2014), 22.

5   Andrzej Zawada (expedition leader), Józef Bakalowski (cameraman), Leszek Cichy, Krzysztof Cielecki, Ryszard Dmoch, Walenty Fiut, Ryszard Gajewski, Zygmunt A. Heinrich, Jan Holnicki-Szulc, Robert Janik (doctor), Bogdan Jankowski, Stanisław Jaworski (cameraman), Janusz Mączka, Aleksander Lwow, Kazimierz W. Olech, Maciej Pawlikowski, Marian Piekutowski, Ryszard Szafirski, Krzysztof Wielicki, Krzysztof Żurek plus five Sherpas led by Pemba Norbu.

6   Andrzej Zawada, 'Mount Everest – the First Winter Ascent', *Alpine Journal* 1984: 54.

7   Ibid., 55.

8   Piotr Drożdż, *Krzysztof Wielicki: Mój Wybór. Wywiad-Rzeka Tom 1* (Kraków: Góry Books, 2014), 104.

9   Andrzej Zawada, 'Mount Everest – the First Winter Ascent,' *Alpine Journal* 1984: 57.

10 Piotr Drożdż, *Krzysztof Wielicki: Mój Wybór. Wywiad-Rzeka Tom 1* (Kraków: Góry Books, 2014), 104.

11 Ibid., 112.

12 Ibid., 113.

13 Ibid., 97.

14 Ibid., 117.

15 Joe Tasker, *Everest the Cruel Way* (London: Hodder and Stoughton, 1981), 3.

16 Ibid., 14.

17 Ibid., 116.

18 Ibid., 130.

19 Conversation recorded in the film *Everest in Winter* (Chameleon, 1981).

20 Adrian and Alan Burgess, *The Burgess Book of Lies* (Calgary: Rocky Mountain Books, 1994), 244.

21 Joe Tasker, *Everest the Cruel Way* (London: Hodder and Stoughton, 1981), 160.

2: MANASLU

1   Stanisław Berbeka, *Dreamland* (Yak Yak, 2018).

2   Ibid.

3   Ibid.

4   Jerzy Porębski, *Manaslu* (Artica, 2014).

5   Ibid.

6   Ibid.

7   Ibid.

8   Ibid.

9   Ibid.

10 Noboru Yamada, 'Asia, Nepal, Manaslu, Northeast Ridge in the Winter', *American Alpine Journal* 1986.

11 Eric Monier, 'Manaslu South Face in Winter', *Himalayan Journal* 48, 1992: 166.

12 Anatoli Boukreev, 'The Roads We Choose, a Himalayan Season', *American Alpine Journal* 1996.

13 Ibid.

14 Ibid.

15 Ibid.

16 Ibid.

17 Élisabeth Revol, 'Attempt of Manaslu (8,163m)', *Boreal*, 10 February 2017.

18 Ibid.

19 Ibid.

3: DHAULAGIRI

1   Bernadette McDonald, *Freedom Climbers* (Calgary: Rocky Mountain Books, 2011), 130.

2   Ibid., 69.

3   Jerzy Kukuczka, *My Vertical World* (Seattle: Mountaineers Books, 1992), 81.

4   Ibid., 81.

5   Ibid., 82.

6   Adam Bilczewski, 'Dhaulagiri 1984–85', *Himalayan Journal* 43, 1987: 21.

7   Jerzy Kukuczka, *My Vertical World* (Seattle: Mountaineers Books, 1992), 85.

8   Ibid., 87.

9   Ibid., 88.

10 Ibid., 90.

11 Ibid., 90.

12 Adam Bilczewski, 'Dhaulagiri 1984–85', *Himalayan Journal* 43, 1987: 21.

13 Jerzy Kukuczka, *My Vertical World* (Seattle: Mountaineers Books, 1992), 92.

14 Ibid.

15 Erhard Loretan, *Night Naked* (Seattle: Mountaineers Books, 2013), 96.

16 The first ascent of the east face was by Voytek Kurtyka, Ludwik Wilczyński, Alex MacIntyre and René Ghilini in 1980.

17 Erhard Loretan, *Night Naked* (Seattle: Mountaineers Books, 2013), 96.

18 Jean Troillet, 'Winter Expedition to Dhaulagiri I, 1985', *Himalayan Journal* 43, 1987: 120.

19 Erhard Loretan, *Night Naked* (Seattle: Mountaineers Books, 2013), 97.

4: CHO OYU

1   Stanisław Berbeka, *Dreamland* (Yak Yak, 2018).

2   Jerzy Kukuczka, *My Vertical World* (Seattle: Mountaineers Books, 1992), 100.

3   Ibid., 102.

4 Maria Coffey, *Where the Mountain Casts Its Shadow: The Dark Side of Extreme Adventure* (New York: St. Martin's Press, 2003), 52.
5 Stanisław Berbeka, *Dreamland* (Yak Yak, 2018).
6 Miguel 'Lito' Sánchez, *Cho Oyu* (Rio Cuarto: Palloni Edicion, 2017), Préface.

5: KANGCHENJUNGA
1 Cherie Bremer-Kamp, *Chicago Tribune*, 31 May 1987.
2 Ibid.
3 Bartek Dobroch, *Artur Hajzer: Droga Słonia* (Kraków: Wydawnictwo Znak, 2018), 171.
4 Piotr Drożdż, *Krzysztof Wielicki: Mój Wybór. Wywiad-Rzeka Tom 1* (Kraków: Góry Books, 2014), 198.
5 Ibid.
6 Ibid.
7 Jerzy Kukuczka, *My Vertical World* (Seattle: Mountaineers Books, 1992), 127.
8 Ibid., 128.
9 Ibid., 129.
10 Piotr Drożdż, *Krzysztof Wielicki: Mój Wybór. Wywiad-Rzeka Tom 1* (Kraków: Góry Books, 2014), 202.
11 Ibid., 208.
12 Ibid., 203.
13 Ibid., 204.
14 Ibid., 204.

6: ANNAPURNA
1 Previous classification by H. Adams Carter in the 1985 *American Alpine Journal* listed thirteen peaks over 7,000 metres and sixteen peaks over 6,000 metres.
2 A Korean team had claimed to reach the summit from the north side in 1984, but based on first-hand information from a French team on the mountain at the same time, their claim was seriously questioned, and finally dismissed by Himalayan historian Elizabeth Hawley.
3 Bartek Dobroch, *Artur Hajzer: Droga Słonia* (Kraków: Wydawnictwo Znak, 2018), 219.
4 Piotr Drożdż, *Krzysztof Wielicki: Mój Wybór. Wywiad-Rzeka Tom 1* (Kraków: Góry Books, 2014), 227.
5 Ibid., 230.
6 Jerzy Kukuczka, *My Vertical World* (Seattle: Mountaineers Books, 1992), 167.
7 Piotr Drożdż, *Krzysztof Wielicki: Mój Wybór. Wywiad-Rzeka Tom 1* (Kraków: Góry Books, 2014), 232.
8 Ibid., 34.
9 Marcello Rossi, 'Simone Moro: The Winter Maestro', www.climbing.com, 13 January 2017.
10 Simone Moro, *Cometa sull'Annapurna* (Milano: Corbaccio, 2003), 115.
11 Ibid., 116.
12 Ibid., 118.
13 Ibid., 124.
14 Simone Moro, 'Annapurna, Attempt and Tragedy', *American Alpine Journal* 1998: 302.
15 Simone Moro, *Cometa sull'Annapurna* (Milano: Corbaccio, 2003), 129.
16 Ibid., 131.
17 Anatoli Boukreev, *Above the Clouds* (St. Martin's Press, 2001), 226.
18 Marcello Rossi, 'Simone Moro: The Winter Maestro', www.climbing.com, 13 January 2017.

7: LHOTSE

1 Andrzej Zawada, 'Winter at 8250 metres: Polish expedition to Lhotse 1974', *Alpine Journal* 1977: 28–35.
2 Ibid.
3 Ibid.
4 Ibid.
5 Ibid.
6 Ibid.
7 Ewa Matuszewska, *Lider: górskim szlakiem Andrzeja Zawady* (Warszawa: Iskry, 2003).
8 Piotr Drożdż, *Krzysztof Wielicki: Mój Wybór. Wywiad-Rzeka Tom 1* (Kraków: Góry Books, 2014), 268.
9 Ibid., 268.
10 Ibid., 269.
11 Ibid., 271.
12 Ibid., 271.
13 Ibid., 272.
14 Ibid., 272.
15 Ibid., 272.
16 Ibid., 275.
17 Osamu Tanabe, 'Lhotse South Face Winter – Near Ascent', *Japan Alpine News*, volume 5, 2004: 3.
18 Ibid.
19 Osamu Tanabe, 'Lhotse South Face Winter Ascent – The Dream Comes True', *Alpine Journal* 2007: 67.
20 Lindsay Griffin, 'Lhotse South Face in Winter – Almost', *Alpinist Online*, 8 January 2007.

8: SHISHAPANGMA

1 Simone Moro, 'Shisha Pangma Winter Expedition', *Mountain RU*, 8 December 2003.
2 Simone Moro, *The Call of the Ice* (Seattle: Mountaineers Books, 2014), 59.
3 Ibid., 60.
4 Simone Moro, 'Shisha Pangma Winter 2004–05', *Mountain RU*, 21 December 2004.
5 Simone Moro, *The Call of the Ice* (Seattle: Mountaineers Books, 2014), 66.
6 Jean-Christophe Lafaille, 'Asia, Tibet, Himalaya, Rolwaling Himal, Shishapangma Main Summit (8,027m), Southwest Face, Solo in December with New Variation', *American Alpine Journal* 2005: 434.
7 Ibid.
8 Krzysztof Wielicki, 'Asia, Tibet, Himalaya, Rolwaling Himal, Winter Ascents of 8,000m Peaks, Commentary', *American Alpine Journal*, 2005: 436.
9 Simone Moro, *The Call of the Ice* (Seattle: Mountaineers Books, 2014), 72.
10 Ibid., 73.
11 Ibid., 74.
12 Simone Moro, 'Asia, Tibet, Himalaya, Rolwaling Himal, Shishapangma, First Winter Ascent', *American Alpine Journal* 2005: 438.
13 Simone Moro, *The Call of the Ice* (Seattle: Mountaineers Books, 2014), 76.
14 Ibid., 79.

9: MAKALU

1 Piotr Drożdż, *Krzysztof Wielicki: Mój Wybór. Wywiad-Rzeka Tom 2* (Kraków: Góry Books, 2015), 21.
2 Ibid., 30.
3 Ibid., 26.
4 Ibid., 184.
5 Ibid., 185.

6   Krzysztof Wielicki, 'Winter Manifesto', *Polski Związek Alpinizmu*, 2002.
7   Jason Burke, 'One Step Beyond', *The Observer*, 9 April 2006.
8   Ibid.
9   Ibid.
10   Denis Urubko, 'Fifty-Fifty: Tales of a Climber's Life', *Alpinist* 37, Winter 2011–12: 72.
11   Denis Urubko, 'Elements Revelry', www.russianclimb.com, 3 February 2008.
12   Denis Urubko, 'Winter Makalu Debrief', www.explorersweb.com, 2 April 2009.
13   Simone Moro, *The Call of the Ice* (Seattle: Mountaineers Books, 2014), 114.
14   Denis Urubko and Simone Moro, 'Makalu Winter Climb', RussianClimb.com, 22 January 2009.
15   Simone Moro, *The Call of the Ice* (Seattle: Mountaineers Books, 2014), 131.
16   Ibid., 137.
17   Denis Urubko, 'Makalu: the First Winter Ascent and Cho Oyu: the Southeast Face', *Japan Alpine News*, volume 11, 2010: 94.
18   Simone Moro, *The Call of the Ice* (Seattle: Mountaineers Books, 2014), 141.
19   Ibid., 142.
20   Ibid., 144.
21   Ibid., 145.
22   Denis Urubko, 'Makalu: the First Winter Ascent and Cho Oyu: the Southeast Face', *Japan Alpine News*, volume 11, 2010: 94.

10: GASHERBRUM II
1   Artur Hajzer, 'You just have to have much bigger balls in winter', www.explorersweb.com, 31 March 2009.
2   Simone Moro, *The Call of the Ice* (Seattle: Mountaineers Books, 2014), 155.
3   Marcello Rossi, 'Simone Moro: The Winter Maestro', www.climbing.com, 13 January 2017.
4   Cory Richards, 'This Photo Captures a Near-Death Experience – and Later Trauma', *National Geographic Magazine*, May 2018: 38.
5   Simone Moro, *The Call of the Ice* (Seattle: Mountaineers Books, 2014), 157.
6   Ibid., 165.
7   Denis Urubko, 'Gasherbrum II, Winter 2011', www.russianclimb.com, 26 January 2011.
8   Ibid.
9   Ibid.
10   Simone Moro, *The Call of the Ice* (Seattle: Mountaineers Books, 2014), 176.
11   Ibid., 178.
12   Ibid., 181
13   Denis Urubko, 'Gasherbrum II, Winter 2011', www.russianclimb.com, 6 February 2011.
14   Ibid.
15   Cory Richards, 'This Photo Captures a Near-Death Experience – and Later Trauma', *National Geographic Magazine*, May 2018: 38.
16   Simone Moro, *The Call of the Ice* (Seattle: Mountaineers Books, 2014), 197.
17   Grayson Schaffer, 'Partly Crazy With a Chance of Frostbite', *Outside Online*, 25 April 2011.
18   Simone Moro, 'Reflecting on Gasherbrum II', *Alpine Journal* 2012: 59–62.
19   Cory Richards, 'This Photo Captures a Near-Death Experience – and Later Trauma', *National Geographic Magazine*, May 2018: 36.
20   Ibid., 36.
21   Ibid., 38.
22   Simone Moro, 'Reflecting on Gasherbrum II', *Alpine Journal* 2012: 59–62.
23   Simone Moro, 'Interview: Simone Moro on Winter K2', www.explorersweb.com, 22 December 2017.
24   Devon O'Neil, 'To Get to the Summit, Cory Richards had to Lose it All', *Outside Online*, 24 August 2017.

11: GASHERBRUM I

1   Louis Rousseau, 'K2 in winter still remains a challenge', www.explorersweb.com, 7 February 2012.
2   Louis Rousseau, 'A Cold Sisyphean Climb', *Gripped*, October/November 2011: 46.
3   Ibid.
4   Ibid.
5   Louis Rousseau, 'Winter GI Commentary', www.explorersweb.com, 3 February 2012.
6   Bartek Dobroch, *Artur Hajzer: Droga Słonia* (Kraków: Wydawnictwo Znak, 2018), 425.
7   Ibid., 426.
8   Ibid., 426.
9   Ibid., 428.
10 Ibid., 434.
11 Adam Bielecki and Dominik Szczepański, *Adam Bielecki* (Warszawa: Agora, 2017), 128.
12 Ibid.
13 Bartek Dobroch, *Artur Hajzer: Droga Słonia* (Kraków: Wydawnictwo Znak, 2018), 467.
14 Adam Bielecki and Dominik Szczepański, *Adam Bielecki* (Warszawa: Agora, 2017), 16.
15 Ibid., 19.
16 Bartek Dobroch, *Artur Hajzer: Droga Słonia* (Kraków: Wydawnictwo Znak, 2018), 468.
17 Adam Bielecki and Dominik Szczepański, *Adam Bielecki* (Warszawa: Agora, 2017), 12.
18 Jochen Hemmleb, *Spuren für die Ewigkeit* (Vienna: EGOTH – Verlag, 2014), 253.
19 Ibid., 253.
20 Ibid., 258.
21 Bartek Dobroch, *Artur Hajzer: Droga Słonia* (Kraków: Wydawnictwo Znak, 2018), 468.
22 Jochen Hemmleb, *Spuren für die Ewigkeit* (Vienna: EGOTH – Verlag, 2014), 262.
23 Adam Bielecki and Dominik Szczepański, *Adam Bielecki* (Warszawa: Agora, 2017), 181.
24 Ibid., 184.
25 Agnieszka Bielecka and Artur Hajzer, 'The Polish Gasherbrum I Winter Expedition', *Alpine Journal* 2013: 19.
26 Jochen Hemmleb, *Spuren für die Ewigkeit* (Vienna: EGOTH – Verlag, 2014), 263.
27 Ibid., 259.
28 Ibid., 265.
29 Adam Bielecki and Dominik Szczepański, *Adam Bielecki* (Warszawa: Agora, 2017), 192.
30 Artur Hajzer, 'Gasherbrum I (8,086m), First Winter Ascent', *American Alpine Journal* 2012: 265.
31 Louis Rousseau, 'Winter GI Commentary', www.explorersweb.com, 3 February 2012.
32 Bartek Dobroch, *Artur Hajzer: Droga Słonia* (Kraków: Wydawnictwo Znak, 2018), 471.
33 Ibid., 473.
34 Adam Bielecki and Dominik Szczepański, *Adam Bielecki* (Warszawa: Agora, 2017), 192.

12: BROAD PEAK

1   Stanisław Berbeka, *Dreamland* (Yak Yak, 2018).
2   Ibid.
3   Piotr Drożdż, *Krzysztof Wielicki: Mój Wybór. Wywiad-Rzeka Tom 1* (Kraków: Góry Books, 2014), 252.
4   Aleksander Lwow, *Zwyciężyć znaczy przeżyć: 20 lat później* (Kraków: Wydawnictwo Bezdroża, 2014) 255.
5   Ibid., 260.
6   Stanisław Berbeka, *Dreamland* (Yak Yak, 2018).
7   Aleksander Lwow, *Zwyciężyć znaczy przeżyć: 20 lat później* (Kraków: Wydawnictwo Bezdroża, 2014), 263.
8   Ibid., 264.
9   Stanisław Berbeka, *Dreamland* (Yak Yak, 2018).

10   Piotr Drożdż, *Krzysztof Wielicki: Mój Wybór. Wywiad-Rzeka Tom 1* (Kraków: Góry Books, 2014), 255.

11   Stanisław Berbeka, *Dreamland* (Yak Yak, 2018).

12   Ibid.

13   Piotr Drożdż, *Krzysztof Wielicki: Mój Wybór. Wywiad-Rzeka Tom 1* (Kraków: Góry Books, 2014), 256.

14   Bartek Dobroch and Przemysław Wilczyński, *Broad Peak: Niebo I Piekło* (Poznań: Wydawnictwo Poznańskie, 2014), 63.

15   Ibid., 63.

16   Bartek Dobroch, *Artur Hajzer: Droga Słonia* (Kraków: Wydawnictwo Znak, 2018), 478.

17   Adam Bielecki and Dominik Szczepański, *Adam Bielecki* (Warszawa: Agora, 2017), 237.

18   Ibid., 239.

19   Bartek Dobroch and Przemysław Wilczyński, *Broad Peak: Niebo I Piekło* (Poznań: Wydawnictwo Poznańskie, 2014), 113.

20   Piotr Drożdż, *Krzysztof Wielicki: Mój Wybór. Wywiad-Rzeka Tom 2* (Kraków: Góry Books, 2015), 241.

21   Adam Bielecki and Dominik Szczepański, *Adam Bielecki* (Warszawa: Agora, 2017), 266.

22   Ibid., 268.

23   Ibid., 271.

24   Ibid., 274.

25   Piotr Drożdż, *Krzysztof Wielicki: Mój Wybór. Wywiad-Rzeka Tom 2* (Kraków: Góry Books, 2015), 242.

26   Adam Bielecki and Dominik Szczepański, *Adam Bielecki* (Warszawa: Agora, 2017), 274.

27   Piotr Drożdż, *Krzysztof Wielicki: Mój Wybór. Wywiad-Rzeka Tom 2* (Kraków: Góry Books, 2015), 244.

28   Adam Bielecki and Dominik Szczepański, *Adam Bielecki* (Warszawa: Agora, 2017), 274.

29   Bartek Dobroch and Przemysław Wilczyński, *Broad Peak: Niebo I Piekło* (Poznań: Wydawnictwo Poznańskie, 2014), 145.

30   Stanisław Berbeka, *Dreamland* (Yak Yak, 2018).

31   Bartek Dobroch and Przemysław Wilczyński, *Broad Peak: Niebo I Piekło* (Poznań: Wydawnictwo Poznańskie, 2014), 148.

32   Adam Bielecki and Dominik Szczepański, *Adam Bielecki* (Warszawa: Agora, 2017), pg. 287.

33   Ibid., 287.

34   Piotr Drożdż, *Krzysztof Wielicki: Mój Wybór. Wywiad-Rzeka Tom 2* (Kraków: Góry Books, 2015), pg. 245.

35   Bartek Dobroch and Przemysław Wilczyński, *Broad Peak: Niebo I Piekło* (Poznań: Wydawnictwo Poznańskie, 2014), 164.

36   Ewa A Rozmowa Berbeka and Beata Sabała-Zielińska, *Jak Wysoko Sięga Miłość? Życie Po Broad Peak* (Warszawa: Prószyński Media Sp. z o.o., 2016), 35.

37   Adam Bielecki and Dominik Szczepański, *Adam Bielecki* (Warszawa: Agora, 2017), 287.

38   Bartek Dobroch and Przemysław Wilczyński, *Broad Peak: Niebo I Piekło* (Poznań: Wydawnictwo Poznańskie, 2014), 317.

39   Ibid., 321.

40   Ibid., 323.

41   Piotr Drożdż, *Krzysztof Wielicki: Mój Wybór. Wywiad-Rzeka Tom 2* (Kraków: Góry Books, 2015), 242.

42   Adam Bielecki and Dominik Szczepański, *Adam Bielecki* (Warszawa: Agora, 2017), 304.

43   Ewa A Rozmowa Berbeka and Beata Sabała-Zielińska, *Jak Wysoko Sięga Miłość? Życie Po Broad Peak* (Warszawa: Prószyński Media Sp. z o.o., 2016), 22.

44   Jagoda Mytych, 'Artur Hajzer – Ice Leader', http://goryksiazek.pl, September 2013.

45   Piotr Drożdż, *Krzysztof Wielicki: Mój Wybór. Wywiad-Rzeka Tom 2* (Kraków: Góry Books, 2015), 255.

46 Ewa A Rozmowa Berbeka and Beata Sabała-Zielińska, *Jak Wysoko Sięga Miłość? Życie Po Broad Peak* (Warszawa: Prószyński Media Sp. z o.o., 2016), 18.
47 Stanisław Berbeka, *Dreamland* (Yak Yak, 2018).
48 Bartek Dobroch and Przemysław Wilczyński, *Broad Peak: Niebo I Piekło* (Poznań: Wydawnictwo Poznańskie, 2014), 325.

13: NANGA PARBAT
1 Captain R.H. Marsh, 'Nanga Parbat: The Accident in December, 1950', *Alpine Journal* 1951: 130.
2 Piotr Drożdż, *Krzysztof Wielicki: Mój Wybór. Wywiad-Rzeka Tom 2* (Kraków: Góry Books, 2015), 226.
3 Dominik Szczepański, *Czapkins* (Warszawa: Agora, 2019), 255.
4 'Nanga Parbat in winter, Moro and Urubko aim to climb route attempted by Messner and Eisendle', www.planetmountain.com, 13 January 2012.
5 www.wspinanie.pl/forum, 7 January 2013.
6 Dominik Szczepański, *Czapkins* (Warszawa: Agora, 2019), 274.
7 'Winter 2014: Daniele Nardi Returns to Nanga Parbat', www.altitudepakistan.blogspot.com, 28 December 2013.
8 Piotr Drożdż, *Krzysztof Wielicki: Mój Wybór. Wywiad-Rzeka Tom 2* (Kraków: Góry Books, 2015), 210.
9 Adam Bielecki and Dominik Szczepański, *Adam Bielecki* (Warszawa: Agora, 2017), 390.
10 Ibid., 396.
11 Ibid., 397.
12 Dominik Szczepański, *Czapkins* (Warszawa: Agora, 2019), 379.
13 Ibid., 385.
14 Tamara Lunger, 'Winter Expedition', www.tamaralunger.com, January/February 2016.
15 Marcello Rossi, 'Simone Moro: The Winter Maestro', www.climbing.com, 13 January 2017.
16 Dominik Szczepański, *Czapkins* (Warszawa: Agora, 2019), 21.
17 Ibid., 23.
18 Ibid., 28.
19 Ibid., 31.
20 Ibid., 42.
21 Ibid., 44.
22 Ibid., 403.
23 Ibid., 403.
24 Ibid., 404.
25 Ibid., 409.
26 Ibid., 410.
27 Ibid., 420.
28 Ibid., 438.
29 Ibid., 443.
30 Derek Franz and Maheed Syed, 'A retrospective on the second winter ascent of Nanga Parbat … ', *Alpinist Online*, 7 August 2018.
31 Dominik Szczepański, *Czapkins* (Warszawa: Agora, 2019), 446.
32 Marcin Jamkowski, 'Rescue on the Killer Mountain', *Outside Online*, 11 April 2018.
33 Ibid.
34 Vinicio Stefanello, 'For Daniele Nardi and Tom Ballard lost forever on Nanga Parbat', www.planetmountain.com, 9 March 2019.

14: K2

1. Peter Beal, 'Escape Route: Chaos Canyon, Colorado', *Alpinist* 37, Winter 2011–12: 90.
2. Steve Swenson, 'K2: the Mountaineer's Mountain', *Alpinist* 37, Winter 2011–12: 40.
3. Robert Macfarlane, *Mountains of the Mind* (New York: Pantheon Books, 2003), 175.
4. Fosco Maraini, *Karakoram: The Ascent of Gasherbrum IV* (New York: Viking Press, 1961), 167.
5. Piotr Drożdż, *Krzysztof Wielicki: Mój Wybór. Wywiad-Rzeka Tom 1* (Kraków: Góry Books, 2014), 252.
6. Ibid.
7. Ibid.
8. Ewa Matuszewska, *Lider: górskim szlakiem Andrzeja Zawady* (Warszawa: Iskry, 2003), 299.
9. Piotr Drożdż, *Krzysztof Wielicki: Mój Wybór. Wywiad-Rzeka Tom 1* (Kraków: Góry Books, 2014), 179.
10. The team comprised Jacek Berbeka, Marcin Kaczkan, Piotr Morawksi, Jerzy Natkański, Maciej Pawlikowski and Darek Załuski from Poland; Gia Tortladze from Georgia; Vassiliy Pivtsov and Denis Urubko from Kazakhstan; and Ilyas Tukhvatullin from Uzbekistan.
11. Piotr Drożdż, *Krzysztof Wielicki: Mój Wybór. Wywiad-Rzeka Tom 2* (Kraków: Góry Books, 2015), 196.
12. Ibid., 198.
13. Piotr Morawski and Grzegorz Glazek, 'Asia, China, Karakoram, K2, Winter Attempt on the North Ridge', *American Alpine Journal* 2003: 403.
14. Himalman, 'Polish Winter Expedition to K2: 2002/3', www.polishhimalayas.wordpress.com, 2 January 2008.
15. Piotr Drożdż, *Krzysztof Wielicki: Mój Wybór. Wywiad-Rzeka Tom 2* (Kraków: Góry Books, 2015), 199.
16. Monika Rogozińska, 'Polish Himalaists Attack K2 in Winter', *RussianClimb.com*, 9 November 2002.
17. Piotr Drożdż, *Krzysztof Wielicki: Mój Wybór. Wywiad-Rzeka Tom 2* (Kraków: Góry Books, 2015), 207.
18. Ludwik Wilczyński, *Ice Warriors* (Katowice: STAPIS, 2019), 97.
19. Mark Jenkins, 'Climber Breaks From Team, Attempts and Abandons Solo Ascent of "Savage Mountain"', www.nationalgeographic.com, 25 February 2018.
20. Alan Arnette, 'Winter K2 Attempt Over – Can it Ever be Done?', www.alanarnette.com, 18 March 2019.

EPILOGUE

1. Denis Urubko, 'Fifty-Fifty: Tales of a Climber's Life', *Alpinist* 37, Winter 2011–12: 77.
2. Élisabeth Revol, 'Attempt of Manaslu (8,163m)', *Boreal*, 10 February 2017.
3. Louis Rousseau, 'A Cold Sisyphean Climb', *Gripped*, October/November 2011, 46.
4. Miguel 'Lito' Sánchez, *Cho Oyu*, (Rio Cuarto: Palloni Edicion, 2017), Préface.
5. Maria Coffey, *Where the Mountain Casts Its Shadow: The Dark Side of Extreme Adventure* (New York: St. Martin's Press, 2003), xvii.

SELECT BIBLIOGRAPHY
AND SOURCES

BOOKS

Adamiecki, Wojciech. *Zdobyć Everest*. Warszawa: Iskry, 1984.

Berbeka, Ewa A Rozmowa and Beata Sabała-Zielińska. *Jak Wysoko Sięga Miłość? Życie Po Broad Peak*. Warszawa: Prószyński Media Sp. z o.o., 2016.

Bielecki, Adam and Dominik Szczepański. *Adam Bielecki*. Warszawa: Agora, 2017.

Boukreev, Anatoli. *Above the Clouds*. New York: St. Martin's Press, 2001.

Burgess, Adrian and Alan. *The Burgess Book of Lies*. Calgary: Rocky Mountain Books, 1994.

Coffey, Maria. *Where the Mountain Casts its Shadow: The Dark Side of Extreme Adventure*. New York: St. Martin's Press, 2003.

Davies, Norman. *God's Playground: A History of Poland (revised edition), Volume II: 1795 to the Present*. Oxford and New York: Oxford University Press, 2005.

Dobroch, Bartek. *Artur Hajzer: Droga Słonia*. Kraków: Wydawnictwo Znak, 2018.

Dobroch, Bartek and Przemysław Wilczyński. *Broad Peak: Niebo I Piekło*. Poznań: Wydawnictwo Poznańskie, 2014.

Drożdż, Piotr. *Krzysztof Wielicki: Mój Wybór. Wywiad-Rzeka Tom 1*. Kraków: Góry Books, 2014.

———. *Krzysztof Wielicki: Mój Wybór. Wywiad-Rzeka Tom 2*. Kraków: Góry Books, 2015.

Fronia, Rafał. *Anatomia Góry*. Kraków: Wydanie I, 2018.

Hajzer, Artur. *Atak Rozpaczy*. Gliwice, Poland: Explo Publishers, 1994.

Hemmleb, Jochen. *Spuren für die Ewigkeit*. Vienna: EGOTH Verlag, 2014.

Isserman, Maurice, and Stewart Weaver, with sketches by Dee Molenaar. *Fallen Giants: A History of Himalayan Mountaineering from the Age of Empire to the Age of Extremes*. New Haven: Yale University Press, 2008.

Kortko, Dariusz, and Marcin Pietraszewski. *Krzysztof Wielicki. Piekło mnie nie chciało*. Warszawa: Agora, 2019.

Kukuczka, Jerzy. *My Vertical World: Climbing the 8000-Metre Peaks*. Seattle: Mountaineers Books, 1992.

Kurczab, Janusz. *Lodowi Wojownicy: Polskie Himalaje Część 2*. Warszawa: Agora, 2008.

Loretan, Erhard. *Night Naked*. Seattle: Mountaineers Books, 2013.

Lwow, Aleksander. *Zwyciężyć znaczy przeżyć*. Kraków: Hudowski & Marcisz, 1994.

———. *Zwyciężyć znaczy przeżyć: 20 lat później*. Kraków: Wydawnictwo Bezdroża, 2014.

Macfarlane, Robert. *Mountains of the Mind*. New York: Pantheon Books, 2003.

Maraini, Fosco. *Karakoram: The Ascent of Gasherbrum IV*. New York: Viking Press, 1961.

Matuszewska, Ewa. *Lider: górskim szlakiem Andrzeja Zawady*. Warszawa: Iskry, 2003.

———. *Uciec jak najwyżej: nie dokończone życie Wandy Rutkiewicz (Escaping to the Highest: The Unfinished Life of Wanda Rutkiewicz)*. Warszawa: Iskry, 1999.

McDonald, Bernadette. *Alpine Warriors*. Calgary: Rocky Mountain Books, 2015.

———. *Freedom Climbers*. Calgary: Rocky Mountain Books, 2011.

———. *Freedom Climbers*. Sheffield: Vertebrate Publishing, 2012.

Sánchez, Miguel 'Lito'. *Cho Oyu*. Rio Cuarto: Palloni Edicion, 2017.

Milewska, Anna. *Życie z Zawadą*. Warszawa: Oficyna Wydawnicza Łośgraf, 2009.

Milewska-Zawada, Anna. *K2: Pierwsza Zimowz Wyprawa*. Warszawa: Selion Sp. Z.o.o., 2018.

Moro, Simone. *Cometa sull'Annapurna*. Milano: Corbaccio, 2003.

Nardi, Daniele and Alessandra Carati. *La via perfetto. Nanga Parbat: sperone Mummery*. Torino: Giulio Einaudi editore s.p.a., 2019.

Piotrowski, Tadeusz. *Gdy Krzepnie Rtęć*. Warszawa: Iskry, 1982.

Reinisch, Gertrude. *Wanda Rutkiewicz: A Caravan of Dreams*. Ross-on-Wye, UK: Carreg Ltd, 2000.

Revol, Élisabeth. *Vivre*. Paris: Éditions Arthaud, 2019.

Rogozińska, Monika. *Lot Koło: Nagiej Damy*. Pelplin: Bernardinum, 2016.

Rutkiewicz, Wanda. *Na jednej linie*. Warszawa: Krajowa Agencja Wydawnicza, 1986.

Szczepański, Dominik. *Czapkins*. Warszawa: Agora, 2019.

Tasker, Joe. *Everest the Cruel Way. The Boardman Tasker Omnibus*. London: Hodder & Stoughton, 1995.

Trybalski, Piotr. *Wszystko za K2*. Kraków: Wydawnictwo Literackie, 2018.

Urubko, Denis. *Skazany Na Góry*. Warszawa: Agora, 2018.

Wielicki, Krzysztof. *Korona Himalajów: 14 X 8000*. Kraków: Wydawnictwo Ati, 1997.

Wilczyński, Ludwik. *Jak dobrze nam zdobywać gory*. Kraków: STAPIS, 2019.

JOURNALS, NEWSPAPERS AND MAGAZINES

Alpine Journal, years: 1951, 1977, 1979, 1984, 2000, 2001, 2012, 2013.

American Alpine Journal, years: 1979, 1980, 1982, 1983, 1984, 1985, 1986, 1987, 1988, 1989, 1991, 1992, 1998, 2003, 2005, 2011, 2012.

Himalayan Journal, years: 1987, 1991, 1992, 1993.

Bremer-Kamp, Cherie. *Chicago Tribune*, 31 May 1987.

Burke, Jason. 'One Step Beyond', *The Observer*, 9 April 2006.

Richards, Cory. 'This Photo Captures a Near-Death Experience – and Later Trauma', *National Geographic Magazine*, May 2018: 36–38.

Rousseau, Louis. 'A Cold Sisyphean Climb', *Gripped*, October/November 2011: 44–49.

Swenson, Steve. 'K2: The Mountaineer's Mountain', *Alpinist* 37 (Winter 2011–12): 38–61.

Tanabe, Osamu. 'Lhotse South Face Winter – Near Ascent', *Japan Alpine News* volume 5 (2004): 3.

Urubko, Denis. 'Fifty-Fifty: Tales of a Climber's Life', *Alpinist* 37 (Winter 2011–12): 70–79.

———. 'Makalu: the First Winter Ascent and Cho Oyu: the Southeast Face', *Japan Alpine News* volume 11 (2010): 94.

Wielicki, Krzysztof. 'Winter Manifesto', *Polski Związek Alpinizmu*, 2002.

FILMS

Berbeka, Stanisław. 2018. *Dreamland*. Yak Yak, Poland.

Fogel, Anson. 2011. *Cold*. Forge Mountain Pictures, USA.

Jewhurst, Allen. 1981. *Everest in Winter*. Chameleon, UK.

Pelletier, Vic. 1995. *K-2 Winter 1987–88*. Les Productions Vic Pelletier Inc., France 3 Montagne.

Porębski, Jerzy. 2008. *Polskie Himalaje: The Ice Warriors*. Artica, Poland.

———. 2014. *Manaslu*. Artica, Poland.

Stauber, Hans Peter. 2012. *Der Letze Weg*: Servus TV, Salzburg, Austria.

Załuski, Darek. 2019. *The Last Mountain*. Ostatnia Góra, Warszawa, Poland.

ONLINE

Arnette, Alan. 'Winter K2 Attempt Over – Can it Ever be Done?' www.alanarnette.com: 18 March 2019.

Griffin, Lindsay. 'Lhotse South Face in Winter – Almost', *Alpinist Online*: 8 January 2007.

Himalman. 'Polish Winter Expedition to K2: 2002/3', www.polishhimalayas.wordpress.com: 2 January 2008.

Jamkowski, Marcin. 'Rescue on the Killer Mountain', *Outside Online*: 11 April 2018.

Korniszewski, Lech. 'Life Passions', *Puls*: 5 January 2007.

Lunger, Tamara. 'Winter Expedition', www.tamaralunger.com: January/February 2016.

Moro, Simone. 'Shisha Pangma Winter Expedition', *Mountain RU*: 8 December 2003, 21 December 2003.

Mytych, Jagoda. 'Artur Hajzer – Ice Leader', www.goryksiazek.pl: September 2013.

O'Neil, Devon. 'To Get to the Summit, Cory Richards had to Lose it All', *Outside Online*: 24 August 2017.

Revol, Élisabeth. 'Attempt of Manaslu (8,163m)', *Boreal*: 10 February 2017.

Rogozińska, Monika. 'Polish Himalaists Attack K2 in Winter', www.russianclimb.com: 9 November 2002.

Rossi, Marcello. 'Simone Moro: The Winter Maestro', www.climbing.com: 13 January 2017.

Rousseau, Louis. 'Winter GI Commentary', www.explorersweb: 3 February 2012.

Schaffer, Grayson. 'Partly Crazy With a Chance of Frostbite', *Outside Online*: 25 April 2011.

Urubko, Denis. 'Elements Revelry', www.russianclimb.com: 3 February 2008.

———. 'Gasherbrum II, Winter 2011', www.russianclimb.com: 26 January 2011.

Urubko, Denis and Simone Moro, 'Makalu Winter Climb', www.russianclimb.com: 22 January 2009.

www.altitudepakistan.blogspot.com: 28 December 2012.

www.czapkins.blogspot.com: 3 July 2016.

www.planetmountain.com: 13 January 2012.

www.wspinanie.pl/forum: 7 January 2013.

INDEX